INDIA

AN HISTORICAL SKETCH

INDIA

AN HISTORICAL SKETCH

GEORGE TREVOR, M. A.

GYAN

Published by

Gyan Publishing House
5, Ansari Road
Daryaganj, New Delhi-110002
Phone: 011-47034999, 9811692060
E-mail: books@gyanbooks.com

Distribution Network
gyanbooks.com
India, USA, Canada, UK, Australia, France

ISBN: 978-81-212-8820-0 (PB)
First Published, 1799

2nd Impression 2023

Printed at: Gyan Press, Delhi.

INDIA AN HISTORICAL SKETCH
Author: George Trevor

INDIA.

AN HISTORICAL SKETCH.

BY THE

REV. GEORGE TREVOR, M.A.

Canon of York; late Chaplain on the Madras Establishment.

LONDON:

THE RELIGIOUS TRACT SOCIETY:

Instituted 1799.

56, PATERNOSTER ROW; 65, ST. PAUL'S CHURCHYARD;
AND 164, PICCADILLY.

CONTENTS.

CHAPTER IV.

AFFGHAN DYNASTIES.

CHAPTER V.

THE MOGULS.

CHAPTER VI.

DECLINE AND FALL OF THE MOGULS.

CHAPTER VII.

EUROPEANS IN INDIA.

PAGE

CHAPTER VIII.

THE BRITISH EMPIRE.

CHAPTER X.

THE BRITISH EMPIRE (*continued*).

CHAPTER XI.

PROGRESS OF CHRISTIANITY.

APPENDIX I.

APPENDIX II.

APPENDIX III.

NOTE.

Since the following pages were committed to the press, "An Act of Parliament for the Better Government of India" has passed (21 & 22 Vic. cap. 106), extinguishing the political powers of the East India Company, and transferring the government to her Majesty. A Secretary of State is appointed for this purpose, assisted by a Council of fifteen members, seven of whom were elected by the Court of Directors, from their own body, before its dissolution, and the other eight are appointed by the Crown, the major part of each section having served or resided in India for ten years. Future vacancies in the Council are to be filled up by the Crown when happening among its nominees, and by the Council itself in the other cases; the qualification of ten years' residence in India being always required for the major part, with the additional proviso, that such residence shall not have ceased more than ten years previously to the appointment. The salaries of the members of Council are fixed at £1,200 per annum each, to be paid out of the Indian revenues.

In India the Governor-General, Governors, and Advocates-General are to be appointed by the Crown; the members of Council by "the Secretary of State in Council;" and the Lieutenant-Governors by the Governor-General, with the approval of the Crown. The civil service is to be open to competition among all "natural born subjects" of the Queen. Naval and military cadets are to be appointed by the Crown; all natural born subjects of her Majesty being allowed to become candidates for examination in the engineers and artillery. The cavalry and infantry cadets are to be recommended by the Council, the Secretary of State's share of the patronage being double that of each member of Council. One-tenth of the whole number of such cadetships are to be reserved, under regulations, for the sons of officers in the Indian military or civil services.

The Secretary of State is President of the Council, with power to appoint a Vice-President. Acts done in the absence of the Secretary of State require his sanction in writing; and his determination in Council is final against the majority, every member having the right to enter his opinions on the minutes. Despatches to India are to be signed by the Secretary of State, having been previously agreed to in Council, or left for perusal in the council-room for seven days.

These regulations, however, are subject to one important exception. In the Secret Department the Secretary of State alone may send orders to any government or servant in India without the knowledge of the Council. This proviso was much debated in Parliament, being in fact a considerable extension of the powers under which the unfortunate Affghan expedition was ordered and undertaken. Under the former system, three members of the Court of Directors were always cognisant of such orders, and had on some occasions remonstrated with effect, though they had not the power of absolutely resisting their transmission. By the present enactment a war may be ordered in India *by a single minister of the Crown,* without the knowledge of Parliament or indeed of any other individual; for the Act does not require the minister to consult the Cabinet, nor even to take the pleasure of the Sovereign. His powers are not limited to sending orders to the Governor-General; they may be addressed, without his knowledge, to "any officer or servant in India."

The only condition imposed by the Act is, that if any order be sent "directing the actual commencement of hostilities *by her Majesty's forces in India,*" the fact of such order having been sent shall be communicated to Parliament (if sitting) within three months after its despatch, and if Parliament be not sitting within a month after its assembly. Such a notification would obviously come too late to arrest any hostilities disapproved of by Parliament; and the Secretary of State might order the Resident at a native court to commence hostilities *by means of the local forces* without notifying the fact at all.

There is another proviso, that the revenues of India shall not be applied to military operations beyond the Indian frontier without the consent of Parliament, but it is to be feared this cannot prevent the repetition of such expeditions as were lately ordered against Persia.

The unlimited authority confided to the Secretary of State in the matter of war, is not extended to the expenditure of the revenues of India; no part of them can be appropriated without the concurrence of a majority of the Council.

All the existing establishments of the Company become those of her Majesty, the naval and military forces remaining as at present constituted, under the designation of her Majesty's Indian Forces, with the same advantages of pay, pension, etc., as were previously enjoyed. The Act takes effect from the 2nd September, 1858, being thirty days from its passing.

This important enactment being limited to the government at home, is necessarily silent upon the future administration of affairs in India, where the natives are really governed. Much interest is felt as to the spirit and principles of the directions by which the local governments will be guided. No definite indications have yet appeared of the course to be pursued on the all-important questions of caste, education, and the increase of facilities for the extension of divine truth. It is earnestly to be hoped that the difficulties attending these questions will not be aggravated by any hasty proclamation, unadvisedly pledging the Queen's name to the maintenance or recognition of existing superstitions; but the subject is one on which British statesmanship exhibits but little of a decided and satisfactory character, and the thoughtful Christian must not fail to commend it, much and often, to the overruling wisdom of the Most High.

LONDON, *September*, 1858.

GLOSSARY.

A, Arabic; C, Canarese; M, Mahratta; H, Hindustanee; S, Sanscrit; T, Tamul.

Ab (H), water; *e.g.*, *Doab*, two waters; *Trimab*, three waters; *Punjab*, five waters.

Abad (H), dwelling or city, as Allahabad (God's house).

Adawlut (H), court of justice.

Ameen (H), a native judge.

Ameer or *Amir* (H), noble or chief.

Amil and *amildar* (H), a native collector of revenue.

Ayeen (H), government laws or regulations, in distinction to those of the Koran or sacred tradition.

Bagh (H), a garden; also a tiger.

Bahadur (H), title of rank.

Bajra (H), a kind of millet (*panicum spicatum*).

Begum (H), a princess (Mohammedan).

Bhang (H), an intoxicating preparation of hemp.

Brahm (S), the Divine essence.

Brahma (S), the personal Creator.

Brahmin or *Brahman* (H), the first of the four Hindu castes.

Bund (H), a dyke or bank.

Byragees (H), religious mendicants, worshippers of Vishnu.

Cadhi, *Cazee*, or *Qazee*, a Mohammedan judge deciding both civil and criminal suits by the Koran.

Caliph or *Khalifa* (H), the successors of Mohammed.

Chowt or *chouth* (H), a fourth part of the government collections demanded by the Mahrattas as the price of forbearing to ravage the country.

Circar (H), a district.

Cot and *cottah* (H), a fort.

Crore (H), ten millions, a hundred lakhs.

Deccan (H), the south.

Deen or *din* (H), religion, especially the Mohammedan.

Desmook (M), a hereditary native officer of police and revenue.

Dewan (H), the chief minister of finance; also a court or council (Divan).

Dharma (S), law divine.

——— *Shastra*, the Hindu code.

Doab (H), "two waters;" a tract of land between two rivers.

Droog (H), a hill fort.

Durbar (H), the royal court or levee.

Dwarpar Yug (S), the third age of the world.

Emir, corruption of ameer.

Fakir (H), a Mohammedan religious mendicant.

Firman (H), a mandate; grant or patent.

Florikin, a small species of the bustard.

Ghât (H), a mountain pass; also a landing place or flight of steps on a river.

Gossain (H), a religious mendicant, worshipping Mahadeo (or Siva), and wearing yellow or orange, his emblematical colour; the term is also applied to vagrants in general.

Guru (S), a spiritual teacher.

Hadjee (H), a Mohammedan who has performed the pilgrimage to Mecca.

Hegira (A), the flight of Mohammed from Medina.

Islam (H and A), the Mohammedan religion.

Istan (H), a termination signifying country, as Affghanistan, the country of the Affghans.

Jaghire (H), a fief or grant of the revenue and government of a district for a time or for life; sometimes renewable to the heir on payment of a fine.

Jemadar (H), a native subaltern officer.

Jowar (H), a kind of millet (*holcus jorghum*).

Kali Yug (S), the fourth, or present age of the world.

Kalpa (S), the day or period for which Brahm assigns the universe to the sacred triad.

Koran (A), the book; *i.e.*, the supposed revelation to Mohammed, collected by the Caliph Omar.

Kshatriya (S), the second or military caste of the Hindus.

Lakh or *lac* (H), a hundred thousand.

Mir or *Meer*, see Ameer.

Monsoon, the trade wind; also the period for which it continues.

Moslem, *Mussulman*, *Musliman*, *Muslim* (H), a believer in Islam or Mohammedanism.

Moulavie, *Moulvie*, or *Moollah* (H), a Mohammedan lawyer or judge; deputy of the cadhi.

Mufti (H), a Mohammedan law officer or scribe.

Muntra (S), a prayer; a magical formula.

Musjid or *Mosque*, Mohammedan place of worship.

Nabob, English corruption of nawab.

Naib (H), deputy or viceroy.

Namaz (H), prayer (Mohammedan).

Nawab (H), plural of naib; used honorifically as a title of rank (Mohammedan).

Nazim or *Nizam* (H), viceroy, or chief administrator of criminal laws (Mohammedan).

Nuggur (H), a town.

Nullah (H), a watercourse, rivulet, or ravine.

Omrah (H), plural of ameer; *ameer-ul-omrah*, chief of the nobles; sometimes "commander-in-chief."

Padisha or *Padshah* (H), a king (Mohammedan); title of Mogul emperors.

Padre (Portuguese), common term in India for a Christian clergyman.

Pagoda, Portuguese word for heathen temple.

Patan, a term applied to the old *Affghan* Mohammedans, as distinguished from the *Moguls*.

Peishwah (M), chief minister of the Mahratta court.

Pergunnah (H), a district or province; less than a zillah.

Perwunah (H), a permit or pass.

Polygar (T), an independent chieftain.

Pundit (S), a Brahmin learned in the Vedas and other Shastras.

Pur, *poor*, or *pore* (S), a town or city, mostly used in composition, as *Sir-ram-pur*, vulgarly *Serampore*.

Purana (S), old: the especial designation of the eighteen books of Hindu traditions and legends.

Raggi (C), a grain, a kind of *panicum*.

Raja and *Rai* (H), a king, a prince (Hindu); given as a title by Mohammedan governments.

Rana (H), corruption of raja.

Ranee (H), feminine of raja.

Rupee (H), a silver coin, worth about two shillings, formerly bearing the impress of the emperor Shah Alum and other native authorities; but in 1835 the "Company's rupee" was issued and made current throughout British India, bearing the effigy of the British sovereign.

Ryot (H), a peasant.

Sastra or *Shastra* (S), scripture.

Satya Yug (S), the first age of the world.

Shah (H), a king, a prince (Mohammedan); used as a title.

Shahzada (H), son of the king.

Shastree, a Brahmin learned in the Shastras.

Shias or *Shiites* (H), one of the great Mohammedan sects; "followers" of Ali, the son-in-law of the Prophet, and esteeming the three caliphs, Abubeker, Omar, and Osman as usurpers. To this sect belong the Persians generally, the royal family of Oude, and most of the lower orders of Mussulmans in India.

Sirdar (H), a chief.

Sirdeshmooki (M), the claim of the desmook, ten per cent. on the revenue exacted in addition to the chout.

Sirkar (H), the state or government.

Soonnees (H), "followers of the traditions," who maintain the lawful succession of the three caliphs before Ali, and pay great deference to the traditions of Islam. The Arabs, Turks, Affghans, and most of the educated Mussulmans of India are of this class, and style themselves *orthodox*, the Shias being regarded as heretics.

Stan, see *istan*.

Subah or *soubah*, a province or government.

Sudder (H), chief, as *sudder adawlut*, the Company's supreme court of justice.

Sudra (S), the fourth, or servile, caste of the Hindus; now vaguely applied also to all the mixed castes.

Sultan (H), a sovereign prince (Mohammedan); also a title borne by the younger members of the royal family, especially Delhi.

Sunnud (H), a grant or diploma.

Syed, *Syud*, or *Said* (H), a descendant of Husein, son of Ali, and grandson of the Prophet.

Tahsildar (H), a native collector of revenue.

Talook (H), an estate usually smaller than a zemindarry, but in north-west provinces presents various peculiarities.

Tank, a term applied in India to an artificial lake or reservoir, large or small.

Treta Yug (S), the second age of the world.

Vaishya (S), the third of the Hindu castes.

Veda (S), "the book," or the Hindu sacred scriptures; properly four, or some say three, but the term is extended to other works.

Vedanta (S), a system of pantheistic philosophy founded on scattered texts of the Vedas.

Vizier (H), the principal minister in a Mohammedan sovereignty.

Vizierut (H), the office of vizier.

Zemindar (H), a landholder; also a collector of revenue for the government over a large district.

Zillah (H), a large district.

INDIA.

CHAPTER I.

THE COUNTRY.

Geography—Area and population—Name—Natural divisions—Rivers and mountains—The Punjab—The Ganges—Hindustan—Deccan—Peninsula—Central India—Ghâts — Bengal—Guzerat—Coast —Languages—Political divisions—British presidencies—Native states—Portuguese and French —Climate—European colonization—Monsoons — Rain—Seasons—Irrigation—Productions—Minerals—Zoology—Sunrise and sunset.

INDIA is the geographical name of that extensive portion of Asia which lies between the Himmaleh, or Himalaya, Mountains and the Indian Ocean. The western boundary is completed by the Suliman range, connected with the Himalayas by the Khyber hills, and extending southward to the Arabian Sea, near the port of Kurrachee. The opposite limit is less perfectly defined by the mountains of Assam, joining the Himalayas on the north, and continued through the range called Yoomadung to Cape Nigris, near the mouths of the Irrawaddy. Each of these mountain-barriers is lined by a mighty river. The Indus rising on the northern face, about the centre of the Himalayas, after flowing for two hundred miles through the territory of Thibet, issues by the deep gorge which divides the snowy range from the Hindu Koosh, and descends along the foot of the Suliman hills to enter the sea by as many as thirteen mouths, spread over a line of coast one hundred and fifty miles in length. At no great distance from the source of the Indus rise the waters which, flowing to the east and rounding the opposite extremity of the Himalayas, constitute the Brahmapootra; which thence holding its course to the south, empties itself by three mouths at the head of the Bay of Bengal.

By the ancient geographers, the name of India was extended over the continent eastward as far as the Pacific Ocean, the whole being divided into "India within the Ganges" and "India without the Ganges."* Modern writers usually confine the term to the limits now described; but British India has already extended beyond the eastern mountains into Pegu, and as the Birman empire is tenanted by a branch of the Hindu race, the ancient appellation might well be resumed, as far at least as the borders of China. Including Pegu, India contains an area of 1,467,183 square miles, with a total population of 180,853,017 souls;† greatly exceeding in both respects all the countries of Europe south of the Baltic.

Like Europe, it is inhabited by different nations, having their own proper names for the territories in which they are settled. As the appellation of a single country, India is a word and an idea wholly unknown to any of its natives.

The name is apparently connected with the Indus, which divided this unknown region from Persia and

* Some of the ancient geographers appear to have confounded the Ganges with the Brahmapootra.

† Official Return, East India House, Feb. 1857.

the world of ancient classical literature. But whether the river was called from the people who dwelt on its banks, or the people from the river, seems to be in doubt. Mr. Elphinstone traces the appellation to the Sanscrit word *Sindh* or *Hindh*, signifying *blue*,* a term applied to the river, as denoting the colour of its waters; but Colonel Tod prefers *Indu*, the Sanscrit for *moon*, which the leaders of the race affected to call their parent.† A third etymology, derived from the Persian word *Hindu*, signifying *black*, seems less trustworthy, not only because the names of nations are to be sought for in their own languages rather than in that of foreigners, but also because the Hindus are in fact the fairest of the natives of India, and were, beyond all doubt, of the Caucasian or white race of mankind. The country is called in Sanscrit *Bharat* or *Bharatkund*, from a dynasty of ancient kings; and also Punya Dhurma, the Holy Land, and *Djam-bhu-dwip*, the "Peninsula of the Tree of Life."

India is, to a great extent, divided amongst its several races by the natural barriers of mountain and river. The mouths of the Indus discharge the united waters of the *Jhelum*, the *Chenab*, the *Ravee*, the *Beas*, and the *Sutlej*, all issuing from the southern face of the western Himalayas, and collected first into the two channels of the *Ghara* and the *Trimab*, and then into the *Punjnud*, which, after a separate course of sixty miles, enters the Indus about four hundred and ninety miles from the sea. From these five rivers the region which they intersect is denominated the *Punjab*, or Five Waters.

* History of India, by Hon. Mountstuart Elphinstone, vol. i.

† Annals of Rajasthan, by Col. Tod.

To the south-west of the Punjab is a low tract of sand and alluvium, denominated, from the great river which forms its principal highway, *Sindh.* With this country was formerly united the adjoining province of *Cutch.* *Guzerat* is defined by the Gulfs of Cutch and Cambay; and from the head of the latter a range of mountains, called the *Vindhyas,* crosses the continent eastward. To the north of these as far as the Himalayas, stretches the territory properly denominated *Hindustan,* or the country of the Hindus; a word which in Europe is often erroneously used as synonymous with India.

On the snowy range, not far from the lake in which the Sutlej takes its rise, is the source of the *Jumna;* and about two degrees to the eastward, from a low arch under the base of a great snow-bed issues, at an elevation of thirteen thousand eight hundred feet above the sea, the stream denominated *Bhageerettee,* which, after joining another called Jahnuvi, breaks through the Himalaya proper, and, augmented by some large mountain torrents, meets another considerable river, the *Aluknunda,* at Devaprayaga, or Deoprag.* From this point, the united waters assume the sacred name of *Ganges,* and traversing Hindustan to the south and east, are finally emptied through a number of mouths into the Bay of Bengal. The Ganges is joined at Allahabad by the Jumna, which, after an independent course of eight hundred and sixty miles, fed by numerous tributaries, rolls its rapid waters, clear as crystal, into the deeper channel of the yet more sacred river, and is lost in its yellow tide. Lower

* That is, the Holy Confluence. These *prayas* are always sacred among the Hindus; the most so is the junction of the Ganges and the Jumna at Allahabad.

down, the *Gogra*, the *Goomtee*, the *Gunduck*, the *Coosey*, with other smaller tributaries, are received on the left, while from the opposite side the *Sone* brings its contribution from the mountains of the south-west.

Arrived within three hundred miles of the sea, the river begins to throw off its arms to the right, two of which again uniting constitute the *Hooghly*, which flows by Calcutta and forms the westernmost mouth of the Ganges. It is by this channel that the holy waters are considered to find their outlet, after a course of more than one thousand five hundred miles from their source. The name of Ganges, however, has been retained by that portion of the stream which proceeds in an easterly direction to meet the Brahmapootra. The delta of these two great rivers is intersected by a net-work of channels uniting them at various points. Besides the Hooghly, the *Podda*, and the *Chundna*, a maze of streams penetrate the low regions called *Sunderbund*, and issue into the sea by more than twenty different estuaries.

The *Nerbudda* is a smaller river, rising at an elevation of only three or four thousand feet, at the eastern extremity of the Vindhyas, and flowing along the foot of these hills to the Gulf of Cambay. The *Kistna* or *Krishna* springs from the Western Ghâts, at a still lower latitude, and making its way eastward crosses the whole country, here considerably diminished in breadth, to empty itself in the Bay of Bengal. The deep precipitous valleys of these two rivers effect the three grand divisions of India. North of the Nerbudda is *Hindustan*; between this river and the Kistna is the *Deccan*, or south country; and below the Kistna, where neither the Hindu nor the Mohammedan invasions extended, the Anglo-Indians apply the term *Peninsula*, though this is also less properly used of the whole continent.

The portion of Hindustan immediately above the Vindhyas, is denominated *Central India*. It is a table-land from one thousand five hundred to two thousand five hundred feet high, supported on the west by the Aravulli range, on the south-east by the lower hills of Bundlecund, and on the other sides gradually declining into the great plain which is watered by the Ganges.

Below the valley of the Nerbudda, along the western coast, at a distance of from thirty to fifty miles from the sea, extends a lofty range of hills terminating in Cape Comorin, and called by Europeans the Western *Ghâts*, but by the natives the *Syadree* mountains. Their elevation varies from two to four or even five thousand feet. The ascent from the coast is steep and precipitous, but on the inland side the mountains slope more gently down to a table-land, which gradually sinks towards the east and north, being supported on the opposite side by a corresponding range of less elevation, denominated the Eastern Ghâts. These latter ghâts extend in like manner along the coast, but at a greater distance inland, from the eastern extremity of the Vindhyas to about two and a half degrees from Cape Comorin, where they are united to the Western Ghâts by the *Neilgherry* group. The higher portion of the table land included in the triangle formed by the Ghâts, the Neilgherries, and the Kistna, is the *Mysore* territory; the lower, north of the Kistna, is subject to the nizam of *Hyderabad*, anciently called the soubahdar of the Deccan.

Bengal on the east, and *Guzerat* on the west, are low regions, lying beyond the mountain system, and not included either in Hindustan or the Deccan. They have each their separate language and population; a remark which applies also to several portions of the long line of coast which, running from one to the other, surrounds the ghâts with a level slip of sandy or alluvial soil. The distinct features of the provinces still further east, *Assam*, *Arracan*, and *Tenasserim*, are yet more strongly marked. Though now included under the dominant influence of a single empire, these great divisions of India are the seats of many different populations who were once distributed into independent kingdoms.

The distinctions are still marked by great diversity of speech. The languages extant and in vernacular use in India are classed by Mr. Elphinstone under two heads, the *Tamul* with its derivatives in the south, and the several tongues of northern India, all descended from the *Sanscrit*. The latter, which is now a dead language, was in all probability the vernacular of the first Hindus; as the southern family may be taken to represent the aboriginal populations less affected by their invasion. The Tamul, a highly polished language, which is indebted to Sanscrit only for a few scientific terms, is still the vernacular of the south-eastern parts of the Peninsula. Its derivatives are the *Canarese* or *Carnarese*, the proper language of the Carnatic; the *Telugu* (called also *Gentoo*), marking the ancient kingdom of Telingana; the *Malayalim*, spoken on the coast of Malabar; and the *Uriya*, in Orissa. These dialects are affected more or less by admixtures of Sanscrit; the largest, as from the locality might be anticipated, being found in the *Uriya*. The derivatives of the Sanscrit are six,—the *Canoujee*, or *Hindee*, in western Hindustan; the *Mithila*, in

Behar; the *Punjabee*, the *Bengalee*, the *Guzerattee*, and the *Mahratta*—the last being the only branch of the family found in the Deccan, and supposed to mark the ancient kingdom of *Marashtra*. Some writers are of opinion that all these also were aboriginal vernaculars, existing before the introduction of Sanscrit, and only more largely affected by the latter than the more distant languages.* The languages enumerated are independent of the dialects of the various hill tribes, omitted as illiterate jargons,—and also of the *Hindustanee*, which is not the speech of any particular nation, but a compound of Persian and Hindee, forming the *Oordu* or camp language of the Mohammedan invaders. It is still the general language of the Mussulman population, and is also the most usual medium of communication between official persons, and between Europeans and Natives throughout India.

Politically, India is divided into British and Native: the former being distributed under the three presidencies of Fort William in Bengal, Fort St. George at Madras, and Bombay. Each presidency was formerly administered by a governor and council, the Bengal Government being supreme, and its governor termed the Governor-General. Of late years the supreme government has been styled the Governor-General and Council of India; and the presidency of Bengal is subdivided under the Lieutenant-Governors of Bengal and the North-Western Provinces. The later acquisitions of the Punjab, Oude,

* For the proper boundaries of these ancient nations, the reader must consult the learned pages of Elphinstone, Wilkes, Tod, Duff, etc. They are by no means accurately retained in the modern application of the terms Carnatic, Malabar, Coromandel, etc.

Berar, and Pegu, are not included in either presidency, but are administered by commissioners under the immediate direction of the Supreme Government.

The total area of British India is 838,019 square miles, and its population amounts to 131,912,238. The Native states are above one hundred and fifty in number, including a total area of 627,910 square miles, and a population of 48,423,630. Of these states, Nepal, Cashmere, and Dholpore, are independent allies of the British Government. The remainder are all more or less under its authority and protection. The principal are the Sikh states, on either bank of the Sutlej; the states of Central India and Rajpootana; those of Orissa, on the southern frontier of Bengal; Hyderabad in the Deccan; Mysore, Cochin, and Travancore, in the Peninsula; and in Western India, the states of Guzerat and Kattywar, the southern Mahratta country, Cutch, and a part of Sindh. An enumeration of the several native states, with their respective populations and areas, will be found in the Appendix.

The Portuguese, once masters of a noble empire, still linger in Goa and two other little towns on the western coast; and the French, who struggled so unscrupulously to crush the rising fortunes of the English, retain the scattered settlements of Chandernagore on the Hooghly, Yanaon in Orissa, Pondicherry and Karical on the Coromandel coast, and Mahé in Malabar. With these insignificant exceptions the "meteor flag of England" flies paramount or alone throughout India.

A country extending for nearly two thousand miles, from north to south, and from the regions of perpetual snow to within eight degrees of the equator, must possess every variety of climate inhabitable by the human species. The variety is increased in India by the inequality of the surface, for temperature is more affected by elevation and proximity to the sea than by the course of the sun. On the Neilgherries, whose summits ascend eight thousand five hundred feet above the sea level, the thermometer ranges from 32° to 68°, as the extreme points, though only 11° from the line: while at Calcutta, situate beyond the tropic, it averages through the year 87°, and often stands at above 100° in the swamps of the Sunderbunds.

Change of climate is effected in some parts with magical rapidity. From the burning plains of Coimbatore the traveller is borne in a single night to a region where his breath clouds the frosty air, the song of European birds is in his ear, and looking from his palanquin he sees the hills covered with verdure to the highest summit, and their sides embroidered with wild geraniums, rhododendrons, hedge-roses, and myrtles. Again, the author has left the hoar-frost lying on the ground as he quitted this enchanting scene at sunrise, and stretched himself at midday by a stream under the shade of the Indian jungle, to rest a few hours, watching the monkeys and parrots, and lulled by that low hum of all living things which marks, more than mars, the deep silence of a tropical noon.

The other great cause of reduced temperature is the neighbourhood of the ocean; the sea breezes at certain seasons alternate with the hot land wind for several hours together, and greatly modify a heat which would otherwise be insupportable. Still the temperature of almost all India is ordinarily too high for the European constitution to endure without many precautions. It is only at the hill stations that it is safe to walk in the sun, whose rays are observed to be hotter in India than in the corresponding latitudes of the United States.* The difference between the shade and the sun is also more perceptibly felt in India, and instead of getting acclimatized by long residence, it is usually found that, after a certain amount of exposure, Europeans become every year more enervated, till they seek refuge and renewal of strength on the mountains, or in a voyage to sea.

In such a climate it is, of course, impossible to employ the white man in laborious occupations out of doors. The only duties of that sort ever attempted are those of the army; and even the private soldier is shielded from the sun, and all midday exercise, to the utmost extent consistent with the exigencies of the service. The officers, with all other classes of Europeans, confine themselves to the house through the heat of the day, or move in covered carriages, or if on horseback, only for short distances, and rarely in the sun. Agricultural labour is wholly confined to the natives, a fact which seems to offer an insurmountable impediment to European colonization. Whoever may be its rulers, India must belong to the indigenous races. It would be only by fusion with the natives, that a settlement of white men could hope to take permanent root in the land, unless, indeed, they were to be sustained, as in tropical America and the West Indies, by the labour of slaves.†

* Allen's India.

† If the acclimatization of both Hindu and Mohammedan colonists seems opposed to this remark, it must be borne in mind that both those races advanced into India by degrees, entering it from countries which, though colder than India, did not offer the decided contrast of European climates, and settling first in the northern provinces, both mixed freely with the native blood as they proceeded towards the south, a process which has continued over a period of time sufficient to alter the complexion and physical constitution of the invaders.

An equally remarkable feature in the Indian climate is the extraordinary supply of rain. During the greater part of the year there is seldom a single shower, but in the months of June, July, August, and September, the fall is more than double the average of England in a whole year. The rainy season, called the *monsoon*, is regulated by the trade winds blowing in one direction for a certain portion of the year, and then shifting to another for the remainder. Over the greater part of India the principal monsoon is from the south-west. Its approach is heralded, about the end of May, by dense banks of clouds appearing in that quarter of the heavens, accompanied by heavy thunder, and lightning far more vivid than is known in Europe. These announcements are followed by torrents of rain, descending first on Cape Comorin, and proceeding rapidly northward over the rest of the country. On the Western Ghâts the fall is often more than two hundred inches in the four months; and over the whole coast it varies from seventy to a hundred inches, the stream descending almost without intermission for a month or six weeks together. On the table-lands and high plain of the Ganges the fall is less. The eastern coast, lying under the shelter of the table-land, is also less exposed to this monsoon, receiving its rain a little later from the Bay of Bengal, after the wind has shifted to the north-east. On that side of India, therefore, there are two monsoons, the most rain falling in the north-eastern, during the months of October and November.

A land from which heat is never absent requires, as the one other condition of agricultural prosperity, water. In India, accordingly, the seasons of spring, summer, autumn, and winter have no existence; the year is divided into the "hot" season and the "rainy" season, with an uncertain period in some parts denominated the "cold weather," but seldom descending below a moderate heat. Over a great part of the country, for three months in the year, even the wind is hot, the ground is parched and brown, dust flies in little hurricanes, the brooks are dry, small rivers hardly maintain a running stream, and the largest are reduced to narrow channels, wandering through broad beds of sand. A thorough change ensues on the breaking of the clouds. The gaping soil drinks in the floods by a thousand clefts, which close up as it becomes saturated to a depth of many feet. A brilliant verdure immediately covers the plains. Birds and animals, no less than human beings, are suddenly invigorated; cascades begin to gleam among the thick foliage of the mountain sides; torrents rush violently down their rocky channels; the *nullahs* are filled with rapid streams, and the swollen rivers often overflow or burst their banks.

The most important labour of agriculture is to regulate and preserve the supply of this indispensable element. Canals and smaller channels of irrigation have been constructed at great cost from the larger rivers, and where no river is available the art of man has contrived huge reservoirs or *tanks*, by building strong dams across the valleys, to detain their waters till they rise into lakes of several miles in circumference. The dam or *bund* of these tanks is fitted with sluices, by which the water is let out upon the fields beneath, and the tanks are usually constructed in a chain, so as to gather again upon a lower level the waters which have escaped after irrigating the higher lands.

Rice, a chief production of India, is grown upon fields entirely flooded with water, and can only be cultivated in situations where the supply is ample. It is the common food in Bengal, Behar, Guzerat, and the level lands of the coast. On the table-land of Mysore the people mostly eat *raggi* (the *Cynosurus corocanus*), a small black grain, in appearance not unlike turnip seed, but larger in size. In the Deccan various kinds of grain are grown in addition to raggi, of which *jowar* and *bajra* are the most common. Hindustan produces abundance of wheat, and throughout India the natives are plentifully supplied with vegetables and fruit; the *brinjal*, tomato, yam, carrot, radish, onion, garlic, spinach cabbage, *nowkohl*, cucumbers, and other gourds, may be mentioned among the former; and of the latter, mangoes, melons, plantains, cocoa-nuts, guavas, tamarinds, custard apples, loquats, jacks, oranges, peaches, grapes, pine-apples, limes, figs, and citrons, constitute a never-ending supply. All, however, are inferior in flavour to the same fruits in the West Indies. Cotton is produced in abundance, and of a quality naturally not inferior to that of America; it is the superior skill in cleaning which gives the latter the advantage in the markets of Europe. The sugar-cane flourishes in the warmer parts, and coffee in the more temperate. Silk, indigo, tobacco, and oil-seeds are largely exported, as also pepper, cardamums, ginger, capsicums, etc. In certain provinces the poppy is cultivated for the manufacture of opium, a drug which occasions a vast amount of misery, debauchery, and death, both in India and China. Tea is extensively raised and manufactured in Assam and other parts of northern India.

The forests are rich in timber and woods for furniture. Bamboos and palms of various descriptions grow in abundance, including the cocoa-nut, of which every part is available to the wants of mankind—the fruit for food, the husks for cordage and matting, the wood for water-pipes, beams, and rafters. The banyan, a forest in itself, spreads its cathedral aisles over a space sufficient to enclose a battalion of soldiers. The sandal adds its fragrant wood, and the Himalayas are laden with magnificent pines.

Among minerals, cornelians, agates, and other precious stones are common. The famous *Koh-i-Nor* was found in the mines of Golconda in the Deccan, but neither diamonds nor the precious metals are now produced in any quantity. Marble abounds in Central India, and rock salt in the Punjab. Coal of good quality exists in considerable quantities in the valley of the Nerbudda, on the Tenasserim coast, and in many other parts. Iron ore is likewise found of a superior kind; the famous blades of Damascus were wrought from the iron of India; and in modern times steel has been produced at Porto Novo, on the coast of Coromandel, equal to that of the royal mines of Sweden.*

The zoology of India embraces the elephant, tiger, panther, leopard, bear, hyæna, wolf, jackal, fox, boar, dog, porcupine, and a multitude of the monkey, deer, and antelope tribes. Lions are found in the western

* The town of Tendukera, on the Nerbudda, is at the present time entirely engaged in iron-making. The ore is of excellent quality, containing forty per cent. of metal, and produced at the rate of from £4 10*s*. to £5 8*s*. per ton cheaper than it can be made in England, with all its mechanical appliances.—*Report to Bombay Government by J. Blackwell, Esq.*

parts of the continent, and in the east the rhinoceros. As beasts of burden, the elephant is employed by princes and public officers, the camel by all classes, and the bullock in droves without number. Horses are common, but small and of little value, save when carefully bred from the stocks of Arabia, Europe, and the Cape of Good Hope. Cattle, sheep, goats, swine, and poultry of all kinds, are kept in large numbers. The wool of the sheep is coarse and wiry, approximating so closely to goats' hair as occasionally to render the two animals not very dissimilar in appearance.

Crocodiles, alligators, serpents of all sorts, scorpions, centipedes, musquitoes, and other venomous creatures, are numerous. Among the birds of prey are eagles, vultures, buzzards, hawks, kites, herons, *toucans*, and crows; while the forest, hill, and plain resound with the cry of peacocks, jungle fowl, grouse of various sorts, quails, parrots, and doves innumerable. The bustard, florikin, partridge, hare, and other game, reward the search of the sportsmen; and few scenes are more healthfully exciting than to traverse the jungle at sunrise, when its feathery inhabitants are all awakening into life and utterance. The trees, of various hues, are rich with brilliant plumage; wild creepers, studded with gorgeous blossoms, swing themselves in ropy festoons from branch to branch; while ever and anon, from the middle of some bamboo brake, a sharp, sudden cry is heard, as

> "With pendant train and rushing wings
> Aloft the gorgeous peacock springs."

The close of day, too, in India, crowds into its brief twilight many objects of interest, described with great truth and feeling in the exquisite little poem from which these two lines are extracted. For the sake of the religious sentiment, no less than its accurate description of nature, the whole is subjoined in the note.* Many are the English hearts which still remember those

* An Evening Walk in Bengal.

" Our task is done; on Gunga's breast
The sun is sinking down to rest;
And, moor'd beneath the tamarind bough,
Our bark has found its harbour now.
With furléd sail, and painted side,
Behold the tiny frigate ride.
Upon her deck, 'mid charcoal gleams,
The Moslem's savoury supper steams;
While all apart, beneath the wood,
The Hindu cooks his simpler food.
"Come, walk with me the jungle through;
If yonder hunter told us true,
Far off, in desert dank and rude,
The tiger holds his solitude;
Nor (taught by recent harm to shun
The thunders of the English gun),
A dreadful guest but rarely seen,
Returns to scare the village green.
Come boldly on. No venom'd snake
Can shelter in so cool a brake.
Child of the sun, he loves to lie
'Mid nature's embers, parch'd and dry,
Where, o'er some tower in ruin laid,
The peepul spreads its haunted shade;
Or, round a tomb his scales to wreathe,
Fit warder in the gate of death.
Come on. Yet pause. Behold us now
Beneath the bamboo's archéd bough,
Where, gemming oft that sacred gloom,
Glows the geranium's scarlet bloom,
And winds our path through many a bower
Of fragrant tree and giant flower;
The ceiba's crimson pomp display'd
O'er the broad plantain's humbler shade,
And dusk anana's prickly blade;
While o'er the brake, so wild and fair,
The betel waves his crest in air.
With pendant train and rushing wings
Aloft the gorgeous peacock springs;
And he, the bird of hundred dyes,
Whose plumes the dames of Ava prize.
So rich a shade, so green a sod,
Our English fairies never trod.

Indian scenes in the dear mother land, where, unlike the gifted author, it has been granted them

"To gaze upon her oaks again."

And deep should be their thankfulness to the gracious

Yet who in Indian bower has stood,
But thought on England's "good greenwood?"
And bless'd, beneath the palmy shade,
Her hazel and her hawthorn glade;
And breathed a prayer (how oft in vain!)
To gaze upon her oaks again?
A truce to thought; the jackal's cry
Resounds like sylvan revelry;
And through the trees yon failing ray
Will scantly serve to guide our way.
Yet mark, as fade the upper skies,
Each thicket opes ten thousand eyes.
Before, beside us, and above,
The fire-fly lights his lamp of love;
Retreating, chasing, sinking, soaring,
The darkness of the copse exploring;
While to this cooler air confest
The broad Dhatura bares her breast,
Of fragrant scent and virgin white,
A pearl around the locks of night.
Still as we pass, in soften'd hum,
Along the breezy alleys come
The village song, the horn, the drum.
Still as we pass, from bush and brier
The shrill cigala strikes his lyre.
And what is she, whose liquid strain
Thrills through yon copse of sugar-cane?
I know that soul-entrancing swell;
It is—it must be—Philomel.
Enough, enough, the rustling trees
Announce a shower upon the breeze;
The flashes of the summer sky
Assume a deeper, ruddier dye;
Yon lamp, that trembles on the stream,
From forth our cabin sheds its beam;
And we must early sleep, to find
Betimes the morning's healthy wind.
But oh! with thankful hearts confess
Ev'n here there may be happiness;
And He, the bounteous Sire, has given,
His peace on earth—his hope of heaven.

Bishop Heber's Narrative, etc. vol. i. p. 185.

Providence which has brought them again in peace, from a region where, with all its beauties, sickness and languor are frequent attendants on the European constitution, and where the Christian heart is painfully reminded, at every turn, of the moral degradation and spiritual darkness of its teeming inhabitants.

Notwithstanding its vast forests and sandy deserts, India is more thickly peopled than the most flourishing portions of the western world. The most populous kingdom in Europe is Belgium, which contains, on an average, 337 persons to the square mile. England contains 304; Ireland 242; France 168, and Scotland only 110. But there are districts in Bengal where the population is as high as 698, and in the north-western provinces 678, to the square mile. The native population has greatly increased under the mild and equitable administration of the British: an augmentation of no less than seventeen millions* being reported

* The following totals are given by Mountstuart Elphinstone, from an official report to the House of Commons in October, 1831:—

Bengal, Lower Provinces	37,500,000
" Upper Provinces	32,200,000
" Berar	3,200,000
	72,900,000
Madras	13,500,000
Bombay	6,800,000
Total British India	93,200,000

Excluding the territories acquired since the date of this calculation, the official returns for 1857 are as follows:—

Under the Lieut.-Governor of Bengal	41,212,562
Under the Lieut.-Governor of N. W. P.	33,216,365
Nagpore, or Berar	4,650,000
Total	79,078,927
Madras (deducting Coorg)	22,301,697
Bombay (deducting Sindh and Sattara)	9,015,534
Total in 1857	110,396,158
Total in 1831	93,200,000
Increase in 26 years	17,196,158

in the official returns during the last quarter of a century. Still, comparing the enormous numbers who are stated to have perished in the continual battles and massacres of the Mohammedan period, with the ruins of vast cities still perceptible in various parts of India, it must be concluded that the population was very large at a remote period of antiquity.

In place of opening, like the uninhabited plains of America, Australia, and southern Africa, a boundless field for European colonization, India is not too large for the races already in possession. Vast additions, no doubt, may be made to the area of its cultivation by reducing the jungle and improving the means of irrigation; but all will be needed for the natural increase of the existing population, under the fostering care of a wise and beneficent government. There is little room for the European immigrant, unless, like the Hindu and the Mohammedan, he is to dispossess and reduce into bondage the existing tenants.

CHAPTER II.

THE HINDUS.

Aboriginal races—Primitive settlements—Patriarchal worship—Early corruptions—Chaldea—Egypt—Canaan—India—Progress of idolatry—Hindu immigration — Their religion — Vedas — Menu — Puranas — Four ages—Monotheism—Morality—Hindu triad—Other gods—Later idolatries—Transmigration of souls—Cruelty—Caste—Brahmins—Military and agricultural castes—Outcasts—Alteration in caste — New castes — Village municipalities.

THE natives of India are commonly regarded in Europe as consisting of two classes, Hindus and Mohammedans; it would be nearly as accurate to divide Europeans themselves into Christians and Jews. These are religious, not national, designations. The Hindus and Mohammedans of India belong to divers nations, while the number of those who adhere to neither religion is nearly double that of the Mussulmans. The *Bheels* of Central India, the *Coolies* and *Dunjas* of Guzerat, the *Ghoonds* and *Coles* of Orissa, the *Shanars* of Tinnevelly, with many other tribes in different parts, are the fragments of an earlier population, which, though driven into the mountains and extremities of the land, has continued to preserve an independent existence, and is still computed at sixteen millions of souls.*

* General Briggs distributes the natives of India as follows:—

Aboriginal races	16,000,000
Mohammedans	10,000,000
Other foreigners	1,000,000
Leaving a *Hindu* population of	143,971,480

India and Europe compared, p. 29.

From the present state of these tribes little can be conjectured of the history and condition of the aboriginal race or races which they represent. Their occupation of India, however, must have been among the earliest settlements of mankind. A country where life is sustained in comfort with little or no protection from the elements, and by a moderate application of unskilled labour, would naturally be populated before the arts and sciences had been discovered, which in colder regions are necessary to obtain food, clothes, and habitation. It may be assumed, therefore, that India was visited by the first wanderers from the dispersion of Babel.

The parent of civilization, and the chief element in the formation of national character, is in all ages religion, and in those early times religion formed the sole distinction among the human family. The worship which Noah and his sons brought out of the ark required neither temples, priests, nor liturgy. Its principal rite was *sacrifice*, that memorial of guilt and expiation, which through every subsequent corruption of religion the human heart could never consent to abandon. But the altars which received the earliest types of the true Lamb of God were erected in the open air, mostly on the tops of hills, in remembrance of Mount Ararat; and the sacrifice was offered by the parent or chief, as the natural head of his children and dependents. The faith of this religion was fixed on the One True God, and the Seed whom he had promised for the destruction of the serpent; whilst its code consisted of the few leading moral and religious principles which have been denominated the seven precepts of Noah.*

* These precepts are as follows:—1. To abstain from idolatry. 2 To worship the true God. 3. To administer judgment in uprightness. 4. To

The first corruptions of this religion arose from the worship of the heavenly bodies, where the primitive astronomers had before planted the memorials of Noah's sacrifice, in the constellations of the ark, the dove, the raven, the altar, and the ram.* Soon after, the elements of nature came to be ranked among "the gods that governed the world;" then the deification of dead men introduced images as their memorials and representatives; these were followed by other idols, in "the likeness of birds and four-footed beasts and creeping things;" then in "the great war of ignorance" which ensued, "men slew their children in sacrifices, or used secret ceremonies, or made revellings of strange rites." These corruptions were followed by a general state of violence and immorality: "They kept neither lives nor marriages any longer undefiled, but either one slew another traitorously, or grieved him by adultery, so that there reigned in all men without exception, blood, manslaughter, theft and dissimulation, corruption, unfaithfulness, tumults, perjury, disquieting of good men, forgetfulness of good turns, defiling of souls, changing of kin, disorder in marriages, adultery, and shameless uncleanness."†

The patriarchal worship was first innovated upon in Chaldea, where the ancestors of Abraham "served other gods."‡ His family, declaring for the religion of Shem, were expelled by the idolaters, but on Abraham's subsequent removal into Canaan, he found

commit no uncleanness. 5. To be guilty of no man's blood. 6. To do as one would be done by. 7. To abstain from flesh, with the blood thereof.

* See Harcourt's "Doctrine of the Deluge."

† See Romans i., and compare the ancient apocryphal Book of Wisdom, chap. xiii. xiv.

‡ Joshua xxiv. 2; Job xxxi. 26—28.

the true worship still maintained by Melchisedec and a portion, at least, of the then possessors of the land. In Egypt also the father of the faithful seems to have encountered none of the religious opposition which he had dreaded. It was two hundred and fifty years later when we read of its being "an abomination to the Egyptians to eat bread with the Israelites." A hundred and thirty years more elapsed before the "new king arose which knew not Joseph." It was probably at this date that the idolatries were introduced which were found in full possession of Canaan, when the posterity of Abraham returned to it, B.C. 1743.* The high places of the patriarchal worship were still sacred to religious uses, but new deities were invoked, the land was polluted with the blood of children slain in sacrifice to Moloch and other demons, and "secret ceremonies with revelling of strange rites" had effected their result in a general "defiling of souls and shameless uncleanness."†

Similar, no doubt, at that time was the condition of the aboriginal inhabitants of India, though there are no means of tracing the history of their settlements, or the progress of their moral and spiritual decay. That some degree of civilization had been reached may

* Shuckford's "Connexion of Sacred and Profane History," corrected to the longer chronology of the Septuagint, as established by Dr. Russell. Abraham removed out of Haran into Canaan 1147 years after the Flood, or B.C. 2113; it is from that period that the 430 years of Israel's sojourn in Egypt are reckoned (Exod. xii. 40). The descent of Jacob was 215 years later, and 130 years after the "new king arose," whom Shuckford supposes to be the first of the "shepherd kings," who had overrun Canaan, and thence burst into Egypt. The bondage of the Israelites endured 85 years, and adding 40 for the wandering in the wilderness, they entered Canaan B.C. 1743, or, according to the shorter chronology of the Hebrew text, followed in the English translation, B.C. 1451.

† See Lev. xvii. xviii.

be inferred from the perfection of the Tamul language, which, attaining to maturity before the introduction of Sanscrit, has not only survived that learned tongue, but contains a literature scarcely inferior to its rival. There are evidences also of a powerful kingdom existing in the south, which long withstood the Brahminical invasion. Still the aboriginal worship, if we may at all judge from what remains of it among their descendants, was a low and grovelling idolatry. The deities were local, and of a malignant, oftener than a beneficent, character. The sacrifices were offered more to avert their wrath than to implore their bounty. Their priests were sorcerers and necromancers, and there is no trace of their possessing any sacred books.

It was probably about the time of the exodus under Moses that the earlier inhabitants of India were invaded by a fairer and more powerful race from beyond the north-western passes, by which they had effected their own entrance into the land. Nothing is known of the countries from which the new immigration proceeded. Sir William Jones supposes it to have come from Iran, others from the Caucasian mountains, and others from the borders of the Caspian Sea, or the plains of the Euphrates. It consisted, beyond question, of a portion of the Caucasian race, and one closely allied to the Celts, who first populated the British isles. This is the people who have received in the land of their migration the appellation of *Hindus*.

They possess records, written like the Jewish Scriptures, after their departure from their first abode, but doubtless compiled from traditions and rites previously received. The earliest of these records are the *Vedas*, believed to have been reduced to their present arrangement in the fourteenth century before the Christian era. The Hindus had been then for some time seated on the banks of the Ganges, and had already reduced to bondage a large proportion of the aboriginal races.* From three to five hundred years later† the *Institutes of Menu* exhibit a regular system of religion and government, observed, or more probably such as its compilers desired to see observed, throughout the Hindu settlements. The *Puranas* were compiled at a much later date, when extensive changes had been effected in the religion of the Vedas. They consist of a number of poems and religious writings of uncertain antiquity, but supposed to have been collected into their present form between the eighth and the sixteenth centuries after Christ.

These works, denominated in general the Dharma Shastras, or Divine Scriptures, are written in Sanscrit, which has long been a dead language, though doubtless the vernacular of the Hindus at the respective periods of their compilation.

The Vedas are always referred to as the highest and most sacred of the Shastras. It is not merely inspiration which is claimed for them; for revelation, it is said, though proceeding from the Divine mind in perfection, must be clouded in its passage through a human medium. To obviate this consequence, the Vedas are supposed to have been revealed to *Rishis*, or saints, exempt from human infirmities, and so capable of infallibly apprehending infallible truth.

* One of the statements in these sacred writings is, that *Indra* (the god of the air or firmament), after destroying the indigenous barbarians, bestowed the fields on his *white-complexioned* friends.

† Sir William Jones dates the compilation at three hundred years after the Vedas; Elphinstone, about half way between the Vedas and Alexander's invasion, that is, in the ninth century B.C. (vol. i. p. 430).

Others go so far as to assert that these depositories of primitive truth proceeded bodily out of the mouth of Brahma, and are in their very substance a portion of the Divine essence.

With all this exaggerated reverence, the Vedas are very little known to the most learned of the Hindus, and wholly secluded from the mass of the people. The dialect is so ancient as to be legible only to the best Sanscrit scholars; while manuscripts are so few and imperfect as to render it doubtful if an entire copy anywhere exists in Hindustan.

An edition is now being published in England by Dr. Max Muller, under the patronage of the East India Company, which will enable the descendants of the divine Rishis to study, beside their sacred rivers, the Shastras edited on the banks of the Isis. The portion now appearing is called the Rig Veda, the oldest of the number, or as some think the only authentic Veda; the others being either of doubtful authority, or compiled from its materials. Of this Veda the first book has been translated into English by Professor H. Wilson, and forms our best account of the religious and social institutions of the primitive Hindus.

The term Vedas includes two classes of compositions, entitled *Muntra* and *Brahmana*: the first being a collection of hymns and metrical prayers; and the latter a kind of commentary, supplying directions for the performance of the sacred rites in which the hymns are used, with illustrative remarks, explanations, and legends. This latter composition is considerably later in date than the *Muntra*, which alone is in fact the original Veda. The prayers and hymns are called *Suktas*, and the collection in which they appear

Sanhita: they are simple compositions, addressed to different divinities, each being ascribed to a *Rishi*, or inspired saint. No directions for use accompany the *Suktas;* and even their authors and the deities addressed are often supplied from subsequent sources. This portion of the Veda is beyond all question of very high antiquity, and some of the *Suktas*, as is evident from the style, are considerably older than others. The Brahmana is no less evidently long posterior in date, when a system of religious and social organization had been elaborated unknown to the primitive compositions. Later still are the treatises connected with and dependent on the Vedas, called *Vedangas*, *Sutras*, *Upanishad*, etc.

The Hindus ascribe the compilation of the Vedas to a period three thousand years before Christ, which, by the common computation of England, corresponds with the last days of Adam; or by the longer and more approved chronology, with the age of Noah.* Internal evidence assigns their arrangement to the fourteenth century before Christ, when the solstitial points agreed with those which are cited in the Vedas.

Like the poets of Greece and Rome, Hindu writers commemorate four ages of the world, which they call *Yugs;* each inferior to its predecessor in happiness, virtue, and power. The Yugs are denominated *Satya*, *Treta*, *Dwarpar*, and *Kali*, and are respectively stated

* According to the present chronology of the Hebrew Scriptures, the world was created B.C. 4004, and destroyed by the deluge B.C. 2349; but the Septuagint Bible exhibits a longer system, which the best authorities of the present day consider to be genuine. This system places the creation B.C. 5411, and the flood B.C. 3155, according to Dr. Hales; or 5441 and 3185, according to the yet more recent computation of Bishop Russell. See his "Connexion of Sacred and Profane History;" Preliminary Dissertation.

at the prodigious duration of 1,728,000, 1,296,000, 864,000 and 432,000 years. The last is the present age, and of its allotted term 4,950 years are already passed. During the first of these ages mankind are represented as universally virtuous, surviving for 100,000 years, and attaining to the stature of twenty-one cubits (thirty-seven feet). In the second, one third of the race were corrupt, and human life was reduced to 10,000 years. One half were depraved in the third, and then 1,000 years was the period of existence. The present is the bad age; when all men are corrupt, and human life is restricted to 100 years.*

If these numbers are to be taken for the *chronology* of the Hindus, nothing could appear less deserving of attention than the writings in which they occur; but they seem to belong to another system, and were perhaps designed as a sort of arithmetical allegory, expressing the *character*, rather than the *duration*, of the periods referred to. The descending ratios of 100,000, 10,000, 1,000, and 100, may indicate only the gradual shortening of human life since the creation of man; as the corresponding proportions of the virtuous and the vicious denote the spread of moral evil, till in the present age "there is none that doeth good, no, not one." On the same principle, the present age being assumed at 432,000 years, the others are found simply by multiplying that number by two, three, and four respectively. The number itself, it will be seen, is the tithe of the sum total of the four *Yugs*, which total is arrived at on a somewhat similar principle. The "divine year," being computed, like the prophetic, at "a year for a day"

* Mill. Book ii. c. 1.

(counting 360 days to the year), is equal to 360 ordinary years; and these multiplied by the perfect number 12,000, makes 4,320,000 years, the sum of the ages, and a *Kalpa*, or "day of Brahma," at the close of which the universe is to be destroyed, and created anew.

In like manner the prodigious stature of men in the first age, and the preternatural number of faces and arms assigned to them, may be meant to indicate moral and intellectual, rather than physical, qualities. At this day, in the puppet dramas of which the natives of all ranks are so fond, it is common to see a figure of a yard long and sumptuously robed, carried in a palanquin by bearers of five or six inches in height. The spectators do not on this account believe that rajas are really taller or stouter, but only in the metaphorical sense *greater* than the rest of mankind.

In confirmation of this view it may be observed that a patriarch, called Satyavrata, or Vaivaswata, is represented as prolonging his existence and his reign through the whole period of the Satya-Yug. This is adduced by Mr. Mill as an evidence of absurd inconsistency; but as the writer could hardly have forgotten that he had himself assigned 10,000 years as the longest limit of human life, the probability is that *Satya* stands for a succession of generations corresponding possibly with those of the antediluvian world. He is represented as escaping with his family from a universal deluge, which had destroyed the rest of mankind; and is the same with the seventh *Menu*, a name identified with Noah.*

* Harcourt's "Doctrine of the Deluge," Tod's "Rajasthan," Maurice's "Hindostan," etc. Col. Tod says, that all the oldest traditions "appear to

The Hindu religion, as exhibited in the early Shastras, was already far advanced on the road to idolatry. Their primary doctrine indeed, according to the Brahmins, is the unity of God. It is repeatedly declared, that there is in truth but one Deity, the Supreme Spirit, the Lord of the universe, and whose work is the universe. A Brahmin, learned in their contents, gave the following as their summary of the Divine character: "Perfect truth, perfect happiness, without equal, immortal, absolute unity; whom neither speech can describe, nor mind comprehend; all-pervading, all-transcending; delighted with his own boundless intelligence, not limited by time or space; without feet, moving swiftly; without hands, grasping all worlds; without eyes, all-surveying; without ears, all-hearing; without any intelligent guide, understanding all; without cause, the first of all causes; all-ruling, all-powerful; the Creator, the preserver, and the transformer of all things; such is the Great One." The *Gayatri*, which is considered the holiest verse in the Vedas, and much referred to in the highest duties of religion, is translated thus:—"Let us meditate the adorable delight of the Divine Ruler: may it guide our intellects."

The principle of Monotheism equally pervades the system denominated from Menu. Of all the duties of man it declares the principal to be, "to obtain from the sacred writings a true knowledge of the One Supreme Being." The Institutes acknowledge further a conscience of right and wrong, implanted

point to one spot, and to one individual, in the early history of mankind, when the Hindu and Greek approach a common focus, for there is little doubt that Adnath, Adismara, Osiris, Baghes, Bacchus, Menu, Menes, designate the patriarch of mankind, Noah."—Annals of Rajasthan, vol. i. p. 22.

by God in the human soul, and proclaim in solemn and appropriate terms a future judgment of good and bad. Perjury, now so common among all ranks of Hindus, is forbidden under the most awful penalties—"Marking well all the murders comprehended in the crime of perjury: declare thou the whole truth with precision."* "Headlong into utter darkness shall the impious wretch tumble into hell, who being interrogated on a judicial inquiry answers one question falsely." Homicide, adultery, theft, robbery, with other acts of violence and contumacy, are no less emphatically denounced.

It was doubtless some retention of the primitive faith and morals which imparted its superior character to Hindu civilization, and gave the people who possessed it an ascendency over the gross idolaters of the land they invaded. It is to be observed, however, that these and other similar statements, which have attracted the attention of Europeans, are derived from the later *philosophical* portions of the Vedas, and are little in harmony with the common faith and worship of the Hindus at any period of time.

The primitive *Suktas* in the first book of the Rig Veda, 121 in number, are all addressed to different deities; 37 to *Agni* the god of fire, 45 to *Indra* the god of the sky, 12 to the *Maruts*, or winds, 11 to the *Aswins* the children of the sun, 4 to the personified Dawn, 4 to the *Viswadevas* or collective deities, and the rest to inferior divinities. All these appear to be resolvable into three, and it is accordingly stated by the native commentator Yanka, that "there are in the Veda three gods, *Agni* on the earth; *Vayu*, or *Indra*, in the sky; and *Surya* (the sun) in heaven." But Professor

* Elphinstone's India, vol. i.

Wilson objects, with reason, to the further gloss, that "all the gods are but parts of one soul, subservient to the diversification of his praises through the immensity and variety of his attributes." These philosophical theories belong to a later period; it does not even appear from any passage hitherto examined in the original Suktas "that their authors entertained any belief in a Creator and Ruler of the universe."

Not less unknown to the true Veda is the well-known theory which represents the Deity (Brahm) as evolving the three personal manifestations of Brahma, Vishnu, and Siva (Creator, Preserver, and Destroyer.)

"The worship which the Suktas describe comprehends offerings, prayer, and praise; the former are chiefly oblations and libations—clarified butter poured on fire, and the expressed and fermented juice of the *Soma* plant, presented in ladles to the deities invoked, in what manner does not exactly appear, although it seems to have been sometimes sprinkled on the fire, sometimes on the ground, or rather on the *Kusa* or sacred grass, strewed on the floor; and in all cases the residue was drunk by the assistants. The ceremony takes place in the dwelling of the worshipper, in a chamber appropriated to the purpose and probably to the maintenance of a perpetual fire, although the frequent allusions to the occasional kindling of the sacred flame are rather at variance with this practice. There is no mention of any temple, or any reference to a public place of worship, and it is clear that the worship was entirely domestic. The worshipper, or *Yajamana*, does not appear to have taken of necessity any part personally in the ceremony, and there is a goodly array of officiating priests,—in some instances seven, in some sixteen—

by whom the different ceremonial rites are performed, and by whom the *Mantras*, or prayers, or hymns, are recited. That animal victims were offered on particular occasions may be inferred from brief and obscure allusions in the hymns of the first book, and it is inferrible from some passages, that human sacrifices were not unknown, although infrequent, and sometimes typical; but these are the exceptions, and the habitual offerings may be regarded as consisting of clarified butter and the juice of the *Soma* plant. The Sukta almost invariably combines the attributes of prayer and praise; the power, the vastness, the generosity, the goodness, and even the personal beauty of the deity addressed, are described in highly laudatory strains, and his past bounty or exploits rehearsed and glorified; in requital of which commendations, and of the libations or oblations which he is solicited to accept, and in approval of the rite in his honour, at which his presence is invoked, he is implored to bestow blessings on the person who has instituted the ceremony, and sometimes, but not so commonly, also, on the author or reciter of the prayer."

"The blessings prayed for are, for the most part, of a temporal and personal description—wealth, food, life, posterity, cattle, cows, and horses; protection against enemies, victory over them, and sometimes their destruction, particularly when they are represented as inimical to the celebration of religious rites, or in other words, people not professing the same religious faith. There are a few indications of a hope of immortality and of future happiness, but they are neither frequent, nor in general distinctly announced, although the immortality of the gods is recognised, and the possibility of its attainment by human beings exemplified in the case of the demigods, termed *Ribhus*, elevated for their piety to the rank of divinities. Protection against evil spirits (*Rakshasas*) is also requested, and in one or two passages *Yama*, and his office as ruler of the dead, are obscurely alluded to. There is little demand for moral benefactions, although in some few instances hatred of untruth and abhorrence of sin are expressed; a hope is uttered that the latter may be repented of, or expiated, and the gods are in one hymn solicited to extricate the worshipper from sin of every kind. The main objects of the prayer, however, are benefits of a more worldly and physical character; the tone in which these are requested indicates a quiet confidence in their being granted, as a return for the benefits which the gods are supposed to derive from the offerings made to them, in gratifying their bodily wants, and from the praises which impart to them enhanced energy and augmented power: there is nothing, however, which denotes any particular potency in the prayer or hymn, so as to compel the gods to comply with the desires of the worshipper; nothing of that enforced necessity which makes so conspicuous and characteristic a figure in the Hindu mythology of a later date, by which the performance of austerities for a continued period constrain the gods to grant the desired boon, although fraught with peril and even destruction to themselves."*

Such is the true character of primitive Hinduism. In still later times, posterior to Menu, it degenerated, partly by admixture with the aboriginal worship, partly by the speculations of Vedantic philosophy, and partly by the natural corruption of

* Rig Veda Sanhita. Introduction, by Professor Wilson.

human nature, into the prolific system of idolatry which has prevailed for many centuries. The scriptures of this later system are the *Puranas*, a collection of poems, composed at various and uncertain dates, and containing much that is inconsistent with the older Shastras and with themselves. Gods are here introduced unknown to the earlier system, dead men elevated to their companionship, and new sacrifices and ceremonies introduced. The land is covered with temples (some of them richly endowed), inhabited by a multiplicity of idols. By the roadside, and on the banks of rivers and lakes, smaller *Swamee* houses make their appearance. Upon every high hill, and under every green tree, the idolatrous emblem is set up; and even in the depths of the forest, an upright stone, with a patch of red paint, indicates a god. This worship is full of ceremonies, processions, pilgrimages, festivals, and penances. Arising in part from grafting the local idolatries of the earlier natives on the system of the Vedas, it is different in different localities; but the seed and germ of all the corruption was in the Vedas from the beginning.

The Vedas are quoted as teaching the transmigration of souls, to receive successive purgations in various states of existence, till the created spirit, which is regarded as an emanation, or piece of the substance, of the Deity, is again absorbed into his essence, and attains supreme bliss by losing individual existence. To anticipate in some degree this ultimate absorption, is the object and virtue of the intense meditation enjoined as the highest exercise of piety.

This doctrine, which was held also by the Druids of Britain and the priests of ancient Egypt, from whom it was acquired by Pythagoras, naturally produces an extravagant tenderness towards the inferior creatures, any one of which may hold the spirit of an ancestor undergoing its ordeal. But it is remarkable that no corresponding feeling towards mankind has usually accompanied its profession. On the contrary, its disciples have been distinguished for cold-blooded indifference to human suffering. Some of the most frightful tortures and massacres ever inflicted have been the remorseless work of men who would place a curtain before their mouth to avoid inhaling some minute insect, or hire beggars to become the pasture-ground of fleas.

The cruelty of the early Hindus is shown in the sanguinary penalties of the Menu code; as the immorality which attended their decline from religious truth, may be gathered from its awful catalogue of minutely classified crimes. Retaliation is the general rule of punishment, often extending to the loss or mutilation of the offending member. Death is a frequent penalty, for some offences inflicted by burning on iron plates and other inhuman tortures. "The punishments of the Hindus," as a lenient critic admits, "are partial and fanciful; for some crimes dreadfully cruel, for others, reprehensibly slight."*

Sympathy would appear to be an emotion only compatible with the true religion. There is no genuine compassion for man where the Image in which he was made is obscured or distorted. The ladies of Pagan Rome made it their amusement to look at gladiators gashing each other with bloody swords, and

* Sir William Jones's Preface to his translation of the Institutes of Menu.

could smile as they refused the signal for mercy, which the vanquished wretch implored with despairing eyes. Inhumanity in equal or greater degree, both in judicial and military proceedings, has at all times been conspicuous in the natives of India. Mild, docile, and even tender in domestic life, their history exhibits a tiger's nature under the surface, often leaping out into horrible atrocities, and seeming to be never sated with blood.

The Hindu character has been further affected from early antiquity by the institution, which is called by Europeans *caste*. This institution is recognised as of divine origin in the Brahmana and in the code of Menu, though it is still doubtful if it existed in the earlier period of the *Suktas*. It is called in Sanscrit *varna*, a word denoting colour, and possibly referred at first to the distinction between the Hindu invaders and the aboriginal races. The European name was given by the Portuguese, in whose language *casta* means a breed, which appears to be an accurate rendering of the native idea. The institution is related thus: "That the human race might be multiplied, Brahma caused the *Brahmins* to proceed from his mouth, the *Kshatriyas* from his arms, the *Vaishyas* from his thighs, and the *Sudras* from his feet. To the Brahmins he assigned the duty of reading the Vedas, of teaching men, and of sacrificing, of alluring others to sacrifice, of giving alms if they be rich, and if indigent of receiving gifts. To defend the people, to sacrifice, to give alms, to read the Vedas, to shun the allurements of sensual gratifications, are in a few words the duties of the *Kshatriyas*. To keep herds of cattle, to bestow largesses, to sacrifice, to read the Vedas, to carry on trade, to lend money at interest, and to cultivate land, are prescribed to the *Vaishyas*. One principal duty the Supreme Ruler assigned to the *Sudras*, namely, to serve the before-mentioned classes without depreciating their worth."

In this distribution of labour itself there is nothing very remarkable; many other nations are mentioned in ancient history as adopting a similar classification, and some such is inevitable when men begin to form themselves into society. Neither is it peculiar to the Hindus to illustrate the division of labour from the members of the human body. The well-known fable of the Belly and the Members is an instance in point; and a still closer resemblance to the language of the Vedas may be traced in St. Paul's description of the Body of Christ.* It might, indeed, almost be thought that some such allegory was present to the mind of the Hindu writer, in which the priest whose lips are to keep knowledge would naturally spring from the *head;* the class which is to bear the sword, from the *arm;* the mercantile and agricultural body, who are the strength of the community, from the *loins;* and the servile classes from the *feet* of the Creator. This might be at first only a figurative way of saying that "God hath set the members every one of them in the body (politic), as it hath pleased him."

The peculiar vice of the Hindu system lay in connecting this division of labour with a separate creation of each class; constituting each, in fact, a *distinct species*, and directly negativing the position, that "God hath made of one blood all men." Other nations, ancient and modern, have disregarded the claims of humanity in practice; the Hindus openly, and as a

* 1 Cor. xii. 12—30.

part of their religion, deny them. It is impious in their eyes to assert that all men are fellow-creatures; it is an offence before God to love their neighbours as themselves.

It will be observed, moreover, from the passage quoted from the Vedas, that the benefits of the Hindu religion are open only to three of the four classes. The lowest and most numerous is wholly excluded both from the sacrifices and the scriptures. It is not only that Sudras are condemned to unending servitude in this life; they are debarred from the hope of any improvement in their condition in another. A Brahmin may neither counsel nor instruct a Sudra; he must not read the Vedas in his presence, nor assist at his sacrifices. To teach him the mode of expiating sin, sinks the Brahmin himself to *Aswamvrita* (hell), while the Sudra who acquires the forbidden lore is to be put to death. This indiscriminate doom, passed on body and soul, supports the conjecture that the three higher castes represent the invading and dominant race, and that the fourth was invented for the mass of natives subjugated to their rule. The Sudra, it is observed, was at liberty to remove to any other country in quest of subsistence; but the higher castes, called regenerate and "twice-born," were on no account to quit the sacred soil in which they had planted their institutions.

The Brahmins are often erroneously regarded as constituting the Hindu *priesthood;* but the priestly office was so far from being esteemed their first and most distinctive privilege, that to the present day it is accounted one of the least honourable which a Brahmin can discharge. This caste was in fact analogous to the tribe of Levi under the Mosaic economy, but *without* the family of Aaron. It comprehended a variety of avocations much more closely connected with secular life than with any religious ministry. It was the learned order, supplying the nation with judges, lawyers, schoolmasters, physicians, astronomers, philosophers, and men of science in general.* The members of this class were, moreover, permitted to engage in the duties of the military, and the mercantile or agricultural castes at pleasure; and in later times, the service of the state, whether as soldiers or civilians, seems to have become their favourite employment.

With those writers who attribute all national decay to the influence of the priesthood, it has been the fashion to represent the Brahmin caste as the great impediment to political strength and progress under the Hindu system. But their influence was more probably productive of good in the early stages of society, when men are usually too much occupied in military and material pursuits to attend to the calls of learning, justice, or piety. It is the Brahmin whom we usually find in Hindu story, like the bishop or the monk in mediæval Europe, withstanding the injustice of the king, and, even with his low views of religious truth, greatly mitigating the barbarity of the age.

The political weakness of the Hindu system was much more probably due to the peculiarity of the military caste being divided from the agricultural. The natural and wiser course of other nations has

* See Dr. Russell's Connexion of Sacred and Profane History, book i. cap. 1. The right reverend author remarks, that "Moses, *in imitation of the Egyptians*, in whose wisdom he was early and deeply instructed, had thought proper to make the learned professions hereditary in the several families of Levi's descendants." A close connexion is known to have subsisted between the Egyptian and the primitive Hindu systems.

been to connect the rule and defence of the commonwealth with its property and possessions. Until the rise of manufactures and commerce has created a different kind of property, the public defence is usually assigned to the owners and cultivators of the soil. Thus, the Hebrews held their lands on condition of military service; every man of competent age being bound to bear arms in defence of his country.* It was the same in Rome and in England, where the yeomanry were especially relied upon of old for the infantry, which forms the principal strength of an army.† It is only when society has made considerable progress, and riches are invested in a variety of securities, that the defence of the community can be safely removed from the general patriotism to the professional charge of an army, regulated and paid by the public. The attempt of the Hindu system to create and maintain a military caste of divine right, apart from the bulk of the population, only deprived the latter of their proper interest in the government and defence of the state, while the Kshatriyas themselves, isolated from the general sympathy, would naturally come into collision with the Brahmins, and be worsted by their superior intelligence and popularity.

The distinctions of caste appear to have been unknown to the aboriginal races of India, and the absence of them is one of the notes of their descendants to the present day. It has been doubted, also, if they existed among the earliest Hindus, since they are not less foreign to Buddhism, which there is

* See the exemptions (proving the rule) in Deut. xx. 5, 8, and Deut. xxiv. 5.

† Lord Bacon's History of Henry VII.

reason to think was the religion of the first leaders of the immigration,* and continues to be the prevailing form in Nepaul and the south of Ceylon, as well as in Burma, Siam, and China. Caste is repudiated also by the religious orders of Gosayens and Yogies; even Brahmins renounce its observance on being admitted into those fraternities. Whenever introduced, it was designed, no doubt, as a wall of brass about the Brahminical creed, but time has innovated on the one no less than the other.

Notwithstanding the pretended difference of species, and the pains that were taken to prevent any mixture of the castes, children did not fail to be born from clandestine intercourse, who were denominated *Chandalas*, or *outcasts*. They were accounted not simply illegitimate, but unclean. Still their existence and numbers could not be ignored. The Sudras also did not everywhere accept the servile position assigned to their caste: persons of distinction, and even princes, are reckoned among them, belonging probably to indigenous tribes, which had embraced the Hindu worship, but refused to submit to its bondage.† There are still temples in India where the sacrifices are performed by Sudra priests, though they are held in great abhorrence by the Brahmins.

The higher castes also appear to have suffered from mutual collision. The Brahmins affirm that both the

* According to Colonel Tod, Bhooda, son of Indu (the moon), was the great progenitor of the Tartars, Chinese, and Hindus: he is said to be *son-in-law* to Vaivaswatoo, Menu, or Noah, and his religion prevailed till the schism of Krishna and the Sooryas (children of the sun and worshippers of Baal). The name of Bhooda, however, is applied to more than one person, and the founder of the present system of Bhoodism was Gaudama, who flourished at Benares in the sixth century B.C., and is regarded as the latest incarnation of Bhood.

† The Mahrattas are apparently such Sudras.

Kshatriyas and the Vaishyas are now extinct; and there is a story in one of the Puranas of their being destroyed by the Brahmins in some religious or civil war. The Rajpoots, indeed, at the present time lay claim to be Kshatriyas, and some mercantile classes boast the appellation of Vaishyas. Still the Brahmins refuse the use of the Vedas to either, maintaining the assertion that their own is the only one of the four divinely instituted castes now extant.

Among Brahmins themselves, too, sects and divisions have grown up, refusing to eat with one another; and their general mode of life is altogether changed from that prescribed in the Shastras. The Brahmin's life is there divided out, like the world, into four ages. During the first, he was to study the Vedas and the ritual under a spiritual guide; in the second, marry and become a householder, employing himself in teaching the Vedas, sacrificing, and receiving or bestowing alms. The flesh of the sacrifices, even beef, is expressly appointed as his food. "When his muscles become flaccid, his hair grey, and he sees his child's child," he was to retire into the forest, and practise the severest austerities. In old age he was released from all forms and ceremonies of religion, and, devoting his remaining days to meditation and abstinence, was to become an anchorite in the house of his son till his removal by death. Such are the injunctions of the Vedas; but these rules are now universally disregarded. Very few of the Brahmin caste understand Sanscrit or read the Vedas; only a small proportion execute the priest's office. The great majority lead a purely secular life, engage in the service of Government, become soldiers, merchants, moneylenders, and agriculturists; in short, employ themselves in the proper duties of the two extinct castes, to the neglect of their own, but without surrendering any of their hyper-priestly claims to the deference of mankind.

In the room of the lower castes, a vast number of mixed and impure classes have grown up, usurping the name of caste. Most of these are really only trades or occupations, which the genius of Hindu institutions renders hereditary, and indolence and superstition combine to make immutable. There is a caste of sweepers, and another for thieves.

All these, without a shadow of support from the authoritative standards of the Hindu creed, are guarded with a jealousy unknown to the Vedas. Their members neither eat together, nor intermarry, nor partake of common rites, making up for the want of legitimacy by an increased rigour of ceremonial. Nevertheless it is observed that the requisitions of caste are, from the nature of the case, variable with the opportunities of gratifying them. Where high-caste men (real or pretended) congregate in numbers, and are deferred to by others, their pretensions become domineering and exacting; but in circumstances where they would encounter only contempt or persecution, the wily Brahmin finds a way to satisfy his scruples without endangering his position or emoluments.*

An institution only second to caste in its influence

* The Shastras expressly prohibit the "twice-born" castes from crossing the Indus, yet the Bengal Sepoys passed the forbidden boundary without a murmur in the expedition into Affghanistan, A.D. 1838. Again, there can be no doubt that the strict requisitions of caste are daily violated in the native's intercourse with his European superiors; but it is only occasionally that self-interest allows him to exhibit the feeling.

upon Hindu society was the *village municipality*. The cultivation of the land—by European chivalry deemed ignoble—was, by the laws of Menu, assigned to one of the higher or regenerate castes. It was undertaken, however, neither by individual proprietors nor peasants, but in a sort of partnership which has not been improperly termed a municipality. The agricultural population at the present day is found located, not in farmhouses and cottages, but in closely built villages, mostly enclosed within a wall.* The lands of the township belonging to each of these villages were defined by a belt embracing the whole, divided into as many parts (usually twelve) as there were public functionaries in the village. The latter consisted in general of a headman, accountant, Brahmin priest, astrologer, watchman, money-changer and silversmith, barber and surgeon, smith, carpenter, potter, washerman, tailor, etc. The priest or the astrologer was also the schoolmaster. Where a running stream, or channel for irrigation existed, there was an officer to regulate the distribution of water; a minstrel or genealogist was sometimes included. Each of these officers enjoyed a portion of the boundary land in freehold; the rest was cultivated on the common account; the crops, after discharging the government assessment, being shared by the villagers in definite proportions. The separate freeholds, with some additional advantage in the partition, constituted the retaining fee, by which a family was secured for each of the requisite vocations. The headman was a

* The same appears to have been the custom of the Israelites in Canaan, whence "the gate of the city," where the people passed out to their labours in the fields, was the place of concourse, and for that reason the seat of justice, as the *forum*, or market-place, was to the citizens of Rome.

sort of magistrate, who is still recognised by the government as the representative of the community in fixing and collecting the revenue assignment. The accountant (also recognised as a government officer) was bound to keep accounts for their inspection.

The effect of this institution, supposed to be anciently universal, was to divide the population into a number of republican municipalities, wholly irrespective of the state government. Land not settled was held to belong to the crown, but once reduced into a township, the right of the sovereign merged into a fixed claim on the produce. By these arrangements the agricultural classes were completely separated from the politics of the realm. The village was, in fact, their "father land." Neighbouring villages were like neighbouring states, and the relations of each to the raja more that of tributaries than subjects. The lands were strictly entailed, with no power in the individual to alienate his share by will or otherwise. The village senate levied the necessary rates for the pagoda, the sacrifices, the walls, the feasts and the charities; and the community, happy in its own little self-governed sphere, had little to desire from the sovereign but military protection and non-interference.

This system, together with the distinctions of caste, have lent an extraordinary vitality and permanency to the private life and popular customs of the Hindu race, but they were fatal to national development and unity, and left the country at all times an easy prey to foreign invasion.

CHAPTER III.

THE HINDUS.

Early government—Solar and Lunar kings—Rama—Ayodhya—Native princes—The great war—Krishna—Chandragupta—Darius—Alexander the Great—Porus—Halt of the Macedonian army—Return of expedition—Descent of the Indus—Condition of Hindus—Character—Civilization—Slavery—Truthfulness.

THE Hindus, from the earliest period of which we have any account, were distributed into a number of independent states. They entered India, probably, as the Celts and Gauls entered Europe, under different leaders and in successive waves of immigration. Possessing common institutions, civil and religious, they were destitute of that central unity which was so strongly impressed on the tribes of Israel. Their states were often confederated for a time under one paramount chief, but never compacted into a permanent monarchy. At every glimpse which the Shastras afford of the primitive polity, we see a number of separate communities ruled by independent and often hostile rajas. The form of government was always despotic; the prince being held in check, however, first by the Brahmins, as the divinely authorized expounders of the Shastras, which supplied the sole rule for every transaction public and private; and, secondly by "custom," a law among all classes of Hindus scarcely less binding, and generally much better understood, than the Vedas. The earliest recorded settlement was planted in a tract situated between "two waters" or rivers, about 100 miles to the north-west of Delhi, and called, from the sanctity of the locality, *Brahmaverta*. The next that is mentioned is *Brahmarshi*, extending towards the Jumna, and including North Behar: in the centre of this latter district the Hindu history commences.

Two royal lines here descended from Satyavrata, Menu, or Noah, the one called *Sooriya*, children of the sun; the other, *Chandra*, children of the moon: the genealogies of each are given in the Puranas, but with many discrepancies.* The Solar dynasty reigned at Ayodhya in Oude; the Lunar at Pratishthana, or Pruyag, situate between the Ganges and the Jumna, and supposed to be the modern Allahabad. These two parallel dynasties are represented as flourishing through the whole of the second and third yugas, together with the first thousand years of the present age. After a succession of mythical or doubtful personages, perhaps about the twelfth or thirteenth century B.C., the throne of Ayodhya was occupied by Dasaratha, whose son, Ram or Ramchundra, is the hero of the oldest Hindu epic, the *Ramayana*. This prince was married to Seeta, daughter of the rajah of *Mithili*, also of the Sooriya race; but his bride having been forcibly abducted by the sovereign of Singul Dwip (or Ceylon), Rama led an army into that island, punished the robber, and recovered his wife without injury.

Such appear to be the historical facts upon which the poet has embroidered his embellishments. Ravana,

* Sir W. Jones framed a list from the *Bhagavat*. Another was collated by Captain Nilford, with the Vishnu and other Puranas; and Colonel Tod has published a third, compiled by a body of learned pundits—all differing.

the offending raja, is represented as prince of the Rakshas, or evil genii, who had obtained the supremacy over the good spirits. Vishnu is invoked by the other gods to become incarnate for his subjugation. The god, who is described as riding on an eagle, dazzling like the sun, assents and Rama is born. He is assisted in his expedition by an army of monkeys led by Hanuman, an incarnation of one of the gods, who tear up the mountains, and construct a causeway from the peninsula to Ceylon. After the recovery of Seeta, Brahma appears to bless their re-union, and Rama finally "ascends to heaven" *by means of suicide*, and is "reunited to the divinity." This is accounted the seventh incarnation of Vishnu.

Valmiki, the author of this poem, is said to have lived in the age which he describes—a point perhaps not sufficiently established; but as he is allowed to be of great antiquity, much value attaches to his work as a testimony to the social condition of the Hindus at a very early period. Ayodhya is described as a city founded by Menu himself; "its streets, well arranged, were refreshed with ceaseless streams of water; its halls, curiously ornamented, resembled the chequered surface of a chess-board. It was filled with merchants, dramatists, elephants, horses, and chariots. The clouds of fragrant incense darkened the sun at noonday; but the *glowing radiance of the resplendent diamonds and jewels that adorned the persons of the ladies relieved the gloom.* The city was decorated with precious stones; filled with riches; furnished with abundance of provisions; adorned with magnificent temples, whose towers, like the gods, dwelt in the heavens—such was their height; palaces whose lofty summits were in perpetual conflict with the clouds; baths, and gardens. It was inhabited by the twice-born, the regenerate, profoundly instructed in the Vedas, endowed with every good quality, full of sincerity, zeal, and compassion."*

Another passage in this poem describes the father of Rama as inviting other princes to assist at an *Asswamedha*, or solemn sacrifice of a horse. The persons enumerated are the rajas of Kasi (Benares), Magadha (Behar), Sindu (Sindh), Surahstra (Surat), Unga (conjectured to be Ava), Savira (supposed to be a district on the Persian frontier), and the princes of the south.† From various notices contained in this poem, the Deccan, and other countries passed through by Rama in his expedition, would appear to have been in a much lower state of civilization than the Hindu kingdoms on the Ganges.

The next passage in Hindu history is that which forms the subject of the second famous epic, the *Maha Bharat*, or Great War. This describes a contest between two branches of the Chandra dynasty for the sovereignty of a territory on the Ganges, north-east of Delhi, still bearing its ancient name of Hastinapoora. Princes are enumerated, as taking part in the struggle, from the Deccan and the Indus, and even beyond the Indus, especially the *Yavans*, thought to be *Greeks*.‡ Fifty-six royal leaders are assembled on the field of battle, which raged for eighteen days with prodigious slaughter;—another proof of the division of India into many separate states, though occasionally combined, as in this poem, under the leadership of some great general on either

* The Land of the Veda. By the Rev. Peter Percival, p. 77.

† Heeren's Historical Researches.

‡ Yavan, the seventh from Japhet, was the parent of the Ionians.

side. The contest was waged between the sons of Pandu, the deceased raja, and their cousins the Kooroos, who denied their legitimacy, a never-failing subject of dispute in Hindu successions. It ended in the victory of the Pandus; but what they gained by arms, they lost through gaming. Yudisthira, the Agamemnon of the poem, departs with his brothers and the beautiful Draupadi into exile on the Himalayas. Their evil deeds prevailing, they drop dead, one after another, by the wayside. Yudisthira is the last, and when Indra comes to admit him to *Swarga* (Paradise), he demands to be accompanied by his faithful dog. The poem follows the hero into the other world; where, arrived in Indra's paradise and finding his enemies there before him, with none of his own party, he refuses to stay; and descending to the shades in quest of Draupadi and his brothers, succeeds in rescuing them from torment. The gods applaud his virtue, and he is permitted to convey them with himself to *Swarga*.

The hero of this poem is Krishna, the great ally of the Pandus, and generally regarded as the eighth incarnation of Vishnu. Krishna, however, is considered by many not so much an incarnation, as the very person of Vishnu in human form; from which it might be thought that this is the only proper *incarnation* believed in by the Hindus;—the others being rather men endowed with some divine power, but in fact distinct persons from the divinity. In a portion of the Maha Bharat, Krishna is described as a child conveyed away by a herdsman from the tyrant who sought to slay him, and brought up among peasants in the country. This is the most favourite period in the story of the god. He is worshipped both as an infant and as a beautiful youth, dancing among the rustics, and captivating at once milkmaids and princesses by his pipe.* Rama and Krishna are the two divinities most popular in India to this day. They were doubtless real personages—deified after death, and then confounded with the Divine Being. The "Great War" is commonly dated about two hundred years before the siege of Troy.

All that can be further gathered of the Sooriya and Chandra dynasties is, that both became extinct at the expiration of a thousand years of the kali yuga. At the same time failed a contemporary dynasty, founded in Magadha at the commencement of the present age; and the throne of that country, after an uncertain period of usurpation, was mounted by Chandragupta, said to be placed on it by a Brahmin, who murdered his predecessor. The name of Chandragupta signifies "protected by the moon." He is called a *Mauriya* and a *Sudra*, indicating, probably, a difference both of race and religion, from the authors of the Puranas. With this raja we emerge from the realms of poetry and conjecture into the light of history. Chandragupta is identified with the Sandracottus of Greek history, and was therefore a contemporary with Alexander the Great, and Seleucus his successor. Some invasions of the Persians, and possibly of other nations, had taken

* The legend of Krishna, though bearing in some leading points an oblique resemblance to the TRUE INCARNATION, is disfigured by abominations too awful to be more than alluded to in these pages. The figures carved upon the cars on which his idol is borne, are described by Dr. Buchanan as the most indecent he had ever seen; and Dr. Allen declares that if offered for sale, as statues or pictures, they would subject the exhibitor or seller to severe but merited punishment in any civilized country; yet more than half the natives of Bengal are worshippers of this god.

place before this time through the passes of the north-west. Darius Hystaspes numbered among his extensive possessions an Indian satrapy, which, though said to be the most valuable of the twenty that paid tribute to his crown, probably did not extend beyond the Punjâb.

Alexander the Great, having conquered the Persians, was fired with the ambition of extending his arms also into India. He crossed the Indus at Attock, as Arrian supposes on a bridge of boats, with an army of one hundred and twenty thousand foot and fifteen thousand horse, and was gladly received by the native prince of Taxila, a city between the Indus and the Jhelum. This prince, called Taxiles from the name of his capital, came out to meet the conqueror with his army and elephants, and conducted him with much pomp into the city, where he was welcomed by embassies from other states. The site of this city has not been verified, but the ruins of an ancient town are yet seen on the route from Attock to Lahore, and near them abundance of Greek and Bactrian coins have been found. A tumulus in the neighbourhood, examined in 1834 by M. Court, a French officer in the service of Runjeet Singh, was surrounded by pillars having their capitals ornamented with *rams' heads*, a favourite emblem of Alexander's. It appeared also that the Hindus used to resort to this tumulus, to offer the first cuttings of the hair of their sons, thus unconsciously perpetuating a rite of classic paganism, and proving the facility with which one sort of idolatry always fraternizes with another.

Taxiles was at feud with a more powerful raja, whom the Greek authors call Porus, supposed to be a corruption of Pooru, the patronymic of one of the

Chandra, or Lunar families. Colonel Tod supposes him to have reigned at Canouj on the Ganges. This prince was now encamped on the eastern bank of the Jhelum, determined to resist alike the native and the foreign enemy. His army consisted of four thousand horse, three hundred chariots, two hundred elephants, and near thirty thousand foot. Alexander, on receiving intelligence of his intentions, marched to meet him, attended by Taxiles, at the head of five thousand native troops. Crossing the river by stratagem, in spite of the precautions of Porus, Alexander attacked the Indians with his cavalry and six thousand infantry; and after some fighting, the elephants becoming wounded and ungovernable, the vast host was completely routed with a loss of twelve thousand killed and nine thousand taken prisoners.* Porus himself, wearing a coat of mail of great strength and beauty, fought bravely till he was taken captive; and his gallant bearing so attracted the esteem of his conqueror, that he was restored to his kingdom, and after being reconciled with Taxiles became a faithful ally of the European invader.

Alexander next pushed forward with a portion of his army through a most populous country† to the Chenab, then called *Chandrabagha* (or Moon's Gift), but by the Greeks denominated *Acesines*. Here he received the submission of another Porus and a prince called Abissares, with a present of money and forty elephants.

After crossing the Ravee, he advanced to Sangala,

* Diodorus Siculus. Arrian gives the killed at little less than twenty thousand foot and three thousand horse, adding that all the elephants were either killed or taken, and the chariots hacked to pieces. Lib. v. 18. He rates the total loss of Alexander at four hundred and ten.

† It contained thirty-seven cities, the least of which had five thousand inhabitants, and many above ten thousand, with a vast number of large villages. Arrian, v. 19.

either the same with Lahore, or not far from its site, and defeated the Cathæans, which some suppose to be a corruption of *Kshatriya*, the military caste. Exasperated by their resistance, Alexander put seventeen thousand to death, made seventy thousand prisoners, and razed their capital to the ground, giving the country to some free Indians who had voluntarily submitted.

At the Beas, just above its junction with the Sutlej, the conqueror's march was arrested by the refusal of his troops to proceed any further. In vain their leader exhorted them to cross the river, descend the Ganges, and sail round Africa to the Pillars of Hercules.* That triumphant progress was reserved indeed for European soldiers, but for Europeans of whom Alexander could have barely heard, as a rude nation of painted savages, wandering in the isles of the northern Atlantic. The ambition of Alexander was inflamed by accounts of a great monarchy on the Ganges, whose king could bring into the field two hundred thousand foot and twenty thousand horse, with thousands of elephants. He called loudly for volunteers to accompany him, exclaiming that the rest might return to Macedon, and say that they had forsaken their king in the midst of his enemies. But all was in vain; he was obliged to retrace his steps; and, after embarking a part of his army on the Jhelum, he proceeded with the remainder and the elephants along the eastern bank to its confluence with the Chenab. Before he embarked he constituted Porus king over all his conquests in India, including seven nations, with above two thousand cities; and then determined to descend the Indus, which he had persuaded himself was the

* Arrian, lib. v. cap. 25.

same river with the Nile, because he had observed crocodiles in both, and beans grew on the Chenab similar to those of Egypt.

From the confluence of the rivers he made an expedition to the west against the *Seevi*, apparently so called from their worship of Siva, whose emblem was branded on their cattle; and another to the eastward, on the Sudracæ, or some of the Sudra caste. The latter were reinforced by the Malli, who seem to have been Brahmins; and upon these the conqueror wreaked his first deadly vengeance. Pursuing them into the desert, he stormed their strongholds, and massacred the inhabitants without distinction. At the capital (thought to be Mooltan) Alexander was himself in no little danger. The besieged having retreated into their citadel, the monarch impatiently mounted the first ladder that was brought, and leaped into the place. He was followed by only three companions, one of whom instantly fell, pierced by an arrow. Alexander and both the others were also wounded; and when the soldiers, mounting by pegs driven into the mud walls, or bursting open the gates, at last poured in, their leader lay senseless on his shield. His life was long in doubt, but rallying, at length he received the submission of the Malli, whose envoys are described as men of lofty stature, riding in chariots, and robed in linen embroidered with purple and gold.

Regaining the Indus, and leaving a colony at its junction with the Chenab, the conqueror advanced along the river through Sindh, planted garrisons in several towns, and finally reached the ocean after many disasters to the shipping. The navigation employed nine months. Nearly four were spent in or near *Pattala* (conjectured to be Tatra or Allore), where he contemplated the formation of docks, harbour and citadel for a great settlement.

In August, B.C. 325, the expedition quitted India. The fleet, under Nearchus the Cretan, proceeded on a voyage of discovery to the Persian Gulf; while Alexander himself, at the head of the land forces, undertook the prodigious exploit of returning by the coast, through Beloochistan. Struggling through the natural difficulties of the road, the extreme heat, and the hostility of tribes who fought desperately with poisoned arrows, the army reached at last the mouth of the Persian Gulf, and was joined by the fleet near the island of Ormuz. From thence the expedition proceeded to Susa, where its two parts were again united. In the second year after, Alexander terminated his life at the early age of thirty-two;—"the solace of his last days being to hear Nearchus relate the story of his voyage, and all that was most observable with respect to the ocean."*

The expedition of Alexander afforded the first opportunity for European observation on the condition of India and its natives. Arrian has carefully collected the statements of Nearchus and Megasthenes, who had visited the court of Chandragupta, and the result is to confirm the testimony of the Hindu writings as to their numbers, religion, and civilization. No less than one hundred and twenty-two several nations are mentioned by Megasthenes, whose cities were too numerous to be easily reckoned. Palimbothra, situated at the confluence of the Ganges and Erannoboas, was defended by a ditch enclosing six acres of ground, having walls with five hundred and seventy towers, and sixty-four gates. The Erannoboas is described as the third river

* Plutarch's Life of Alexander.

in India, inferior only to the Ganges and the Indus. This seems to point at the Jumna and the ancient fortress of Allahabad; but some authors make the modern Patna to be the city alluded to.

The Hindus are described by the Greeks as tall, slender, well proportioned, and lighter than other nations; riding on camels, horses, and asses, the richer sort only mounted on elephants, and honoured with an umbrella. The population was divided into seven classes; of which one appears to indicate the aboriginal races, and two others the public officers of high rank; the remaining four are the regular Hindu castes.* The prohibition of intermarriage, the hereditary character of trades, the vegetable diet, shoes with thick soles, and ear-rings in the men's ears, are noted. Their beards were dyed of different colours, and their garments were of surprising fineness and whiteness. The practice of burning the dead is also mentioned, with the voluntary incremation of widows. Their numbers and bravery were shown in their engagements with the invaders, in which the latter suffered far more severely than in Persia. Considerable progress had been made in the arts of civilized life. Agriculture occupied then, as it does now, a high rank in public estimation. The husbandman's employment was considered sacred; to root up or injure the young crops was a crime which no native prince would commit †

On the whole, the Greeks appear to have received a very favourable opinion of the Hindus. They are

* Arrian numbers them thus:—1. Sophists (or Brahmins). 2. Husbandmen (or Vaisyas). 3. Shepherds, living on hills and hunting game; the exact description of some of the aboriginal tribes at this day. 4. Artificers and tradesmen (Sudras). 5. Soldiers (Kshatriyas). 6. The revenue officers; and 7. The ministers of state.

† Orders to the same effect were given by Sivajee, the modern reviver of Hindu power in the Deccan.

described as sober, moderate, peaceful, *singularly truthful*, averse to slavery in any form, and ardently attached to liberal institutions. Some portions of this picture may, undoubtedly, be suspected of too high a colouring. On the other hand, Mr. Mill has laboured with perverse ingenuity to reduce the Hindu character and civilization almost to the level of barbarism. On his reflections Professor Wilson passes the following judicious strictures:—"It may be admitted that the Hindus were not a civilized people, according to Mr. Mill's standard; but what that standard is he has not fully defined. Civilization is used by him, however, as a relative term; and in this sense we may readily grant that the Hindus never attained the advance made by modern Europe. It is not just to institute such a comparison; for, to say nothing of the advantages we possess in a pure system of religious belief, we cannot leave out of consideration the agency of time. The Hindus, by the character of their institutions, and by the depressing influence of foreign subjugation, are apparently what they were at least three centuries before the Christian era; years have done nothing for them, everything for us. We must therefore, in fairness, compare them with their contemporaries, with the people of antiquity, and we shall then have reason to believe that they occupied a very foremost station amongst the nations. They had a religion less disgraced by idolatrous worship than most of those which prevailed in early times. They had a government which, although despotic, was equally restricted by law, by institutions, and religion. They had a code of laws, in many respects wise and rational, and adapted to a great variety of relations, which could not have existed except in an advanced condition of social organization. They had a copious and cultivated language, and an extensive and diversified literature; they had made great progress in the mathematical sciences; they speculated profoundly on the mysteries of man and nature; and they had acquired remarkable proficiency in many of the ornamental and useful arts of life. Whatever defects may be justly imputed to their religion, their government, their laws, their literature, their sciences, their arts, as contrasted with the same proofs of civilization in modern Europe, it will not be disputed by any impartial and candid critic, that, as far as we have the means of instituting a comparison, the Hindus were, in all these respects, quite as civilized as the most civilized nations of the ancient world, and in as early times as any of which records or traditions remain."*

These remarks are sustained by general agreement among the best writers. Descending to particulars, it may be observed that the aversion to slavery, ascribed to the Hindus by the Greeks, must be understood as limited to the fighting and agricultural castes with whom they came in contact, or else as referring to political and personal slavery. Serfdom, or prædial bondage, was certainly the condition of large classes of the earlier natives.† With respect to the "singular truthfulness" of the ancient Hindus, it is certain that truth is highly commended in the Vedas and Institutes of Menu, and not less so that a total disregard of its sanctions has long been among the

* Mill's History, by Wilson, vol. ii. pp. 232-3.

† General Briggs accounts it one of the certain proofs of the "Iranian" descent of the Hindus, that "they invariably reduced the enemies they subdued to the condition of agrestic, not domestic, slavery."—*India and Europe Compared*, p. 4.

most prominent traits of Hindu character. Nothing in subsequent history is more common than breach of truth, though plighted with the most binding solemnities. No oath has ever been devised sacred enough to deter the natives of India from perjury. To violate a capitulation seems to be thought almost a lawful stratagem in war, and in the intercourse of business a lie is the rule and truth the exception. All classes, in short, of Hindus, from the raja to the peasant, appear to have anticipated the jest of a modern diplomatist, that the gift of language was designed to *conceal* the sentiments of mankind. It must be concluded that either the Greeks formed a too favourable estimate from the few instances falling under their own observation; or that the Hindu character has degenerated in truthfulness during the two thousand years in which it has been subjected to the double yoke of idolatry and foreign domination.

In the division of the Macedonian empire, which followed Alexander's death, Seleucus obtained Bactria (between Balkh and the Punjab) and with it Alexander's claims upon India. He renewed the invasion, and fought a great battle with Chandragupta, who then governed a large part of central and northern India. A treaty of peace was afterwards concluded between the kings, and strengthened by a matrimonial connexion. The capital of Chandragupta's realm was Palibothra, from which a royal road extended to the Indus and another to Baroach, in Guzerat.

This kingdom continued for eight centuries till about A.D. 450, in which period the country is described as prosperous and happy; commerce, arts, literature, and husbandry flourished; the Sanscrit attained its perfection, and literature was patronized at court. The last sovereign of the Magadha kingdom was of the Buddhist religion, which may possibly have been the faith of Chandragupta and of all the Lunar line. Some of the large Buddhist cave temples were constructed at this time. The Brahminical system, which is closely connected with the worship of the sun (and possibly, therefore, with the Sooriya dynasties), succeeded in expelling the Buddhists; and it was, perhaps, during these religious wars that the kingdom of Magadha was overthrown. Possibly also this is the era of the later idolatrous system which supplanted the religion of the Vedas, and was destined, ere long, to feel the sword of a much sterner form of Monotheism.

Other kingdoms mentioned in the Puranas are Pandya,* whose capital was at Madura, in the southern extremity of the peninsula, probably as early as B.C. 500; and Chola, which, about the time of the Christian era, included the whole of the Tamul country. Vicramaditya reigned in Malwa B.C. 56, and established his era over the whole of Hindustan. Chera, including Travancore, with part of Malabar and Coimbatore, lasted for about a thousand years from the Christian era. A colony of Brahmins from Hindustan was planted at Kerala, on the coast of Malabar and Canara, in the first or second century after Christ; but beyond these scattered notices and the conjectures founded on existing institutions and literature, the history of the Deccan is wrapped in darkness. The same obscurity envelopes the rest of India, from the cessation of Greek history to the commencement of the Mohammedan.

* A confused story is related in Arrian's history of India, from the earlier Greek writers, of one *Pandæa*, the daughter of Hercules, to whom her father gave all the kingdom of the south, with a great treasure of *pearls*.

CHAPTER IV.

AFFGHAN DYNASTIES.

Islam—Koran—Mussulman rites, faith, and morals—Rise and progress—Invasions of India—Sindh—Ferocious spirit of the war—Death of Kausim—Expulsion of the invaders—Mahmoud of Ghizni—Somnath—Death of Mahmoud—Character—New inroad of Affghans—First Mohammedan kingdom—Mussulman dominion—Hindu submission—System of government—Law of the Prophet—Provincial governors—Revolutions—Forcible conversion — Civilization — Kuttub-Minar — Slave emperors — Sultana Reza—Second Patan dynasty—Arbitrary power—Cruelty of natives—Incursions into the Deccan—Third Dynasty—Mohammed III.—Expulsion from Deccan — Bengal — Bahmanee kings — Feroze Toghluk — Public works—"Firebrand of the universe."

THE Mohammedan religion, by its disciples called Islam,* dates itself from the Hegira, or flight of the prophet from Mecca A.D. 622. Its one authentic standard is the Koran,† which presents a corruption of the Mosaic revelation, as the Vedas do of the patriarchal. The contents of this book are partly borrowed from the Old Testament Scriptures, adulterated by the puerile superstitions of the Babylonian Jews, and partly from the wild legends of the Arabian desert. Mohammed, who was an illiterate man, is supposed to have been aided in its compilation by Sergius, a Nestorian monk. Other Christian heretics have been also named as his assistants; but beyond recognising "Jesus the son of man" as the highest

* That is, "Salvation," much as "the Gospel," is used to designate Christianity. *Mussulman* or *Moslem*, more properly *Musliman* or *Muslim*, signifies a "believer in Islam."

† Or Scripture: *Alcoran* is the same word, with the definite article prefixed.

of prophets, there is little in the Koran to connect it with any form of Christianity. The Jews, who were numerous in Arabia, have a tradition that it was composed by twelve of their doctors.*

The creed of Islam was summed up in the dogma which Mohammed pretended to see written by the throne of the Most High, and on the gates of the seven heavens;—"There is no god but God, and Mohammed is his prophet." Being composed after the dispersion of the Jews, and for the use of a different branch of the descendants of Abraham, the Koran recognized no priesthood, hereditary or official. It was itself the one source of knowledge, and every man who could read and understand the sacred text was authorized to expound it to others. The public worship consisted of prayers and preaching in mosques, open to Mussulmans without distinction of rank or class: the women only were restricted to the porches, and that upon social more than religious considerations. The prescribed ceremonies of Islam were circumcision, with frequent ablutions, fasting, and almsgiving. It effected a union, or rather identity, of Church and State. The magistrate was to enforce its universal reception by the sword, and the standard of the faith was also the sole code of civil and criminal law.

The most prominent feature of this religion, in respect to the Divine Being, was the assertion of a rigid Monotheism, though the God of the Koran is by no means so spiritual or so holy a being as the divinity, upon whom the educated Brahmin was taught to meditate in the Shastras. Among men, Islam was chiefly known by its intense hatred of all vestiges of

* Chamberlain's Dictionary, Art. "Mahometanism."

idolatry, and a fierce persecution of every other religion. In other respects it was both vicious and ignorant, licentious and superstitious, revelling in the prospect of a sensual paradise hereafter, and at the same time placing the affairs of this world in subjection to astrology and witchcraft.

Such a system was well suited to grow and extend itself in the countries where it first appeared. The barbarian always trembles before a message from the unseen world: and the scenery of the Koran was designed to fascinate the rude minds of the Arabian desert. The comparative simplicity of its doctrine and ritual would be a relief to spirits wearied by a round of dark and brutish superstitions. The sinner's True Refuge had been well nigh lost to view in the heresies and dissensions of the Eastern church; so that when backed by the enthusiastic arms of warlike proselytes, fighting for empire no less than religion, it is little wonder that the creed of Mohammed rapidly overspread Persia, Syria, Egypt, and the adjacent countries.

From the two sides of the Persian Gulf, a commerce had long been carried on with the opposite coasts of Western India. There was everything in this land to attract the ardour of Mussulman proselytism. India was now pre-eminently a land of idols. In the dark interval since the cessation of Greek intercourse, the whole pagoda system, as still extant, had come into operation; its festivals and processions were celebrated with a pomp which has been unknown since the Mohammedan subjugation. The Hindus were also rich, without political cohesion or military power, and greatly inferior to the Arabs in physical strength. Their women had been long esteemed beautiful. Slaves and booty, glory and piety, contributed in equal proportions to fire the lust and avarice, the ambition and the zeal, of the followers of the Arabian Prophet.

Their first appearance in India was about A.D. 664, when Mooltan was invaded from Kabul. At this time Sindh was a powerful kingdom, extending from Kandahar to the sea, and including the Punjab, Cutch, and Guzerat. The sandy desert, which now stretches on both sides of the Indus, was intersected by canals, rich with grain-fields, and dotted with towns and villages. The prevalent religion in this fruitful area appears to have been Buddhism, which was supplanted by a line of Brahmin monarchs, commencing with a usurper named *Chach*. The second of this line, Raja Daher, sustained several Arab incursions with success; but in the reign of the Caliph Walid (A.D. 711) a more determined attempt was made to plant the standard of the Prophet on the shores of India. An army of six thousand men was despatched from Bagdad under Mohammed Kausim, a youth of great beauty, who, though only seventeen years of age, had been designated to victory by the decree of the astrologers. The expedition landed at Debal, a seaport of Sindh*, near a fortified pagoda, which was captured, in spite of a desperate defence by the Brahmins and a strong garrison of Rajpoots. The defeated party were commanded to receive the Mussulman religion, but the Brahmins refusing the males above seventeen were put to the sword, and the women and children reduced to slavery.

Proceeding up the Indus, enriched with booty, the invader was encountered above Hyderabad by an army

* Supposed to be the modern Kurrachee.

of fifty thousand men, commanded by the raja in person. Though not a sixth of their number, the Mohammedans utterly routed this vast host, and the raja and his son were slain in the engagement. Still the spirit of the vanquished natives was far from being subdued. The city held out under one of the widowed queens, till the provisions were exhausted; and then ensued one of those scenes of unavailing courage and despair which not unfrequently illustrate the page of Hindu history. The women and children were first sacrificed in flames of their own kindling; the men performed their ablutions, and, with solemn ceremonies, took leave of one another and of the world. Then, throwing open the gates, they rushed out, sword in hand, and hurling themselves on the weapons of the enemy, perished to a man.*

The war was continued in the same ferocious spirit on both sides, till Sindh and the southern Punjab were reduced. The conditions of the Koran were uniformly enforced—acceptance of the Mussulman faith, or tribute to the utmost means of payment. Resistance was punished with instant death to the men, and their wives and families were carried away as slaves. Having laid a foundation in terror, Kausim succeeded by more moderate means in forming alliances with some of the native rulers, and was preparing greatly to enlarge his conquests, when the warrant for his own death arrived from the caliph.† Soon after a general insur-

* Elphinstone.

† The reason assigned for this decree affords a striking illustration of the spirit of the age, both Mussulman and Hindu. Kausim had sent the beautiful daughter of the raja to Bagdad, as the most acceptable present he could offer to the Commander of the Faithful. On being admitted to his presence the princess declared herself unworthy of the royal alliance, from having been dishonoured by the general in Sindh. Fired by the insult, the caliph instantly issued an order that Kausim should be sent to the presence

rection of the Hindus expelled the invaders, and recovered all that had been wrested from their possession.

The next invasion of Mohammedanism came from another quarter, and was prosecuted to more permanent results. About the year of our Lord 967, Subactajee, originally a Turkish slave, became governor, under the sovereign of Persia, of the province of Kandahar, the capital of which was Ghizni. He defeated the raja of Lahore in several engagements, and having annexed the whole of the Punjab to the Affghan dominions, left them to his son Mahmoud A.D. 997. The latter, asserting his independence of the Persian throne, became himself the most powerful monarch in Asia. A devout Mussulman, he aspired to the character of an apostle of his religion. In twelve successive expeditions into India, during a reign of thirty-five years, he carried fire and sword among the idolaters, dethroned and slew several princes, plundered and burned their cities, stormed the forts, massacred the garrisons, ravaged the fields, and carried away so many natives into captivity, that the price of a slave was reduced at Ghizni to a couple of rupees.

These incursions were resisted by a confederacy of the native powers, at the head of which are mentioned the rajas of Lahore, Oujein, Gwalior, Kalinga, Canouj, Delhi, and Ajmere. All classes were roused to self-defence: the women sold their jewels, melted down their ornaments, and hastened with contributions to the sacred cause. But the sultan (Mah-

sowed up in a bullock's hide. The mandate was received by the unhappy victim, who immediately gave directions for its literal execution. In this fantastic shroud he was carried for three days, before death released him from his sufferings. When the corpse arrived at Bagdad the tyrant showed it in triumph to the Hindu princess, who exultingly told him he had destroyed his best friend, that her accusation was false, but in its success she had avenged the wrongs of her father and her country.

moud was the first who bore that appellation) was uniformly victorious. His last expedition was directed against the temple of Somnath, situated on the promontory of Guzerat in the neighbourhood of Din, one of the three remaining possessions of the Portuguese, whom Ferishta calls the idolaters of Europe.

This *Pagoda*—to adopt the Portuguese designation generally received in Europe—was "endowed with the revenue of two thousand villages; two thousand Brahmins were consecrated to the service of the deity, whom they washed each morning and evening in water from the distant Ganges. The subordinate ministers consisted of three hundred musicians, three hundred barbers, and five hundred dancing girls, conspicuous for their birth or beauty. Three sides of the temple were protected by the ocean, the narrow isthmus was fortified by a natural or artificial precipice, and the city and the adjacent country were peopled by a nation of fanatics. They confessed the sins and the punishment of Canouj and Delhi; but if the impious stranger should presume to approach their holy precincts, he would surely be overwhelmed by a blast of the divine vengeance. By this challenge the faith of Mahmoud was animated to a personal trial of the strength of this Indian deity. Fifty thousand of his worshippers were pierced by the spear of the Moslems; the walls were scaled, the sanctuary was profaned, and the conqueror aimed a blow of his iron mace at the head of the idol. The trembling Brahmins are said to have offered ten millions sterling for his ransom; and it was urged by his wisest counsellors that the destruction of a stone image would not change the hearts of the Gentoos; and that such a sum might be dedicated to the relief of the true believers. "Your reasons," replied the sultan, "are specious and strong; but never, in the eyes of posterity, shall Mahmoud appear as a merchant of idols." He repeated his blows, and a treasure of pearls and rubies, concealed in the belly of the statue, explained in some degree the devout prodigality of the Brahmins. The fragments of the idol were distributed to Ghizni, Mecca, and Medina. Bagdad listened to the edifying tale, and Mahmoud was saluted by the caliph with the title of Guardian of the Fortune and Faith of Mohammed."*

Such is the graphic account of the historian; but truth compels the confession that it has but a scanty foundation in fact. *Nath* is the name of the *Linga*—a plain pillar, which is the type of Siva, supposed in this case to be erected by Soma, the moon. The earlier Mohammedan writers describe the idol as a straight, solid block of stone, three cubits long, without features of any kind. They relate that the stone was broken to pieces, but are silent on the proffer of a ransom and the treasure contained in the interior; in fact, the stone was not hollow.

Mahmoud died at Ghizni A.D. 1030, after enriching his capital with a vast amount of booty from India, as well as with magnificent buildings, imitated from Hindu architecture. A mosque, so beautiful as to be called the "Celestial Bride," attested his religious ardour, and a university filled with books and curiosities his love of learning.

By the Mohammedans the sultan is represented as the model of a brave, fortunate, and religious prince; to the Hindus he was the incarnation of avarice, injustice, and cruelty.† He died lamenting

* Decline and Fall, cap. lvii.

† The story often adduced as an instance of kingly magnanimity and justice exhibits (even if true) a terrible picture of the misery of a people

his inability to inflict upon them further injuries. A short time before his end he had the gold, jewels, and other spoil of which he had deprived them, brought out and arranged before him, weeping bitterly at the thought of seeing them no more. The next day he held a review of all his troops, elephants, camels, horses, and chariots, and having feasted his eyes for awhile on the "glorious pomp," again burst into tears, and retired in grief to his palace. There is little interest in following the details of his Indian expeditions, or those of his successors. In spite of their religious zeal, the main object was plunder, and little was really effected for the extension of the Mussulman faith or empire beyond the Punjab for a considerable period.

Ghizni was abandoned for Lahore as the capital of the Affghan empire in the early part of the twelfth century, but it was not till its close that Hindustan became the seat of a Mohammedan throne. In the interval civil war had desolated the capital of Mahmoud, and destroyed its stolen magnificence. The house of Ghor succeeded the Ghiznevides, and new incursions of Affghans, Arabs, Turks, and other

among whom such crimes were common, and their punishment so rare as to be recorded with admiration. A peasant, whose home and honour had been violently invaded by a Turk who had conceived a passion for his wife, invoked the justice of the king. Mahmoud proceeded in person to the house on the next visit of the adulterer, and with his own hand (after extinguishing the lamp) cut off his head in the dark. Then calling for a light, he examined the corpse, and thanked God it was *not* his nephew. He had suspected no one else would be so bold, and executed his purpose before he knew, lest justice might be biassed by affection.

"I am no heretic, O king," exclaimed another who was brought before this orthodox sultan, on a charge which usually involved confiscation, if not death; "but I confess that I am *rich*—can you not take my property without injuring my reputation?" The king heard the proposal with great *good humour*, took the bribe, and gave him a certificate under the royal signet of his perfect orthodoxy.

Tartars, were made across the Sutlej in quest of spoil, more than dominion.

They were resisted as before by confederacies of native princes, headed by the principal rajas: at one time no fewer than one hundred and fifty kings, with their forces, amounting to three hundred thousand horse, three thousand elephants, and a countless host of infantry, are said to have combined to arrest the progress of the invaders. But these vast armies are usually unmanageable; a sudden assault, conducted with vigour on some selected portion, throws the rest into confusion, and once disordered, the army becomes a mob, whose numbers only increase the carnage. Several provinces were in time overrun and annexed to the Affghan dominions; Delhi, Canouj, Benares, and Gwalior, were captured and plundered. The rajas of Ajmere and Guzerat suffered severely, and a military supremacy was at last established over Hindustan, as far as Bengal. The chief author of these conquests was Kuttub-ud-deen, another Turkish slave, who, after leading the Affghan armies to victory, was invested with the government of his conquests. The Affghan monarch dying in 1206, Kuttub declared himself independent, and assumed the royal title at Delhi.

The new empire was now to be wholly sustained from the country it had seized upon, which was henceforth converted into one continued scene of warfare and plunder. The Mussulmans were not like the Hindu immigration, numerous enough to expel and supplant their predecessors; nor like the British at this day, the representatives of a superior power, possessing abundant resources of its own. They were simply a military class, hating and hateful to the religion, the traditions, and the customs of the population on which they were quartered, and from whose resources they were determined to subsist. The limits of their empire varied with the means of aggression, while its authority was at every moment contingent on the ability to enforce it. In some provinces the Hindu dynasties were annihilated, and Mohammedan governors ruled in their place. In others the rajas remained under a tribute, which was paid with reluctance, and withheld whenever payment could not be immediately enforced. The two races were committed to a never-ending struggle, which on ordinary calculations could end only in the extermination of the smaller. The Mussulmans, however, were constantly recruited by adventurers from the Scythian desert, having all to gain and nothing to lose; and the Hindus, more than any other race in the world, seem to have formed themselves for submission to a foreign yoke. Their civil and religious institutions were unfavourable to political combination and national liberty. The priesthood was venal, and devoid of sympathy with the people; the military caste was feeble or extinct; the agricultural and mercantile classes supine and destitute of patriotism. The genius of their very religion was to worship power,* as that of Islam was to exercise it. Both races were alike insensible to moral obligation; both alike believers in the decrees of a blind destiny. It was the *fate* of one to rule, and of the other to be ruled; so the conquerors

* In the Puranas and ancient poems it is common to find the gods themselves perplexed, if not subdued, by the superior power of evil genii or men. It is even thought that by means of sacrifices a wicked man can acquire a merit with the gods *against their will*, extending to the destruction of their moral government. This monstrous conception supplies the groundwork of Southey's poem, the Curse of Kehama.

maintained their hold, but the sword was never out of their hand, and their footsteps were planted in blood.

The Mohammedans governed entirely by martial law—defined by the highest of British authorities as the absence of all law but the will of the commander. Their position was that of a camp in an enemy's country. Their system reposed all power in the person of the sultan, without any of the checks imposed upon the Hindu raja from the authority of the Brahmins, the municipal rights, or the customs of the nation. The Koran was the single code, divine and secular; and of its provisions the sultan or his officer was equally judge with the moulavie or the cazee. This law afforded but a precarious protection to the Mussulman subject; for the infidel the Koran itself had no law but tribute or death.

The character of the law, and the freedom of speech enjoyed by its expounders, are exhibited in the following passage from the life of Alla-ud-deen, a great patron of civilization in the Mohammedan sense, and who enriched his capital (according to Ferishta) with a university containing forty-five professors of the sciences, with teachers of poetry, philosophy, medicine, divinity, astrology, music, morality, languages, and all the fine arts then known to the world. "The sultan one day said to cazee Mogees-ud-deen that he wished to know the law in some matters concerning the duty of sovereigns. As the sultan had always shown a contempt for the cazees, and called them hypocrites and villains, ready to give any opinions to please those who would reward them, the cazee was much alarmed, and replied, 'I fear from what your majesty has requested, that my last hour has come; if so, and it be your majesty's will, I am ready to die; and it will only be unnecessarily increasing my crime, if I must be punished for speaking the truth, according to the word of God.' The sultan inquired why he was so much agitated, and he replied, 'If I speak the truth, and your majesty is offended, it may cost me my life; and if I speak what is false, and your majesty should ascertain the truth, I may then be put to death for deceiving you.' The sultan replied, that he need not fear to answer his inquiries according to the clear and strict laws of the Koran. The sultan then proposed several inquiries, of which the first was, 'From what class of Hindus is it lawful to exact obedience and tribute?' To which the cazee replied, 'It is lawful to exact obedience and tribute from all infidels, and they can only be considered as obedient who pay the poll-tax without demurring, even should it be obtained by force; for, according to the law of the Prophet it is written regarding infidels, 'Tax them to the extent they can pay, or utterly destroy them.' The learned of the faith have also enjoined the followers of Islam to slay them or to convert them to the faith, a maxim conveyed in the words of the Prophet himself. The Imam Huneef, however, subsequently considers that the poll-tax, or as heavy a tribute imposed upon them as they can bear, may be substituted for death, and he has accordingly forbidden that their blood be unnecessarily shed. So that it is commanded that the poll-tax and tribute should be exacted to the utmost farthing from them, in order that the punishment may approximate as nearly as possible to death.' The sultan, smiling, remarked, 'You may perceive that, without any aid from your learned books or consulting any cazee, I have always been practising, of my own accord, the principles of the Prophet."*

For the administration of government beyond the imperial presence, the Mohammedan system knew no better expedient than to lodge the same powers in the governors of provinces and their subordinate agents; each, like military officers, exercising entire and absolute authority, but responsible to his immediate superior. The function principally expected of the governor was to replenish the imperial exchequer: to enable that governor to gratify his master's wants, and his own, was the prime duty of the subordinate authorities. As long as their respective quotas were made good to the treasury, little inquiry was instituted into other parts of the administration.

The only practical check on any portion of the system was the dread of assassination or rebellion: the people might be goaded into insurrection by the rapacity of their task-masters, or a governor might take up arms against the imperial authority. These remedies were not unfrequently resorted to. A violent death was the most usual termination to a Mussulman reign; and the revolt of a governor was the ordinary result of popularity and power. Hence the empire was seldom free from the convulsions of revolution and civil war. It was further agitated by frequent struggles on the part of Hindu princes to regain their dominions, or by the flight of a whole district population to the jungle, in order to escape the rapacity of the Mussulman tax-gatherer. Blood flowed in torrents upon all these occasions, and, in the words of the Mohammedan historian, "the mise-

* *Ferishta.*—Gleig's History of India.

ries of the country exceeded all power of description."*

Nothing surely but the most resolute prejudice could have induced an English writer to represent such a dominion as a benefit to the Hindus in comparison with their own.† Granting the superiority of the ritual and creed of Islam, they were proposed to the Hindu only at the point of the sword. Their compulsory reception involved the destruction at once of his remaining conscience, and of all that was dear to him in social existence. Death was often accepted in preference, and no tyrant was so dreadful to the Hindu as a religious one. The communication of Mohammedan civilization would have been dearly purchased at such a price could it be conceded that their civilization was superior to that of the Hindu.

* Ferishta.

† See Mr. Mill's General Reflections, with Professor Wilson's Comments, in the second volume of his history. Mr. Mill's admiration of Mohammedanism seems to result from a twofold antipathy to Hindu civilization and to English law. His whimsical panegyrics are carried to the length of commending the superior facility with which *rebellion* was resorted to as a check on despotism by the Mussulman, as compared with the Hindu population. Another philosophical historian, whose enthusiasm is kindled in favour of Islam by its denial of the Holy Trinity and the absence of a clergy, includes among "the calm and rational precepts of its legislator," the reduction of the boundless license of polygamy to *four* legitimate wives or concubines, and the punishment of adultery by death, and of fornication in either sex by one hundred stripes. He adds, "The order, the discipline, the temporal and spiritual ambition of the clergy, are unknown to the Moslems; and the sages of the law are the guides of their conscience and the oracles of their faith. From the Atlantic to the Ganges the Koran is acknowledged as the fundamental code, not only of theology but of civil and criminal jurisprudence; and the laws which regulate the actions and the property of mankind are guarded by the infallible and immutable sanction of the will of God." Yet in the very next sentence we are informed that whenever the "institutions of the desert" are found ill adapted to the wealth and numbers of Ispahan and Constantinople, that is, whenever any one of sufficient weight wishes the "immutable sanction" to be changed, the cadhi respectfully places on his head the holy volume, and substitutes a *dexterous interpretation* (!) more apposite to the principles of equity (!) and the manners and *policy of the times.—Gibbon's Decline and Fall*, cap. 50.

But these Affghan invaders were fresh from the steppes of Tartary, and continued to be recruited from the tribes of their parent desert. Like the Goths in Europe they acquired civilization from the people whom they subdued in war. Mahmoud of Ghizni enriched his capital from the spoils or the imitation of Hindu art, and there can be little doubt that the Patan kings of Delhi were indebted for much of their magnificence to the wealth and intelligence accumulated in that ancient seat of royalty some centuries before the Arabian Prophet strove to elevate the barbarians of his native desert.*

The historians of the period are all Mohammedans, who regard the progress of the empire from their own point of view. Yet they stigmatize many of the

* "Ere yet the Pyramids looked down upon the valley of the Nile, when Greece and Italy, those cradles of European civilization, housed only the tenants of the wilderness, India was the seat of wealth and grandeur. A busy population had covered the land with marks of its industry, rich crops of the most coveted productions of nature annually rewarded the toil of the husbandman, skilful artisans converted the rude produce of the soil into fabrics of unrivalled delicacy and beauty, and architects and sculptors joined in contributing works the solidity of which has not in some instances been overcome by the revolution of thousands of years. The princes and nobles of India, unlike the wandering chieftains of the neighbouring countries, already dwelt in splendid palaces, and clothed in the gorgeous products of its looms, and glittering with gold and gems, indulged a corresponding luxury in every art and habit of their lives. Poets were not wanting to celebrate the exploits of their ancestors, nor philosophers to thread the mazes of metaphysical inquiry and weave the net of ingenious speculation, with as much subtlety and perhaps with not less success than has attended the researches of subsequent inquirers."—*Thornton's History of India*, vol. i. p. 3. If this picture should appear in parts a little highly coloured, and rather antedated in being carried back *before the Pyramids*; yet it presents a far truer representation of the state of India at the Mohammedan invasion, than Mr. Mill's prejudices have allowed him to receive from the evidences undoubtedly in his possession. Delhi, under the name of Indraprastha or Inderput, was one of the earliest Hindu capitals; its foundation is attributed to Yudisthira at the fabulous antiquity of 3,000 years before Christ. It is certainly older than all records, and probably as old as Jerusalem.

sultans as a disgrace to human nature, while of those whom they admire it is easy to perceive that a widely different judgment would be formed by a Hindu observer.

The foundation of a Mussulman empire in India was commemorated by the erection of a superb pillar, which is yet standing, called from its author, the Kuttub Minar. That emperor, however, only commenced the erection, leaving his successor Altumsh to finish it. Altumsh is one of the few emperors to whom the Mohammedan historians accord the united commendations of valour, prudence, and piety. He received the high honour of investiture from the successor of the Prophet, the caliph of Bagdad; an honour purchased by diligent persecutions of the idolaters. A magnificent temple at Oujein, formed on the same plan with that of Somnâth, which was three hundred years in building, and was surrounded by a wall of one hundred cubits high, fell before his zeal; and a brazen statue of the celebrated raja Vicramaditya,* with other images of stone and brass, was brought to Delhi, and broken before the gate of the principal mosque.

Kuttub and his more immediate successors are denominated the slave emperors, having been all Turkish slaves brought out of Tartary, and purchased at the Mohammedan court.† Among them appears the name

* Vicramaditya, or Vickram, was raja of Oujein, then called Ananti, B.C. 56. He is said himself to have worshipped the infinite and invisible God, but at the same time to have erected temples and endowed shrines to the deities generally worshipped by his subjects. He invaded the Deccan, but was compelled to withdraw by Shalewahan, who reigned at Pytan on the Godavery, and forms the theme of many marvellous traditions. The eras of these two princes are used by the natives in Hindustan and the Deccan respectively to the present day.

† For the history of these tribes see Gibbon.

of a woman, the Sultana Rezia, who received the education of a prince from her father Altumsh, and at his death was preferred before her brother in the succession to the throne. Ferishta says, "The strictest scrutineers could find no fault in her, but that she was a woman." Nevertheless the mutinous and intriguing nobles could not be restrained from transferring the power to her rejected brother, and after two defeats in the field, she was captured and put to death with her husband. A similar fate befel no less than five others of the slave emperors, as the penalty of the profligacy and oppression which alienated their Mussulman adherents. The four who were allowed to descend to an unbloody grave, were preserved in no mercy to the Hindus.

Under Mohammedan rule, the character of the government was always determined by that of the sultan. The property, honour, and life of the subject hung wholly upon his lips. At his word, a slave might be invested with the vizierut, and a haughty noble was suddenly stripped, and bastinadoed, or even hurried to the stake, while his wives and children were thrust out to beggary and dishonour. Historians record it for a signal virtue when the prince condescended to admit of remonstrance. More commonly the nobles and "sages of the sacred law" were silent or consenting to the royal caprice, till, when the cup was full, an intrigue was hastily formed in the court, and the dagger or the bowl effected an exchange of tyrants. This remedy was beyond the reach of the Hindu subject, nor were his the wrongs to nerve the hands that wielded it.

One of the four slave emperors who died a natural death was Nasir-ud-deen, a prince who led the life of a dervish in private, while displaying unbounded magnificence in public. The fall of ten thousand Rajpoots in one battle in this reign attests the impatience with which the foreign yoke was borne. Another was Bulbun or Balin, renowned for giving shelter to twenty princes at one time who had been expelled from their dominions; but still more notorious, in the impartial page of history, for putting one hundred thousand Hindus to death, in consequence of one revolt.*

The slave dynasty was succeeded by that of the Khiljees; under the earliest of whom the Mohammedans made their first irruption into the Deccan, A.D. 1294. Like the early incursions into Hindustan, it was a mere predatory expedition, attracted by the wealth ascribed to the princes of the south. Deoghur, the capital of Ramdev, styled by the Mohammedans ruler of the Deccan, but in reality only raja of Marashtra, was besieged and ransomed.† The commander returning enriched with booty, consummated his triumphs by assassinating his uncle and sovereign who went out to meet him, and ascending the throne of Delhi. On a renewal of

* In suppressing some disorders at Juanpore and Benares, the same sultan caused many thousands of men, women, and children to be killed in one common massacre. He was occupied for three years in suppressing a rebellion in Bengal, and his cruelty to the prisoners excited the horror of the Mussulmans themselves. Yet it was after much deliberation, that the cazees and muftis agreed to a round robin in remonstrance, and with still greater difficulty that their remonstrance obtained a hearing. The bulk of the sufferers on these occasions were of course Hindus, though the leaders in the crime were usually Mohammedans.

† Ferishta enumerates the spoil as consisting of 15,000 lbs. of pure gold, 175 lbs. of pearls, 50 lbs. of diamonds, rubies, emeralds, and sapphires, 25,000 lbs. of silver, 4,000 pieces of silk, and a long list of precious commodities. Allowing what we please for the exaggeration of the historian, who wrote late in the fourteenth century, this account sufficiently proves the extent of pre-Mussulman civilization, or, at least, of the Mussulman's own estimate of it.

the war in the Deccan, Ramdev again submitted, and Warangole, the capital of Telingana, was annexed after the same fashion. A few years after, Canara was invaded, and the raja taken prisoner; the plunder on this occasion is stated at a million sterling. All these wars were conducted with a cruelty which outrages human nature; yet, as their author jestingly remarked, they were in instinctive obedience to the precepts of the Koran.

This bloody dynasty ended in a succession of assassinations, by which the whole family were extinguished; and a third Affghan (or Patan) monarchy was inaugurated (A.D. 1321) in the person of Ghazi Khan Toghluk, governor of the Punjab. The predatory expeditions were continued into the Deccan, but on one occasion the Mussulmans sustained a great defeat under Jonah Khan before Deoghur. This prince afterwards ascending the throne, by the title of Mohammed the Third, revenged himself on the infidels by causing a large district in Hindustan to be surrounded with troops after the manner of an Indian hunt, and then closing his soldiers in upon the centre, slaughtered every human being within the circle. This barbarity, it appears, was more than once repeated; there was a general massacre also of the inhabitants of the great city of Canouj.

At another time this monarch resolved to remove the seat of his government from Delhi to Deoghur, which he named Dowlutabad.* He commanded the inhabitants of the former city, men, women, and children, to remove to the new capital, a distance of more

* That is, The City of Riches. Deoghur signifies "The Sacred Rock." The fort is a mass of rock, considered by the natives impregnable. This city, now in ruins, was situated about eight miles from Aurungabad.

than seven hundred miles. Delhi was left desolate; but changing his mind in two or three years, the tyrant issued his edict for a similar wholesale emigration back to Delhi. A few succeeded in regaining their former abodes; famine, sickness, and suffering did their work with the remainder. This emperor, who at one time was animated by frantic schemes of conquest,* and actually reduced the Carnatic with a large part of the Deccan, by the wild ferocity of his administration brought the empire to the verge of ruin. He tampered with the currency, and augmented the taxation to such a degree, that the fertile fields of the Dooab between the Jumna and the Ganges were abandoned by the cultivators, who fled to the woods. Famine desolated the district; the provinces revolted on every side; Bengal became independent; and the rajas of Telingana and the Carnatic formed a confederacy, which in a few months expelled the Mohammedans from every place in the Deccan except Dowlutabad.

In this city a new Mussulman sovereignty was now to be erected. A portion of Mohammed's mercenary troops, consisting, as those armies usually did, of Tartars, Affghans, and Moguls, had revolted from his obedience and seized upon Dowlutabad. Here they elected a sovereign, who was soon replaced by another of the insurgent chiefs, named Hussoun Khan A.D. 1347. The new sultan had once been the slave of a Brahmin at Delhi, called Gungoo. Assuming the name of Alla-ud-deen, he added, in honour of his former master, who had predicted his greatness, the appellations Gungoo Bahmanee; the Brahmin him-

* Besides raising armies for the conquest of Transoxania and Khorassan, he prepared one for the subjugation of China, and sent 100,000 horse through the Himalayas to explore the frontier, which, it is said, they actually reached, but scarcely a man survived to describe the retreat.

self was invited from Delhi, and placed over the royal treasury. Such was the foundation of the Bahmanee dynasty, which for some centuries enjoyed the empire of the Deccan.

Meantime the throne of Hindustan was mounted by Feroze Toghluk (A.D. 1351), who, during a reign of thirty-eight years, reduced the disordered finances to a sounder state, and greatly improved the administration of justice. Abstaining from further interference in Bengal and the Deccan, beyond requiring a small annual present, he succeeded in pacifying the remaining portions of the empire. It is under this emperor that we first read of any rational attempt to develop the resources of the country. In addition to other public works, he constructed fifty dams across rivers, to promote irrigation, and thirty reservoirs, or tanks, for the same purpose. He had the further honour of commencing the great works of irrigation in the north-western provinces, by cutting a canal from the Jumna, or one of its tributary streams, to Hansi and Hissar. His primary object, it is true, appears to have been the increase of imperial luxury, by supplying the fountains, watering the gardens, and filling the wells, of a favourite hunting seat. The canal also was so unskilfully constructed that it ceased to flow in half a century after his death; and the neighbourhood of Hissar returned to its former sterility.* Still the design is worthy of notice, as evincing, after a dreary century and a half of Mussulman misrule, some attempt at discharging one of the real duties of government.

* Colonel Baird Smith's Sketch of the Irrigation System of Northern and Central India; in Appendix B to his two volumes on "Italian Irrigation."

The greatest virtues, however, could not cure, they could only temporarily arrest, the inherent vices of Mohammedan despotism. The emperor was constrained by the intrigues of the vizier to abdicate in favour of a son (A.D. 1385), who was soon deposed by another conspiracy, and driven into exile. A frequent series of violent deaths and imprisonments had vacated the throne four times in rapid succession. A child had been placed on it by the turbulent omrahs. A rival Patan throne had been erected at Juanpore over the territories to the east of the Ganges. The Mahrattas had appeared in the field; the distant provinces were in insurrection; and a civil war raged in the capital, when the horizon of Delhi began to reflect the glare of the approaching "firebrand of the universe."

CHAPTER V.

THE MOGULS.

Origin—Zenghis Khan—Mission to court of Delhi—Punjab invaded—Repulse at Delhi—Timour Beg—Capture of Delhi—General massacre—Anarchy—Empire divided—House of Lodi—BABER—Battle of Panniput—Enthroned at Delhi—Powers of India—Patan rule—Degradation of the natives—State of the empire—Prospects—Murmurs of the army—War with the Patans—Rana Sanka—Baber's penitence—Speech to the army—Defeat of the Rajpoots—Rajpoot despair—Reunion of the empire—Death of Baber—Expulsion of his son—Shere Shah—Extensive dominions—Return of Humayun—Akbar—Toleration—Land-tax—Revenue settlement—Mohammedan exactions—Religious tenets—Extent of the empire—Resistance of Mewar—The Deccan—Dissolution of the Bahmanee empire—Subjugation of Ahmednuggur—Akbar's magnificence—Court luxuries—Treasure—Death by poison—Subahs of the empire.

THE great Scythian desert between China and the Caspian Sea has formed, from the earliest ages, the seed-plot whence the cultivated portions of mankind have been replenished with the human plant. It was inhabited on the west by the Turks, on the east by the Manchus, and by the Moguls or Monguls in the centre,—nations widely differing in language and feature, though often comprehended under the indiscriminate appellation of Tartars.*

The Turks were the first to rise to dominion: after the dissolution of their great northern empire in the sixth century they still formed powerful divisions, and

* "Tartar" and "Tartary" as commonly used in Europe are (like "India") geographical terms not recognised by the natives of the countries referred to. *Tatar*, as it is more correctly written, is the proper appellation of a single tribe of the Mogul nation.

the thrones of Asia were often filled by soldiers or slaves of Turkish extraction. Of this race was Mahmoud of Ghizni, whose dominions at his death extended from the Sutlej to Ispahan. The armies of the more civilized Turks were constantly recruited from the tribes which still roamed the ancestral desert; and when Mahmoud's powerful hand was removed, those warlike shepherds broke in upon their own account. Persia was wrested from his posterity by the ruder Turks of the house of Seljuk,* and these in turn, after yielding to the seductions of Mohammedan civilization, experienced a similar fate from the barbarians of the prolific desert.

In the thirteenth century the divided tribes of the Mogul race were united, and led to conquest by Zenghis Khan and his four sons. Under the standard of their great khan, seven hundred thousand Moguls and Tartars marched from the Caspian to the Indus, never halting till a tract of many hundred miles, adorned with the habitations and labours of mankind, had been reduced to a state of ruin which five centuries have not been able to repair.† The hordes of Zenghis Khan did not cross the Indus; but a portion of them settling in the countries to the west of that river—which after his death became the dominion of his son Zagatai—embraced the religion of Mohammed, and were finally incorporated among the Arabs and Persians. Mixing with the principal Turkish families, and renouncing all intercourse with the idolatrous Moguls of China and the desert, they assumed, with the possessions, the name and language, of the Turks. In India, however, the word *Mogul* has ever since been

* The present sultan of Constantinople is descended from a branch of this family.

† Decline and Fall of the Roman Empire.

used indiscriminately of the Mussulmans of Persia and the north, and they were regarded, not without reason, as the deadly enemies of the Affghan dynasties.

The beginning of their intercourse assumed a friendly aspect. A grandson of Zenghis sent an embassy to Nasir-ud-deen, which was received with all the magnificence which that monarch knew how to assume in public, though his private life was that of a dervish. Fifty thousand horse, twenty thousand infantry, two thousand elephants, and three thousand "carriages of fireworks," are enumerated in the retinue of the vizier who went to meet the envoy. Five princes from beyond the Indus, fugitives from the Mogul arms, and many subject rajas of Hindustan, stood round the throne on which the sultan received his greeting. The display was, perhaps, as imprudent as Hezekiah's. In the next reign the Moguls invaded the Punjab, and the invasion was renewed in greater force under the first of the Khiljees.

Similar assaults continued to harass the empire: the Moguls swarmed upon its frontier, and confidently promised themselves the eventual conquest of Hindustan. In 1303, they reached the gates of Delhi, whither the country people, driven before their ravages, rushed in vast numbers for shelter. Alla-ud-deen, who was not wanting in courage or ability, gave them battle at the head of an army of three hundred thousand horse, two thousand seven hundred elephants, and infantry without number. After a severe and obstinate fight, the Moguls were defeated and driven back across the Indus. A considerable number of these Mohammedans, it seems, had entered the service of the Delhi sovereign, all of whom were now dismissed, and becoming troublesome from destitution, they were destroyed to the number of fifteen thousand. Still the Moguls returned in greater numbers than ever. They were bought off with an enormous sum of money only to come back when the bribe was expended. A chief at last arose under whose leading they became scarcely less formidable than the hordes of Zenghis himself.

Timour Beg—or, as he was nicknamed, Timour *Lenc* (Lame) corrupted by Europeans into Tamerlane—was the son of a chief who rode at the head of ten thousand horse in the vicinity of Samarcand. Driven in early life as an outlaw into the desert, he there organized a force which eventually overran Persia, Tartary, India, Syria, and Asia Minor. His expeditions resembled the inroads of a freebooter more than the march of a conqueror. Timour destroyed existing governments without establishing any authority on their ruins: conducting his incursions in the savage spirit of Zenghis, he departed laden with spoil, and left the scenes which he had desolated to the further miseries of anarchy and famine.*

Being informed of the divisions and weakness of the Delhi empire, Timour crossed the Indus by the ordinary passage at Attock, traversed the Punjab, and, plundering and slaying as he went, appeared before Delhi A.D. 1398. As he approached he spread terror before him, by ordering the massacre, in cold blood, of all the prisoners in his camp, to the number, according to the Mohammedan historians, of one hundred thousand. Mahmoud, the young sultan, venturing out to meet him in the field, was defeated with prodigious slaughter, and pursued to the gates of Delhi. Thence he

* It is in vain that some writers appeal to the book called the *Institutes of Timour* in proof of his just ideas of government; these were the institutions he designed more than established for his own possessions: to the world at large he was the mere barbarian described in the text.

fled to Guzerat, leaving Timour to be proclaimed as his successor in all the mosques of the city.

Mussulman as the conqueror was, he put the capital to the ransom prescribed by the Koran for unbelievers, apparently without discriminating between the disciples of Islam and the idolatrous Hindus. The nobles and bankers refused to pay; but the followers of Timour were better versed in their ancestral mode of warfare than in distinctions of race or religion. They plundered what they chose, and killed all who resisted. Timour was in his camp celebrating his accession with a great festival. His mirth continued for five days, during which the city was given up to pillage and massacre. Many of the higher ranks killed their wives and daughters to save them from the violence of the Mogul soldiers. The houses were set on fire, the streets were choked with the slain, and a large part of the capital was reduced to ashes.

After a stay of fifteen days, Timour, with true Mussulman piety, offered up praises in the mosques for his success, and then departed, laden with plunder, and dragging numbers of men and women into slavery. From Delhi he proceeded to Meerut, threw down its walls, and put every soul to the sword. Thence he ascended the Ganges as far as Hurdwar, and still marking his way by fire and blood, at last quitted Hindustan, after inflicting, in the short space of five months, an amount of destruction only credible to those who have studied the gloomy records of Oriental, and especially of Mohammedan, conquest.

Delhi remained for some time in ruins; at last Mahmoud returned and died in the government, A.D. 1412. A turbulent period ensued, during which the empire was reduced to a few miles of territory immediately adjacent to the city. Guzerat and Bengal became independent Mohammedan kingdoms. A rival throne was erected in Hindustan at Juanpore, ruling over the country to the east of the Ganges. Another Mussulman government established itself in Mewat, within fourteen miles of Delhi; and yet another in Malwa. The Rajpoot princes regained independence in Mewar, Marwar, Ajmeer, and Gwalior. Lastly, the Punjab, with the country as far as Sirhind, was in the possession of Beholi, a chief of the Affghan tribe of Lodi.

This chief, in the year 1450, obtained the throne of Delhi, and during a long reign of thirty-eight years, succeeded in restoring a portion of its authority. His son, Secunder, was favoured with equal fortune, and, by the Mohammedan historians, is ranked among the best of their emperors. Still we are not permitted to lose sight of the spirit in which the dominion now contested among the Mussulmans was ever administered to the unfortunate Hindus. A Brahmin being reviled in this reign for worshipping idols, replied that all religions, if practised with equal sincerity, were equally acceptable to God. For this impiety he was condemned by a council of moulvies to the alternative of circumcision or death: he evinced the sincerity of his faith by embracing the latter.

The third and last monarch of the house of Lodi was named Ibrahim. The position of a family raised to the throne by the assistance of others of an equal rank is at all times precarious, and the new emperor had neither the tact nor the disposition to conciliate the chiefs who laid claim to his gratitude. The Affghan nobles, hitherto permitted to sit in the royal presence, were required to stand before the throne with folded arms in the attitude of other subjects. The members of his own family were the first to rebel. A brother assumed the title of king in Juanpore; and, though taken and put to death, left his throne to successors, who maintained the war till all domestic dissensions were swallowed up in another and more successful invasion of the Moguls.

The possessions of Timour had been divided among various princes of his posterity, and at the close of the fifteenth century the territories round Samarcand, the ancient capital, were distributed into four kingdoms, governed by four brothers at the same time. The smallest was Ferghana, situated to the north-east of Samarcand, on the very edge of the desert. The sultan dying suddenly (A.D. 1494), left his petty throne to his son Zehir-ud-deen Mohammed, surnamed *Baber* (or the Tiger), at the early age of twelve. On the father's side Baber was the lineal descendant of Timour, and so claimed the Turkish name and blood. His mother traced her descent to Zenghis Khan, and her brothers still ruled the Moguls of the desert.

Expelled from his paternal territory, Baber, after many adventures, at last succeeded one of his uncles on the throne of Kabul, and there began to prepare for the conquest of Hindustan. He made several incursions into the Punjab, trying to open negotiations with the Affghan governors, and claiming as his own the territories which from old times had belonged to the Turks.* He met at first with but little success; but the dissensions with Ibrahim becoming more embittered, Baber was encouraged (A.D. 1526) to advance beyond the Sutlej and take the road to Delhi. He was met at Panniput, where the fate of Hindustan has

* Memoirs of Baber.

been often decided, by a much larger force, commanded by the emperor in person.

Baber confesses the terror and alarm which now seized upon his troops. He was comforted, however, by observing that the emperor was young and inexperienced in war, negligent and unskilful in his movements, and lacked the spirit to encourage his soldiers by gratuities out of his great treasures. Ibrahim, confiding in superior numbers, commenced the attack at daylight; but by mid-day his forces were utterly broken and routed. Baber speaks of it as an easy victory, computing the enemy's loss at fifteen or sixteen thousand men, while the natives reckoned it at forty or fifty thousand. Ibrahim was slain in the battle, and the Mogul dynasty was enthroned in Delhi.*

At this time India contained five Mussulman kingdoms, besides many Hindu principalities. The Patan empire of Delhi had included Hindustan and the Punjab, but was now divided in two parts by the recent erection of the "kingdom of the east." Guzerat had been seized, on the death of Feroze Shah, by his cup-bearer. Malwa was under the rule of a Khiljee sultan. A Syud family was on the throne of Bengal, and the Bahmanee sultans ruled in the Deccan. These five, Baber observes, were all powerful princes, possessed of formidable armies. Though Mussulmans, they were divided by sect and race,

* "It may seem one of the strangest caprices of fortune that the empire which he founded in India should have been called, both in the country and by foreigners, the empire of the *Moguls;* thus taking its name from a race that he detested. This arose, not so much from his being a descendant of Chengis Khan, as from his being a foreigner from the north; and from the age of Chengis Khan downwards, all Tartars and Persians (and indeed every Mohammedan with a whitish face) in the loose colloquial language of India, seem to have been denominated Moguls."—*Erskine's Memoirs of Baber.*

and often at war with one another. Of the Hindu princes the two most powerful were the raja of Beejanuggur in the Deccan, and the Rana Sanka of Mewar, the acknowledged head of the Rajpoot princes, who had augmented his dominions by a number of provinces revolted from the sultan of Malwa. There were several other rais and rajas on the borders and within the limits of Hindustan, many of whom, on account of their remoteness and difficulty of access, had never been reduced to the Mussulman yoke.*

Upwards of five centuries had now elapsed since Mahmoud of Ghizni began the work of subjugating India, and three since a separate Mohammedan empire was established at Delhi. An incredible amount of slaughter and misery had been inflicted on the natives, in the attempt to sustain the foreign dominion. It had been a period of almost incessant civil war; yet so far from consolidating a power under which the land might find repose, and be recompensed for its sufferings by a superior administration of government, the invaders had themselves divided into new and hostile combinations, while the native princes were still struggling bravely, and in some parts successfully, for their honour, their dominions, and their religion.

Baber, who was a keen and intelligent observer, has left us in his memoirs the means of estimating the amount of civil improvement introduced during these centuries of Mussulman domination. He observes that none of the provinces of Hindustan possessed any artificial canals for irrigation, as were common in Persia. He notes the decay and disappearance of large cities, which had been inhabited for many years, through the flight of the population, sometimes before

* Baber's Memoirs.

the face of an invading army, but not unfrequently from the exactions of the Mussulman government. Among the Hindus he could find "no genius, no comprehension of mind, no politeness of manner, no ingenuity or mechanical invention, no skill or knowledge in design or architecture." Yet the Hindu is no way inferior to the Mohammedan in natural ability; and in the present day is found to possess a quicker apprehension, with a far more flexible intellect. They had no good food in their bazaars, no baths or colleges, no candles, no torches, not a candlestick; even in the royal palace of Delhi the emperor was lighted by filthy *Deûtis;* half-naked natives holding in one hand an iron tripod having a piece of cotton bound about one of its legs, and in the other a gourd filled with oil, which they poured from time to time on the lighted cotton. The whole description exhibits a population poor and depressed, whom no attempt had been made to elevate either materially or morally.

The revenues of the dominions acquired by the conquest were returned at "fifty-two crores" of dams* or about a million and a half sterling; one-sixth part of this however was enjoyed by "some rais or rajas to confirm them in their obedience." The royal coffers still contained a vast amount of treasure, which Baber liberally distributed among his followers. He sent presents also to the sheiks of Khorassan, Samarcand, Mecca, and Medina, with all his relations and friends, and a sharokeh† to every individual in his own kingdom of Kabul.

The low amount of revenue returned to the conqueror sufficiently indicates the narrow dimensions to

* A dam is equal to the fortieth part of a rupee.

† The sharokeh was about tenpence or elevenpence in value.

which the empire was reduced. It seems probable also that the expedient for confirming the obedience of the rais and rajas, referred to in his memoirs, was extensively applied, and that in many parts the revenues continued in the hands of the Hindu rulers, subject to such annual tribute, or occasional subsidies, as the emperor could find means to exact. The Mussulman dominion was still a mere military supremacy, which all these centuries had not been able to consolidate into a fixed and permanent government.

The new emperor found his conquest by no means so inviting, on nearer inspection, as it had appeared at a distance. "Hindustan (he writes) is a country that has few pleasures to recommend it." The horses, the flesh, the fruits, the water, the climate, were all inferior to those of Kabul. His eye, accustomed to the mountains and romantic passes of the Hindu Koosh, recoiled with disgust from the broad uninteresting plain of the Ganges. He crossed the Jumna from Agra to look for a spot where he might construct a pleasure garden, with artificial streams supplied by water-wheels, and laid out on a regular and elegant plan, after the fashion of Lahore; but the whole prospect "was so ugly and detestable that he repassed the river, quite repulsed and disgusted."

Disagreeable as the country appeared, Baber found it no easy task to become its master. Everywhere, except at Delhi and Agra, the inhabitants fortified themselves against his approach, and the governors of towns refused to submit. He was opposed in Central India by the raja of Mewar, aided by some of the Patan chiefs. Dholpore, Gwalior, Biana, Sambal in Rohilcund, and other strong places, were fortified against him. Canouj, with the country to the eastward, was in the possession of the Sultan Mohammed, who even crossed the Ganges and advanced to threaten Agra. A still more formidable opponent appeared in the Rana Sanka, "the pagan," as Baber indignantly complains, who had sent ambassadors to Kabul inviting his approach and promising assistance, but who now took advantage of his opportunity to make a stand for himself.

It was in vain that Baber employed his arts and his muse in the endeavour to conciliate the rebellious Mussulmans:* in vain he boasted of the Turkish superiority. Promises and threats were alike disregarded. Even in Agra and Delhi the townspeople shunned and disliked his followers, while in the country the inhabitants fled before them, leaving neither grain nor provender to supply their wants. The villagers took to thieving and robbery, and the roads were impassable. The army lost heart, and murmured. Many of the begs and best soldiers began to prepare for their return to Kabul. Baber, however, declared his inflexible determination to persevere in the war, and being joined by the forces which Ibrahim had despatched against his rebellious vassals in the east, he rewarded their allegiance by liberal grants from the possessions to be recovered in Oude and Juanpore.

It was determined to attack the Mussulman enemy

* Baber considered himself no mean proficient in Persian and Turkish poetry. To a khan who held out in Biana, the most famous fort in Hindustan, he wrote "extempore the following fragment":—

"Contend not with Turks, O Mir of Biana;
The speed and bravery of Turks are surpassing;
Now is the time to present yourself and to lend an ear to counsel.
What is the use of telling a man of what is before his eyes?"

But "the man, confiding too much in his position," refused his terms, and Baber could not enforce them.

first. Humayun, the conqueror's son, was sent in command, while Baber amused himself by setting an example in Agra how a *charbagh* (pleasure garden) ought to be laid out. His garden contained a number of buildings on which the name of Kabul was bestowed, to perpetuate by the side of the Jumna the memory of his mountain home.

Meantime, the Patan forces of the east, not venturing to await the onslaught of Humayun's army, retreated across the Ganges, whither they were quickly pursued. Juanpore was taken, and Ghazipoor beleagured by the Moguls, when they were recalled in haste to the assistance of Baber against the Rajpoot princes. Seizing his opportunity, the Rana Sanka was advancing on Delhi and Agra, aided by ten independent rajas united in a last rally against the Mussulman arms. Mahmoud, the brother of the deceased emperor Ibrahim, appeared at the same time at the head of ten thousand horse to support his pretensions. Altogether the hostile forces exceeded two hundred thousand men: on the other hand, some outstanding Mussulman chiefs surrendered their forts, and submitted to Baber on the approach of the infidels. The Rajpoots, however, defeated two detachments sent against them, and the accounts of their valour, with the predictions of an "evil-minded astrologer,"* threw the Mogul army

* The character of Baber, with his quaint mixture of simplicity, self-indulgence, good nature, and good sense, largely coloured by the superstition which forms a principal element in Mussulman piety, is well exhibited in his own account of his subsequent treatment of this man.

"Mohammed Singh, the astrologer, whose perverse and seditious practices I have mentioned, came to congratulate me on my victory. I poured forth a torrent of abuse upon him; and when I had relieved my heart by it, although he was heathenishly inclined, perverse, extremely self-conceited, and an insufferable evil speaker, yet, as he had been my old servant, I gave him a lac as a present, and dismissed him, commanding him not to remain within my dominions."

into a panic. In this emergency "the Tiger" displayed an edifying spectacle of Mussulman penitence and zeal. In spite of the prohibitions of the Koran he was not only fond of wine, but drank openly and habitually to the most disgraceful excess. He now solemnly renounced this sin, destroyed his gold and silver goblets, and poured out his stores of wine on the ground. He further vowed in case of victory to remit the stamp tax from his Mussulman subjects, and called upon his ameers to follow his example in letting the beard grow untrimmed, till the holy war should be crowned with success.

These religious precautions were supported by every secular exertion. Observing the universal discouragement of his troops, the sultan called the ameers and officers together and addressed them in the following spirited language :—

"Noblemen and soldiers! Every man that comes into the world is subject to dissolution. When we are passed away and gone, God only survives unchangeable. Whoever comes to the feast of life must, before it is over, drink from the cup of death. He who arrives at the inn of mortality must one day inevitably take his departure from that house of sorrow—the world. How much better is it to die with honour than to live with infamy!

'With fame, even if I die, I am contented;
Let fame be mine, since my body is Death's.'*

The most high God has been propitious to us, and has now placed us in such a crisis, that if we fall in the field, we die the death of martyrs; if we survive, we rise victorious, the avengers of the cause of God. Let us, then, with one accord, swear on God's holy

* These verses are from the Shahnâmeh of Ferdausi.

word, that none of us will even think of turning his face from this warfare, nor desert from the battle and slaughter that ensues, till his soul is separated from his body."

At these words master and servant, small and great, all with emulation, seizing the Koran in their hands, swore in the form that had been given. The plan succeeded to admiration, and its effects were instantly visible both on friend and foe. The Rajpoots were defeated after a sharp but decisive struggle, in which the raja of Oodipoor, with six other princes and a number of inferior leaders, was slain. "The lowest hell," such is the language of the official despatch, "was rendered populous by the numbers of infidels who delivered up their lives to the angels of death."

After this victory Baber assumed the title of Ghazi, Conqueror of Infidels, and strove to disguise his ambition by writing below the imperial titles a *quatrain* from his prolific muse, which is thus translated:—

> "For love of the faith I became a wanderer in the desert,
> I became the antagonist of pagans and Hindus.
> I strove to make myself a martyr,
> Thanks to the Almighty, who has made me a Ghazi."

While the conqueror thus confidently appealed to the God of the Koran, the vanquished pagans exhibited their devotion with at least equal resolution. Chanderi, a strong fort of the Rajpoots, was besieged, and the garrison, after exhausting their means of defence, resolved on the last dreadful sacrifice, which both honour and religion esteemed preferable to the tender mercies of the proselytizing Mussulman. A sword was placed in the hand of the chief, and one after another the women and children, contending for precedence, came and stretched out their necks for the fatal blow. Then throwing turmeric powder over their garments, as on the day of a festival, the men rushed out with sword and shield to court a soldier's death at the hand of the enemy. Not a man escaped.

Several similar massacres ensued, but Baber experienced little further difficulty in completing his conquest. The Rana Sanka's son surrendered his fort, and delivering up a crown and golden girdle taken from Ibrahim's brother Mahmoud, submitted to become tributary to Baber. Nazret Shah, king of Bengal, also submitted after some resistance. It was only among the Patans of the east that any show of opposition was maintained. These had defeated one of Baber's generals, and after electing Mahmoud their sultan, captured Behar, and for a moment seemed likely to dispute the progress of the new invader. But at the approach of Baber in person their forces broke and dispersed; the chiefs successively gave in their adhesion, and the Mussulman empire was again united under the throne of Delhi.

Baber survived his conquests only five years. The account of his death will complete the view already given of his character. Humayun, his eldest son, whom he fondly loved, fell dangerously ill. A Mussulman doctor informed the afflicted emperor that the Almighty might vouchsafe to receive a man's most valuable possession in exchange for the life of his friend. "My *life*," exclaimed Baber, "is, next to Humayun's, the dearest possession both to me and to him. I freely devote it in exchange for my son's." He was entreated to recall the vow, and substitute a diamond of inestimable value, but he refused. Having walked three times round the dying prince, after the Mussulman practice of thrice waving a present round the person to whom it is offered, he retired to engage in prayer. From his closet he was heard to exclaim twice, "I have borne it away;" and the historians assure us that from that moment Humayun began to recover, while the emperor's health visibly decayed. He died on the 26th December, 1530, leaving a character, of which the best and truest feature recorded by an admiring biographer, is his marked "unlikeness to other Asiatic princes."*

Humayun succeeded to the throne so readily vacated, together with life, by a father's affection; but succeeded only to lose all which that father had acquired. Ferid Shere, an Affghan prince, after making himself master, first of Behar, and then of the kingdom of Bengal, was obliged by Humayun to acknowledge the supremacy of the throne of Delhi; but soon after found means to inflict a series of defeats on the emperor, which finally drove him beyond the Indus, and compelled him to take refuge in the court of Persia. There, at the disgraceful cost of renouncing his hereditary faith, and embracing the tenets of the Shiite sect, he was enabled to recover the dominion of Kabul, while his rival ascended the throne of Delhi by the style of Shere Shah.

Though stigmatized as a usurper by the Turkish historians, this monarch was a native of India, and one who reunited its forces to the expulsion of a foreign family, which had only been fourteen years contending for, rather than enjoying, the empire. His dominions were more extensive than had for some ages belonged to any sovereign of Hindustan, reaching from the mouths of the Ganges to the Indus. From end to end of this great empire he constructed a road through Bengal and the upper provinces, with caravanserais at every stage, and wells at shorter intervals.

* Erskine's Supplement.

Provisions and attendants were supplied for travellers with due regard to their caste; and the road was shaded by rows of trees on either side. At his death, which took place five years after his accession, the empire fell first to one son, and then to another, till, according to the usual destiny of eastern kingdoms, it became distracted with anarchy. Humayun now returned with an army from Kabul, and, aided by the great talents and courage of his son Akbar, succeeded in recovering the throne. His death shortly after (A.D. 1554) placed Hindustan under the sway of perhaps the only just and impartial monarch whom the Mohammedan annals record.

The misfortunes of Humayun are ascribed by his Mohammedan biographer to his virtues. "Had he been less mild and religious, he would have been a more successful prince." With much greater truth it might be affirmed that the glory of Akbar is principally owing to his want of that which Mohammedans call religion. He would have been, assuredly, a far worse man, and a worse monarch, if he had been a more consistent disciple of the Koran. He succeeded to the throne at fourteen years of age, and was only eighteen when he assumed the administration of affairs. He soon perceived that, notwithstanding the many centuries during which Mussulman zeal had laboured to make disciples to Islam by force, the mass of the Hindus were still as wedded as ever to the paganism of their forefathers. The proselytes were few in number and devoid of influence: not the slightest impression had been made on the native idolatry by all the ferocity of Mussulman monotheism. And what Akbar considered of more importance, the idolatrous Hindus were, for the most part, peaceable and obedient subjects, while the Mohammedans were perpetually at war with each other, no less than with the natives. The young emperor had the sense to determine on a more equitable system of government; and all religious persecution was discouraged and forbidden.

Though by no means deficient in military skill, nor insensible to the necessity of consolidating and defending his empire by the power of the sword, Akbar discovered, also, that the safety of the throne was quite as closely concerned with the state of the revenue as with military prowess. The rude and barbarous policy of the Koran had kept the Mohammedan dominion, through all these centuries, in the original condition of a camp quartered upon the enemy. If the infidel's life were spared, it was all he had a right to expect; Mussulman piety demanded at least the confiscation of his property. All personal property, that was not buried from sight, was plundered out of hand, while real property was subjected to an amount of taxation which left the Hindu cultivator hardly the means of sustaining existence. The land-tax had always supplied the principal revenue of the crown; but under Hindu government the proportion of the state was limited to a definite share of the produce, so that a property remained to the owner, over and above the tax and the cost of cultivation. This property the Mussulman administration simply confiscated; the conqueror asserted his own claim to the fee, and confounding taxes with rent reduced the natives to the condition of farmers, or labourers, under the foreign landlord.

In this double capacity of proprietor and sovereign of the realm, the emperor was represented by his viceroys, each of whom levied the revenue of his province, raised his own troops, and was to appear at their head when summoned to the standard of the sovereign. These viceroys, wholly ignorant of finance, were accustomed to lease their revenues to some Hindu banker, who varied the assessment and tortured the cultivators at discretion, in order to make up the stipulated sum. From the moneys so obtained the viceroy first paid his soldiers and himself, and remitted the balance, or a stipulated tribute, to the imperial exchequer. One consequence of this system was, that the military command and the control of the finances were vested in the viceroy much more than in the emperor. The forces and the sinews of war were but feebly directed from Delhi, and they contributed at least as often to the anxieties or overthrow of the throne, as to its magnificence and defence.

Akbar changed the system at once by requiring the revenue to be all remitted to the imperial exchequer, and issuing from thence the pay of the troops. He then revised the whole revenue settlement, abolishing a number of vexatious imposts, and reducing the land revenue to a fixed tax. For this purpose he caused the cultivated lands to be measured and divided into suitable districts. That such elementary measures should remain to be done, in the sixth century of Mohammedan dominion, supplies abundant evidence of the iniquitous character of that rule. The credit of the improvement, however, is unjustly ascribed to Akbar by historians whose prime object was to exalt the house of Timour. The system had, in fact, been devised and partially introduced under Shere Shah; and the author and principal agent in the reform was the Hindu raja Todar Mul, who herein only strove to re-establish the ancient principles of native finance. Akbar's merit consists in adopting a scheme which, while relieving the subject, largely increased the revenue and authority of the crown, and, further, in raising the government share, which Shere Shah had consented to fix at a fourth, to one-third of the produce.*

"The Mohammedan rulers," remarks Col. Wilkes, "combining, in a character full of extravagant contradiction, the worst extremes of the savage with some prominent features of civilized man, did not effect at one blow the extinction of the ancient proprietors; these unfortunate persons resisted—in their way—the successive exactions which were imposed by flying to the woods, from whence they were recalled by persuasion, by false promises, by hunger, or by force, to renew the culture of their lands; but the plain and undeviating principle of the government was to extort the utmost sum that could be levied without the certainty of thereby diminishing the revenue of the succeeding year."†

Akbar fixed and methodized these exactions, but never lost sight of their *principle*. His institutes vary, and even contradict themselves, in different places, on the proportion of the produce, or its money equivalent, to be levied as land tax; but it is hardly doubtful that they never designed to restore to the Hindu subject the property of which he had been deprived. Some authorities represent the general rule as dividing the produce *equally* between the government and the holders of the land, which was in

* The assessed revenue settled by Akbar in the fortieth year of his reign (A.D. 1597), for a period of ten years, amounted to about eleven millions sterling: a striking contrast to the million and a half returned (but not realized) in 1526.

† The South of India, by Lieut.-Col. Mark Wilkes, vol. i. p. 166.

effect to make the former proprietor, and the latter only peasants and husbandmen. Others say, that when the payment was made in money the fourth was accepted. The question was certainly involved in doubt; and in the relative situation of the parties a doubt was not likely to be resolved in favour of the subject.*

Akbar is still more remarkable for his religious than his financial innovations. In early life he had visited the tombs of the saints and talked of a pilgrimage to Mecca; but as his intellect grew and matured itself in the study of government, it naturally revolted from the puerilities of the Koran. He was certainly not a Mussulman, but it is difficult to give a positive definition of his religious views. He showed a great desire to become acquainted with different systems; studied Sanscrit and the sacred books of the Brahmins, inquired about Christianity, and even sent to Goa for Roman Catholic missionaries, who visited him both at Agra and at Lahore, to expound their doctrines. The emperor was, in fact, one of those learned deists who regard themselves as superior to all religions. He worshipped the sun with the Brahmin, repeated the *namaz* in the mosques, and discoursed with the Christian on spiritual and eternal life. The tenets of the Jew and the Zoroastrian were reviewed by the imperial philosopher with equal impartiality, and the same inward self-elation. But, whether it be that they who set themselves above all religion are usually the victims of some low superstition, or that the mind which has no

* See the note of Col. Wilkes on the passage last cited, where it will be seen that the *Ayeen-e-Akberi* is far from deserving the commendations bestowed upon it by the champions of Mohammedan civilization.

God does in fact worship itself, there are many intimations that Akbar desired to be received both as "the prophet and the deity of a new religion."* He composed from his own name a sort of masonic parole and countersign, designed perhaps to parody the famous Mussulman watchword, which may be translated, "There is no God but God, and Akbar is his caliph."†

With respect to Christianity it is difficult to pronounce whether Akbar was really desirous of investigating its claims, or only amused himself with the credulity of the friars. He professed to be enraptured at a portrait of the virgin Mary, and gravely declared their chapel, ornamented with trappings *borrowed from the Hindus*, to be a striking proof of the divinity of their religion.‡ He even prostrated himself to the crucifix, as he had done to the sun. He once proposed to test the claims of the Bible and the Koran, by selecting a moulah and a friar to leap into a furnace, each with his own Scripture in his hand; considerately offering that the moulah should make the experiment first. The friars rejected the ordeal, and finding that he persisted in holding out himself as the true object of worship, at last retired again to Goa.

With all this love of civil and religious reform, Akbar was not inferior to any of his race in mili-

* Col. Wilkes.

† "*Alla Akbar; Jil e Jillalehool,*" were the terms of this celebrated phrase. The former being the title assumed by the emperor on his accession to the throne; the other formed from his previous name, *Jillal-u-deen*, or, "the New Light of Faith."

‡ Very different was the estimate afterwards formed by closer or more honest observers of the worship of the Portuguese. The subahdar of Bengal made a report to Shah Jehan, who, after declaring of the Hindu gods that an army of divinities who could not benefit their worshippers were unfit to be endured, had contemptuously tolerated the popular superstitions; but the laconic answer was, "Expel *those* idolaters from my dominions." The religious images of the *Christians* were at once seized and destroyed.

tary prowess. He entirely extirpâted the party of Shere Shah, whose two nephews had obtained sovereignty in the Punjab and the eastern provinces. Malwa was subdued and annexed to the empire. His own brother, who had been appointed viceroy in Kabul, attempting to rebel, was completely defeated near Lahore. Guzerat, where the sovereignty had fallen to pieces from internal divisions, submitted to his arms with little resistance. Bengal and Orissa were reduced after a brief struggle. Kashmere was conquered, and Kandahar exchanged a nominal for a real subjection. From Bengal to the Indus the countrywas reunited under the Mogul throne.

The Hindu states could not long escape the supremacy of Akbar. Partly by arms, partly by fomenting the dissensions of the Rajpoot princes, he overcame Marwar, Amber (Jeypoor), and Mewar. The two former rajas accepted subordinate authority under the emperor, and what was felt as a more bitter humiliation, contributed each a Rajpoot princess to the imperial seraglio. Mewar alone disdained the double indignity. But the Rana Oodi Sing was unequal to the task of his father Sanka, and fled towards Guzerat. Chittore was besieged, and its commander shot by Akbar's own hand. The saffron-coloured robes were again assumed by the despairing garrison, the women cast themselves into the flames which consumed the body of the chief, and the men, to the number of eight thousand, threw themselves on the Mussulman weapons. When the conqueror entered Chittore, thirty thousand of its inhabitants perished, by order of a monarch who was styled by his courtiers "the guardian of mankind!"*

* Tod's Annals of Rajasthan.

The Rana, hid in the fastnesses of the Aravulli hills, still refused to submit, and began the foundations of the city of Oodipoor, which eventually became the new capital of Mewar. A desolating war ensued, in which his successor, Pertab Singh, after enduring several defeats, with the loss of thousands of his gallant Rajpoots, was so far from being subdued that he recovered a large portion of his hereditary domains, and the family continued independent till the following reign.

Akbar now finding himself master from the mountains to the confines of the Deccan, prepared to add the latter region also to his empire. The Bahmanee sultans (whose capital was Beder or Ahmedabad) had reduced under their sway the Hindu rajas of Telingana and Beejanuggur (or Carnata), stripping them of a part of their dominions, and rendering them tributary for the rest. Berar had also been included in their empire, which after being often at war with the Mussulman sovereignties of Guzerat, Kandeish, and Malwa, finally extended itself from sea to sea, by the conquest of Goa on the one hand, and Orissa on the other. This great Deccanee empire then experienced the fate of other Mohammedan monarchies. The Ameers declared themselves independent in their respective governments, and in the year 1526, five several kingdoms had been constituted, at Beejapoor, Ahmednuggur, Berar, Golconda, and Beder.* These sovereigns were engaged in constant hostilities with each other, and with the sultan of Guzerat, to whom Malwa and Kandeish owned a

* It was about the time of the dissolution of the great Bahmanee empire that the Portuguese appeared on the coast of Malabar, and took possession of Goa.

species of subjection. A temporary union of the shahs of Beejapoor, Ahmednuggur, and Golconda, in 1564, effected the final extinction of the great Hindu monarchy of Beejanuggur, and the conquerors soon after absorbed into their own dominions the two kingdoms of Ahmedabad and Berar.

Such was the condition of the Deccan when Akbar despatched an army for its subjugation, directing his sons, then viceroys of Guzerat and Malwa, to co-operate with all the forces of those dominions. Kandeish submitted without resistance, and after two campaigns the kingdom of Ahmednuggur was subverted, and incorporated with the Mogul empire A.D. 1598.

These acquisitions completed the glory of a reign, whose magnificence was displayed at the great festivals of the vernal equinox, and the padishah's birthday. "The festivities lasted for several days, during which there was a general fair, with processions and other pompous shows. The emperor's usual place was in a rich tent, in the midst of awnings to keep off the sun. At least two acres were thus spread with silk and gold carpets, and hangings as rich as velvet embroidered with gold, pearls, and precious stones could make them. The nobility had similar pavilions, where they received visits from each other, and sometimes from the emperor. Dresses, jewels, horses, and elephants, were bestowed upon the nobles. The emperor was weighed in golden scales against gold, silver, perfumes, and other substances in succession, which were distributed among the spectators. Almonds and other fruits of gold and silver were scattered by the emperor's own hand, and eagerly caught by the courtiers. On the great day of each festival the emperor was seated on his throne in a noble palace surrounded by his nobles, wearing high heron plumes, and sparkling with diamonds like the firmament. Many hundred elephants passed before him in companies, all most richly adorned, and the leading elephant of each company with gold plates on his head and breast, set with rubies and emeralds. Trains of caparisoned horses followed, and after them rhinoceroses, lions, tigers, panthers, hunting leopards, hounds, and hawks, the whole concluding with an innumerable host of cavalry, glittering with cloth of gold."

From the sack of Hindu towns and temples, and the hoards of similar plunder found in the palaces and citadels of the Mohammedans whom he subdued in war, Akbar had heaped together an incredible amount of treasure. His son affirmed that Timour, the spoiler of the world, never accumulated a tenth of the amount. Four hundred pairs of scales were kept at work in Agra, weighing gold and jewels, and in five months the total had not been found. Eight large vaults are said to have been filled with coin, jewels, gold and silver statues (which Akbar was not Mussulman enough to destroy), plate, bullion, tapestries, brocades, weapons, and manuscripts, to the value of nearly seventy millions sterling. The crown, made after the fashion of the Persian diadems, had twelve points surmounted by diamonds of the purest water, with a pearl of extraordinary size and value in the centre; it was priced at above two millions sterling. The throne was ascended by silver steps, on which four silver lions supported the canopy of gold, the whole adorned with jewels, and worth (it is said) thirty millions of English money. Allowing for every exaggeration, the spoil was enormous, and tells an awful tale of the rapine and bloodshed by which it was acquired.

Akbar expired in October, 1605, from the effects of a poisoned cake, which he had prepared for the Raja Maun Sing of Jeypore.* He had reigned forty-nine years, being mostly contemporary with queen Elizabeth.

At his death the empire was divided into fifteen viceroyalties, called subahs, each governed by a subahdar; for Akbar, with all his enlightenment, could not elevate the inherent barbarism of Mohammedan despotism to the rank of an organized government. The names of the subahs were, Allahabad, Agra, Oude, Ajmere, Guzerat, Behar, Bengal, Delhi, Kabul, Lahore, Multan, Malwa, Berar, Kandeish, and Ahmednuggur; all capitals of large districts, once the seat of independent royalties, and now for the first time united under a single "umbrella."

* Tod's Annals of Rajasthan.

CHAPTER VI.

DECLINE AND FALL OF THE MOGULS.

Jehangir—Noor Jehan—Shah Jehan—Submission of Rajpoots—Slaughter of imperial family—Oriental magnificence—New Delhi—Agra—Peacock throne—Conquests in the Deccan—Sons of Shah Jehan—Dara—Aurungzebe—Shuja—Moorad—Defeat of Dara—Dethronement of Shah Jehan—Moorad made away—Aurungzebe emperor—Deaths of Dara, Mohammed, and Shuja—Subjugation of the Deccan—Aurungzebe's persecutions—Sevajee—Rise of the Mahrattas—Death of Aurungzebe—His character and dying sentiments—Sikhs—Cruelties—Nizam of the Deccan—Shao Raja—Bajee Rao—Sirdeshmookee and Chowt—Mahrattas in Guzerat and Malwa—Defeat of the nizam—Nadir Shah—Progress of the Mahrattas—Ahmed Shah—Battle of Panniput—Defeat and dispersion of the Mahrattas—Retirement of Ahmed Shah—Dissolution of the Mogul empire.

The founders and consolidaters of empire claim a place in history which is not conceded to those who simply enjoy, or dissipate, the acquisitions of their predecessors. Yet the son and successor of Akbar demands attention on another and peculiar ground. Nothing more clearly evidences the prolonged barbarism of the Mohammedan rulers, than the absence of any allusion in their history to the influence of the tender feelings, which supplied the grace of Persian poetry, and illumined the unlettered manners of medieval chivalry. Jehangir is the only Mohammedan monarch, whose reign was influenced by an affection which, in other lands, has, even more than ambition or avarice, decided the fate of empires. The object of his love was Noor Mahal, or as she was called after her marriage with the emperor, Noor Jehan. Descended from Persian parents of noble family, though reduced in circumstances, she attracted attention at once by beauty, accomplishments, and extraordinary ability. She was born in the desert near Kandahar, where the poverty of her parents compelled them to expose her at the foot of a tree to the chances of the road. The mother fainted with anguish when the spot where she lay had receded from view, and the father returning found the infant involved in the coils of a hideous serpent, which he hastened to destroy. At this moment a caravan arrived, by whose assistance the wretched family were enabled to proceed to Kandahar.

Eventually the father rose to a post in the household of Akbar, and his wife and daughter becoming visitors in the royal harem, the beauty of the latter attracted the notice of the heir-apparent. Akbar, to avert evil consequences, bestowed the young beauty in marriage on a distinguished Persian, whom he endowed with a jaghire in Bengal. On the accession of Jehangir, he endeavoured to prevail on the husband to consent to a divorce; but failing in the dishonourable proposal, procured him to be assassinated. The dearly bought prize was conveyed to the royal seraglio; but from remorse or some other feeling on the part of the emperor, she remained unnoticed and unprovided for during four years, in which she supported herself by the sale of needlework and paintings. The fame of these productions reaching the emperor's ears, occasioned an interview, which revived all his former passion, and Noor Mahal was immediately installed sultana. Her influence obtained the vizierut for her father, with high employment for her two brothers. They conducted the affairs of the empire with prudence and success, while the monarch, enslaved to the charms of his wife, permitted her to effect a most beneficial change in his cruel and intemperate disposition.* Her taste and skill were manifested in reforming the ladies' dresses, and in planning public edifices and gardens, from the product of which she is said to have first extracted the famous *attar* of roses.

So long as Noor Mahal's father lived, the empire shared the satisfaction of the monarch, and in the language of the day, the light of the harem—Noor Mahal—had some pretensions to be styled the light of the world—Noor Jehan. Upon his death, however, the imperial beauty, spoiled by power and indulgence, began to exercise a calamitous influence over the fate of the empire. She engaged, both by intrigue and open warfare, in the troubles which embittered the closing years of her husband's reign. She fought for him, when inveigled into the custody of her enemies, as she had accompanied him in happier days to the sports of the jungle. Mounted on the elephant from whose back she had shot four tigers with her own hand, the sultana showed herself in the field of battle, with a granddaughter seated in her lap, actively combating the foe. Both were wounded and the driver killed, when the infuriated animal dashed into the river, and with difficulty gained the opposite bank with his burden. The empress was found calmly dressing the wound of the terrified infant.

Defeated in the field, Noor Jehan resolved to

* The emperor's eldest son, Khosru, had raised the standard of revolt at the beginning of the reign, and on his defeat was brought in chains of gold before his father, who wreaked his revenge upon his friends with terrible ferocity. Some were sewn up in raw hides and exposed to a lingering death, others flayed alive, while no less than seven hundred were impaled in a row from the gate of Lahore. Khosru himself was brought daily to witness their agonies, and while borne along the ghastly line on an elephant, was exhorted by an attendant to receive the salutations of his servants.

share the captivity of her lord, but was arrested on the way, with an order for her execution, wrung from the weak-minded Jehangir during their separation. She asked but to kiss the imperial hand before she died. Admitted to his presence the sentence was at once reversed, and she determined to effect by artifice an object which force had failed to achieve. Succeeding in dexterously separating the monarch from his guards at a review, she carried him off in the midst of a contingent raised by herself. Jehangir died shortly after at Lahore, and the queen, throughout a widowhood of twenty years, secluded alike from amusement and business, wore only plain white garments, and in 1646, was interred in the sepulchre prepared by her order for her husband and herself at Lahore.*

The next emperor bore the name of Shah Jehan. He was a younger and favourite son of Jehangir by a Rajpoot princess, and had obtained high honour in his father's lifetime, by completing the subjugation of his maternal connexion, the Rana Umra Sing of Oodipoor, whose crimson banner had waved independent for more than eight centuries.† The prince

* In the little book called "British Rule in India," Miss Martineau has mistaken the burial place of this affectionate pair for the famous Taj Mehal at Agra, which covers the remains of *Shah Jehan and his wife*. In some other respects also she has misapprehended the names and incidents of Indian history.

† The Rana Umra Sing submitted to the Mogul arms, after sustaining seventeen defeats, on promises of the most honourable treatment. He was to retain his dominions under a nominal tribute to the empire; but when required to receive the imperial firman outside his capital, the spirit of the unconquerable Rajpoot recoiled from the humiliation. Assembling the chiefs, he made the teeka (the sign of sovereignty) on his son's forehead, and retired into private life. The "tallest and strongest of the princes of Mewar" never again quitted the palace in which his shame was hidden from the eyes of men, but was often visited by his conqueror, Prince Khoorum, afterwards Shah Jehan.—*Annals of Rajasthan.*

made use of his power to assume the royal titles, and marched in arms against his father. Being defeated, exiled, pardoned, and again received into favour, he was a second time plotting his father's deposition, in league with Noor Jehan's brother (to whose daughter he was married), when the aged emperor's death saved him from a new crime. He had previously caused his elder brother, Khosru, to be assassinated; and now, finding the throne bequeathed by their father to another brother who had married the daughter of Noor Jehan, he scrupled not to add his murder to the list. The infant son of the elder brother, proclaimed by the conspirators as a temporary expedient while Shah Jehan was collecting his forces, was removed in the same manner; and having thus made his way to the throne, the emperor secured it by despatching, by the dagger or the bowstring, the whole of the male posterity of Timour, with the exception of his own sons.

These proceedings, calmly recorded by the Mussulman historians as matter of state necessity, do not prevent their celebrating his reign as a model of justice and good government. Even Mill, however, is obliged to admit, in a note on this great and glorious monarch, that, "knowing more of the circumstances of his reign, we know better what the general eulogies of the oriental historians mean." He adds a remark from the French physician Bernier, who describes his arrival at Shah Jehan's court, "with the little money which remained to him after several encounters with robbers." These are the incidents which afford a glimpse into the true condition of the people.

The reign of Shah Jehan carried to its summit that oriental magnificence which so dazzled the eyes of

Mohammedan historians, and even in Europe invested "the Great Mogul" with a halo of romance. The ancient city of Delhi, whose buildings and gardens had extended above thirty miles along the banks of the Jumna, being desolated by repeated ravages, Shah Jehan founded the new town, which still bears his name, A.D. 1631. Enclosed by the river and a wall of seven miles in circumference, New Delhi or Shah Jehanabad was adorned with a palace and mosques and aqueducts, in a style vastly exceeding all former Indian architecture. The palace is described by Bishop Heber as a kingly residence, far surpassing the Kremlin, and inferior only to Windsor Castle. It stands on the Jumna, defended by the old river fort of Selimghur, constructed by the Patan sovereigns, and is enclosed on the sides towards the city by a wall of red granite forty feet high, flanked with turrets and cupolas. The interior, beautiful even in its present decay, was filled with the costliest and most elegant works of oriental taste and luxury. Pavilions of white marble, surmounted by cupolas, with the pillars and arches exquisitely carved and ornamented with arabesques gilt and inlaid, having the ceilings adorned with a rich foliage of silver, stood in gardens planted with flowers, and cooled with fountains and cascades. The Motee Musjid, or private mosque for the palace, was a marvel of Mohammedan art. The great mosque of the city (Jumma Musjid) rose majestically from a rocky platform, thirty feet higher than the general level of the city, where the splendid edifice, two hundred and sixty-one feet in length, surrounded by an open arcade, and approached by magnificent flights of steps, dominated over the surrounding streets, crowned with cupolas and minarets This mosque was six years in building, and cost £100,000 of English money. A watercourse ran through every principal street, fed from a canal which drew its supply from that of Feroze Shah, at seventy miles distance, the waters of the Jumna at Delhi being strongly impregnated with nitre. On the left bank of the river, opposite the palace, stretched a vast preserve and pleasure ground, surrounded by the stately palaces of the nobles, and watered by another canal of one hundred and thirty-five miles in length.* After several invasions and a century of neglect, Delhi is still a magnificent oriental city: in the meridian of its splendour it filled all spectators with admiration.

The "Great Moguls" had a residence scarcely less dear to them in Agra. The Motee Musjid, or Pearl of Mosques, in the interior of which nothing but white marble is seen; and the Taj Mehal, or Mausoleum of Shah Jehan and his consort Mumtazi Mahal, adorn this favourite capital. The latter occupied twenty thousand men for twenty-two years in its erection. It is crowned by a dome seventy feet in diameter and two hundred and sixty feet in height, surmounted by two gilt globes and a crescent. The interior of the dome is profusely clustered with fruit, flowers, and foliage, in marble and mosaic, to represent the blooming bowers of Paradise; each flower is said to contain a hundred precious stones.

In these abodes of luxury the prodigious treasures of the empire were displayed in more variety of forms than under any former prince. The pomp and prodigality of the padishah were especially manifested in the celebrated peacock throne, which took its name

* Both canals were constructed by Ali Merdan Khan, who had been governor of Kandahar, under the king of Persia, and, dreading his tyranny, yielded the place to Shah Jehan, who employed him in high offices, civil and military.

from a figure of that bird, standing amid a dazzling blaze of diamonds and precious stones, having its train spread, with the natural colours represented in sapphires, emeralds, rubies, and other appropriate jewels. The common belief was that this single piece of imperial furniture cost six millions and a half of our money. Notwithstanding all this lavish expenditure, Shah Jehan left a treasure in money of twenty-four millions sterling. The annual revenue of the empire had also augmented to thirty-two millions.*

The chief political exploit of this reign was the further subjugation of the Deccan; where, as in every region afflicted by Mohammedan usurpation, the natives continued to be desolated by the oppression and internecine warfare of their governors. Shah Jehan arrived at Dowlatabad with an enormous army, and at once attacked the kingdoms of Golconda and Beejapore, giving orders to exercise every possible severity, "because war"—such was his humane reflection—"is the scourge of humanity, and compassion only serves to prolong its evils." One hundred and fifteen towns and fortresses were taken, with the usual horrible treatment of the vanquished party. The two sovereigns were compelled to sue for peace, and, as its condition, resigned their territories to receive them again as tributaries of the Mogul. The emperor's son Aurungzebe, being left in command at Dowlatabad, soon after treacherously attacked the king of Golconda; Hyderabad was taken and burned, but the riches, which had tempted the attack, were mostly consumed in the flames. Peace was again sealed by the marriage of the king's beautiful daughter with the

* Elphinstone, vol. ii. p. 435.

son of Aurungzebe. No treaty or oath, however, could restrain a Mogul prince, when an opportunity offered for rapine. The king of Beejapore dying, Aurungzebe besieged the capital, and was on the eve of taking it, when his attention was recalled to affairs more nearly concerning himself at Agra.

The barbarous expedient of destroying all his male relations had promised Shah Jehan an exemption from the conspiracies and revolts so frequent in the history of his race and creed. But he ought to have remembered that the treasons by which he had brought his father's grey hairs with sorrow to the grave, might be directed from a similar quarter against his own. After a reign of thirty years, he was himself to feel " how sharper than a serpent's tooth it is to have a thankless child." Four sons and three daughters constituted the family of Shah Jehan. Dara, the eldest son, was of an open and generous, but rash, imprudent disposition. He resided near the emperor as heir-apparent, and stood deservedly high in his favour. The second son Shuja was subahdar of Bengal; more prudent than his elder brother, but far inferior both in caution and ability to the deep and dissembling Aurungzebe, who was the third son and held the soubah of the Deccan. Morad, the youngest, was in charge of Guzerat; brave, affable, and popular, but credulous, heady, and intemperate. All were men of capacity, who, instead of being nursed in the effeminate habits of an oriental seraglio, had won distinction in the field, and educated themselves for empire in the conduct of public affairs.

In religion Dara was addicted to the deistical views of Akbar; Shuja had embraced the tenets of the Shiite sect; but Aurungzebe was not merely orthodox, he had affected from an early age a character for extraordinary piety. He talked of renouncing the world, and only panted for the opportunity of taking the pilgrimage to Mecca, and devoting himself to a life of austerity and prayer. To every brother, under an oriental despotism, the sons of the reigning monarch look as either a victim or a butcher, seeing but one choice between the musnud and the grave.* Dara, who was not deficient in penetration, was wont to say that he had no fear of any of his brothers *but the pious one.*

The eldest prince had attained the age of forty-two, when the emperor was seized with an illness pronounced to be mortal. The heir-apparent at once assumed the reins of government, endeavouring to keep the state of affairs from the knowledge of his brothers, and giving orders to put the imperial forces in readiness for the field. His precautions were far from unnecessary. Shuja advanced from Bengal at the head of an army, which he had prepared with this contest in view. He was defeated, and compelled to retreat to Bengal, by Dara's son Soliman. Meanwhile, Aurungzebe concerted a more cautious attempt with Morad, whom he had invited to ascend the throne, protesting for himself that when he had placed his brother in the position of which no other was worthy, he should retire into obscurity, and prosecute a life of religion.

The two brothers advanced with their respective forces. They had crossed the Nerbudda, and defeated the raja of Oodipore, who endeavoured to dispute their further passage, when they learned to their dismay that the emperor had recovered his health and

* Elphinstone, vol. ii., p. 381.

resumed the reins of authority. They were loth to retreat from a design which promised success; and, as they lingered, Dara hastily marched against them at the head of his father's army, and forced them to an engagement. The issue hung long in doubt, till Dara having incautiously dismounted from his wounded elephant,* his troops were discouraged, and fled. Aurungzebe, in the presence of the united armies, fell upon his face and praised God for the victory; then saluting Morad as emperor, he began ostentatiously to prepare for his own pilgrimage to Mecca.

The conspirators advanced towards Agra, where the emperor ordered the gates to be closed against them. Aurungzebe, who was now diligently plotting with his father's omrahs, and justly confided in his matchless powers of dissimulation, wrote to the emperor with the strongest professions of loyalty and obedience: these his father, himself no unskilful dissembler, accepted in the same spirit, affectionately inviting him to the presence, with the design of making him a prisoner. The two diplomatists plied each other for several days, but the elder hypocrite was no match for the younger. Aurungzebe succeeded in introducing his son Mohammed, with a small guard, to the citadel, prevailing on the emperor at the same time to withdraw his own troops. The deluded monarch sat upon his throne, expecting the approach of his repentant

* It appears from the time of Alexander the Great to have been held indispensable in an Indian army (and the numerical majority of all the Mohammedan armies, as now of the British, consisted of Hindus) that the general should be always seen at their head, mounted on his war elephant. Several battles are noted to have been lost in consequence of his disappearance. Aurungzebe himself was once on the point of committing the mistake which proved fatal to Dara, but, as he moved from his howdah, an officer exclaimed, "You descend from the throne;") the cautious prince smiled, and resumed his seat on the wounded animal.

child. He was told that Aurungzebe had turned aside to pay his devotions at the tomb of Akbar, and indignantly demanding of Mohammed what was the meaning of such behaviour, the reply was, "My father never intended to visit the emperor." "Then why are you here?" the monarch retorted. "To take charge of the citadel," calmly answered the youth; and Shah Jehan saw that his reign was over. In vain he tried to bribe his grandson with the offer of the imperial crown at his demise. Mohammed hesitated for a moment; then hastening from the apartment, left the old man a prisoner. He lived for seven years longer, but never again quitted the citadel, nor saw the face of either of his sons. Old as he was, his death was probably hastened by poison. Meantime, Aurungzebe disposed of his brother Morad by causing him to be seized while in a state of intoxication, and carried a prisoner to the castle of Agra. Then, with an affectation of reluctance not inferior to our third Richard, he suffered himself to be adorned with the ensigns of royalty in a garden near Delhi, A.D. 1658.

Dara was soon driven beyond the Indus, and returning was treacherously captured and conveyed to Aurungzebe, who, after publicly exposing him in the streets of Delhi, caused him to be put to death. Shuja, advancing on the capital, was again defeated and forced back. The young Mohammed, who had been betrothed to his daughter, now became dissatisfied with his father's recognition of the service which had secured him the throne. He was induced by the entreaties of his affianced cousin to desert to his uncle; but the emperor was too strong for them both. By his artifices he inspired Shuja with a distrust of his nephew, which compelled the prince to retire from Bengal, and yield himself in despair to his unforgiving father. He was instantly immured in the fort of Gwalior, the *bastille* of Hindustan, where he languished for several years, and died soon after receiving his liberty. Shuja himself finally sought refuge in Arracan, where the raja put him and all his family to death. Soliman, the son of Dara, was next added to the prisoners in Gwalior, and Aurungzebe found himself (like his father) without a rival among the posterity of Timour.*

His protracted reign was chiefly occupied in the final subdual of the Deccan. He succeeded first in reducing the kingdoms of Golconda and Beejapore to capitulation by arms, and then, by the perfidy which was always in his hands a more favourite and a more deadly weapon than the sword, in seizing upon their persons, and annexing their dominions to his own. The prince Shah Aulum was placed in confinement for remonstrating against his father's unprincipled violation of honour; but the emperor had the satisfaction of finding his dominions extended to the farthest limits of the Carnatic, and himself, after a struggle protracted through seven centuries, during the greater part of which the invaders had been divided among themselves, and the land had been never free from pillage and slaughter, at last the sole Mussulman monarch of India. The gourd, however,

* The prisoners at Gwalior were allowed no drink but a decoction of opium, called the *ponsta*, which gradually enfeebled their health of body and mind, and acted as a slow but certain poison. Soliman was so well acquainted with the deadly process that he begged to be beheaded rather than sent to this fortress. His uncle endeavoured to reassure him with his customary hypocrisy, but Bernier tells us that the prince was actually done to death in this detestable manner; and that Shah Jehan, the infant son of Morad, and many others, perished from the same cause.

had not sprung up over his head before the worm was prepared which was to eat into its heart and destroy it.

Aurungzebe was animated by a zeal for the ascendancy of his faith only second to his ambition for territorial empire. The toleration of Akbar and the contempt of Shah Jehan, who, after one or two attempts upon idolatry, decided "that he who wants subjects must take them with all their religious baubles," were exchanged for a bigoted persecution of the infidels and their religious rites. Hindus no longer found the path of civil or military distinction open in the Mogul service, and the long-standing feud of race and creed was embittered by a sense of personal proscription. The capitation-tax upon infidels, that most odious and oppressive impost of Mussulman bigotry which Akbar had remitted, was again vigorously enforced; and the idolatrous processions, which Shah Jehan had scornfully tolerated, were strictly prohibited by the fiercer zeal of Aurungzebe. Force, too, was unscrupulously employed for the conversion of the Hindus. The children of some of the highest natives were seized and circumcised, while pagodas at Benares and elsewhere were broken down, or converted into mosques. Insulted and trampled upon with unrelenting intolerance, the worm began to turn; and a leader appeared both willing and able to raise the lowest of the despised Hindu castes to equality with the haughty Moguls.

In the service and under the protection of the more tolerant kings of Ahmednuggur and Beejapore, lived a Hindu called Shahjee, holding the jaghire of Poona, with at one time a high command in the Carnatic. He was married to the daughter of a great

Mahratta chief, by whom he had an only son, named Sevajee, who resided on the paternal domain at Poona, while his father was employed in the armies of the Deccan. Sevajee was educated by a Brahmin in the bitterest detestation of the faith and empire of the Moguls. Having raised a body of horse, he contrived to seize on several strong forts in the western ghâts, and speedily became master of the Concan, with the coast from Goa to Daman. He was induced, however, to present himself before the emperor at Delhi, where instead of the honours that had been promised him, he was by order of Aurungzebe placed among the inferior ameers. Stung by the perfidious insult, he contrived to effect his escape in a hamper, and after assuming the disguise of a religious mendicant, privily reached his own country. There he assumed the royal title, committing himself with all his tribe to a deadly feud with the Moguls.

In 1677 he marched at the head of forty thousand horse to aid the king of Golconda against Beejapore. These hostilities greatly aided the rising power of the Mahrattas. At his death, which took place in 1682, Sevajee's dominions comprehended along the western coast an extent of four hundred miles in length, by one hundred and twenty in breadth. His son Sambajee had the honour to afford a refuge to Akbar, a younger son of Aurungzebe, who had revolted and fled from his arms. At a later date the Mahratta chief was surprised and carried as a prisoner to Aurungzebe, who, with the usual brutality of a pious Mussulman, ordered the pagan to be tortured and butchered in his own presence.

Sambajee was inferior both in character and popularity to his father Sevajee, but on receiving intelligence of his execution the Mahrattas rose in vast numbers under various chieftains, and issuing from the mountains began to plunder the imperial dominions. The Mogul forces attacked and reduced their forts; but keeping the field and eluding an encounter, the Mahratta horse continued to pillage, and so increased in riches, numbers, and power, as to attract or compel the zemindars to join them. The whole of the Deccan was ravaged by these incursions, and the harassing struggle was protracted, without advantage to the imperial arms, up to the death of Aurungzebe.

This emperor and his father are better known than any former Mohammedan rulers, from the visits paid to their courts by European travellers. Their letters and diaries also have been preserved. We have thus the means of forming a truer estimate, both of their private motives and public policy, than can be gained from the inflated accounts of Mussulman writers, dazzled by external pomp, ignorant of the true principles of government, and indifferent to the miseries of the infidel. The following is a summary, drawn by no unfriendly hand, of the character of Aurungzebe:—"He was a man of a mild temper and cold heart; cautious, artful, and designing; a perfect master of dissimulation; acute and sagacious, though not extended in his views; and ever on the watch to gain friends, and to propitiate enemies. To these less brilliant qualities he joined great courage and skill in military exercises, a handsome though not athletic form, affable and gracious manners, and lively and agreeable conversation. He was so great a dissembler in other matters, that he has been supposed to have been a hypocrite in religion. But although religion was a great instrument of his policy, he was beyond all doubt a sincere and bigoted Mussulman. He had been brought up by men of known sanctity, and had himself shown an early turn for devotion; he at one time professed the intention of renouncing the world, and taking the habit of a fakir; and throughout his whole life he evinced a real attachment to his faith in many things indifferent to his interest, and in some most seriously opposed to it. His zeal was shown in his prayers, and reading the Koran, in pious discourses, in abstemiousness (which he affected to carry so far as to subsist on the earnings of his manual labour), in humility of deportment, patience under provocation, and resignation in misfortunes; but above all, in earnest and constant endeavours to promote his own faith, and to discourage idolatry and infidelity. But neither religion nor morality stood for a moment in his way when they interfered with his ambition; and though full of scruples at other times, he would stick at no crime that was requisite for the gratification of that passion."*

To this estimate of the impartial historian, may be added the monarch's own retrospect of his life, made at a period when the impulses of ambition, the flatteries of a court, and the frauds of hypocrisy fade away in the receding distance, and terrified conscience too surely anticipates the everlasting doom. The following are extracts from the letters of the dying Mogul to his sons:—"Wherever I look I see nothing but the Deity. I know nothing of myself, what I am, and to what I am destined. The instant which passed in power has left only sorrow behind it.

* Elphinstone, vol. ii. p. 521.

I have not been the guardian and protector of the empire. My valuable time has been passed vainly. I had a patron in my own dwelling (conscience), but his glorious light was unseen by my dim sight. I brought nothing into this world, and, except the infirmities of man, carry nothing out. I have a dread for my salvation, and with what torments I may be punished. Though I have strong reliance on the mercies and bounty of God, yet regarding my actions fear will not quit me; but when I am gone, reflection will not remain. My back is bent with weakness, and my feet have lost the powers of motion. The breath which rose is gone, and left not even hope behind it. I have committed numerous crimes, and know not with what punishments I may be seized. The guardianship of a people is the trust by God committed to my sons. I resign you, your mother, and son, to God, as I myself am going. The agonies of death come upon me fast. Odipore, your mother, was a partner in my illness, and wishes to accompany me in death; but everything has its appointed time. I am going. Whatever good or evil I have done, it was for you. No one has seen the departing of his own soul, but I see that mine is departing."

How painful is the thought that no ray of gospel light ever beamed on the thick darkness so affectingly portrayed in these words. The Christian, however poor, is assuredly more to be envied than this renowned but despairing monarch.

Aurungzebe assumed the imperial diadem a month before the death of Oliver Cromwell, and expired on the 21st of February, 1707, when the British throne was occupied by queen Anne. In the eleven years which followed his decease, as many princes of his descent came to a bloody end, five having actually ascended, and the remainder being competitors for the throne. There is little use in recalling their names or their crimes.* The Mogul dynasty was fast hastening to its close, and its mortal agonies were the immediate consequences of the cruelty and intolerance of the monarch, whom its historians delight to celebrate as its greatest honour.

Aurungzebe left the empire involved in a religious war with the Rajpoot states. A new enemy soon appeared in the Sikhs, whom, from a peaceable sect, Mussulman persecution had converted into a formidable banditti. The founder of this sect was a Hindu of the Kshatriya caste named Nanuk, who, having been early instructed in the Koran, compiled out of its pages, and the traditions of his ancestral creed, a new Scripture, called, in the dialect of the Punjab, the *Grunth*, that is, like the Bible and the Koran, *the Book*. After a century of quiet growth, inculcating doctrines of peace and universal toleration, their spiritual chief was wantonly put to death A.D. 1606, the year after Akbar's decease. His followers instantly took up arms, and having been expelled from Lahore, took refuge in the northern mountains. Their leader or *Guru* Govind, about the year 1675, conceived the idea of forming them into a religious commonwealth, which was animated by a deadly animosity against their Mohammedan persecutors. The

* "Oh, wonderful God!" exclaims even the Mohammedan annalist, "how did thy divine justice manifest itself in the several events of this revolution! Feroksheer, in the days of his power, strangled his own brothers, murdered numbers of innocent persons, and blinded others; he was, therefore, destined to suffer all these cruelties before he died." The principal actors in this troubled period were two *Syud* brothers (descendants of the Prophet), named Hussein Ali and Abdullah Khan, who filled the highest situations at court, and performed the part of "king makers." One was finally assassinated, and the other slain in battle.

Hindu deities and the Brahmins were respected; the slaughter of kine was strictly forbidden; but all other prohibitions of food and liquors, with the distinctions of caste, were wholly abolished. Every individual, on his admission to the sect, took the vow as a soldier, to carry steel at all times on his person, wear blue clothes, and allow the hair and beard to grow.

Under the first successor of Aurungzebe this formidable body burst from their mountain retreats, and ravaged the banks of the Sutlej with the utmost cruelty. Mosques were destroyed, moollahs butchered, and all the barbarities practised upon Mussulmans which the Koran prescribes for unbelievers. The Moguls retaliated with equal ferocity. The Sikh leader, Bandar, after a long predatory career, was captured and brought to Delhi. In this city, the theatre of so much magnificence and horror, he was exposed in an iron cage, with the heads of his followers stuck on pikes around him, and a dead cat among them, to show that not even a domestic animal should be preserved from extermination. The prisoner was required to stab his own infant, and refusing, it was butchered before his face, and the heart torn out and thrust between his teeth. He was himself torn to pieces with red-hot pincers, and his followers hunted down like wild beasts. Such was the character of Mussulman civilization about the time of the accession of George I.

The Mogul empire was now rent with dissensions, amid which the power of the Mahrattas steadily advanced to its subversion. Asof Jah, a Turkish chief who had gained distinction in the wars of Aurungzebe, after filling the highest posts in the court of Delhi, disgusted with the intrigues of the favourites, retired with the title of the Nizam ool Moolk to his vice-royalty of the Deccan, and there assumed an independence which descended to his posterity. The nizam was for some time engaged in fomenting the dissensions and arresting the progress of his Mahratta neighbours; but in the end both powers united in the spoliation of the throne of Delhi.

The son of Sevajee, whom Aurungzebe had so cruelly murdered at Delhi, left a child who, falling into the emperor's power, was placed with unwonted compassion in the seraglio, under the care of one of the young begums. Aurungzebe never spoke of the great Mahratta chief by any other epithet than "thief" and "robber;" but, pleased with this boy, he bestowed upon him in jest the nickname of *Sahoo*, shortened into Shao, signifying *no* robber. The youth's proper appellation was the same as that of his grandfather Sevajee, but for some reason he preferred to bear the Mogul nickname, and from his use of it came the English practice of denominating the Mahratta sovereign as the Sahoo or Shao Raja.

Shao obtained his liberty on the death of Aurungzebe. After some family discord, occasioned by the usurpation of his uncle during his captivity, he eventually reunited the Mahratta clans under his lead, and became firmly seated on the throne of Sattara, the capital of the nation. His *peishwah*, or prime minister, was a Brahmin, named Balajee Wishwanath, who was succeeded by his son Bajee Rao, the most able of all the Mahratta nation. Sevajee had established a claim on the revenues of the Beejapore kingdom, in right of his father, who had purchased the office of *desmookh* which, under all the old Hindu governments, was entitled to a share in the collections.

On the subversion of that kingdom by Aurungzebe, he demanded and obtained, in satisfaction of this claim, a payment of ten per cent. on the revenues arising within its limits: this was called the *sirdeshmooki*. Another claim, called *chowt*, was levied by the powerful Mahratta after plundering Surat (A.D. 1670); it amounted to one-fourth of the revenue, and exempted the district from plunder as long as it was regularly paid. This kind of black-mail was afterwards enforced by every Mahratta chief to the extent of his power. The practice was to ravage and spoil without mercy where the demand was resisted, but to preserve perfect order and good faith as soon as it was submitted to. The rule of Sevajee, however, was universally observed, that a *cow*, a *woman*, and a *husbandman* were at no time to be molested.

These claims of *sirdeshmooki* and *chowt* were gradually extended by the power of the Mahrattas, till the nizam was obliged to concede them over the whole of the Deccan. The court of Delhi for some time withheld its ratification; but in the interval between the murder of one emperor and the elevation of another, when two princes, whose names are erased from the records, successively gained and lost the slippery eminence, firmans were obtained conceding both claims over all the six subahs into which the Deccan was divided, and further granting in *swurajee*, or sovereignty, all the territory possessed by Sevajee at the time of his death.*

This concession little availed the declining empire. The peishwah crossed the Nerbudda, and extended the *chowt* to Guzerat and Malwa. His demands were raised as the emperor was found unable to resist.

* Duff's History of the Mahrattas, vol. i. p. 450.

All Malwa was claimed in jaghire, and the peishwah appeared at the gates of Delhi itself A.D. 1737. The nizam, roused at the progress of his dangerous ally, deserted the Mahratta cause, and marched to the support of the tottering throne, but his allegiance was resumed too late. He was defeated at the head of the united Mogul armies, and obliged to concede all the demands of the victorious Mahratta. At this juncture the progress of conquest and decay was suddenly arrested by a visitation hardly second in horror to the invasion of Tamerlane.

Nadir Kuli, the greatest warrior Persia has produced, " the boast, the terror, and the execration of his country," was now on the throne of Ispahan, and had extended his arms to the frontiers of India. Seizing the pretext of some slight from the court of Delhi, he resolved to replenish his exhausted finances from the Mogul exchequer. Advancing without resistance through the Punjab, he defeated at Kurnaul all the forces which the divided state of the empire could bring into the field, and compelled the emperor Mohammed to join the invading army, and march with him to Delhi. Both kings took up their residence in the palace; but on the second day, a report having been spread of Nadir's death, the populace fell upon the Persians and destroyed some hundreds. Nadir presenting himself to allay the tumult was attacked from the houses, and one of his chiefs killed at his side. Giving way to passion, he ordered a general massacre. Twenty thousand men obeyed the mandate, and the slaughter raged from sunrise till the day was far advanced, attended by all the horrors of rapine, lust, and revenge. Nadir sate in gloomy silence within the mosque of Roku-u-dowla, till the tears of Mohammed obtained an order to spare his unhappy subjects. The number of the slain is variously stated from thirty thousand to one hundred and fifty thousand.

The massacre over, the pillage began. All the imperial treasury and jewels, with the peacock throne, were seized; the effects of the nobles followed; then of the inferior officers and common people. Guards were placed to prevent escape, and every one was plundered to the full extent of his means. Torture and blows were liberally applied to discover concealed treasure. "It was before a general massacre: now it was the murder of individuals."

Having exhausted all attainable sources of wealth, the conqueror marched away, carrying with him a treasure in money stated at from eight to thirty millions sterling, with untold millions in gold and silver plate, stuffs, and jewels of inestimable value. Before he went he made a treaty with Mohammed Shah, seating him on the throne and enjoining all the Indian nobles to obey him. He concluded the ceremony by exchanging turbans with the Mogul, thereby receiving and adding to his plunder the celebrated Koh-i-noor diamond, which the emperor wore in his head-dress.

The departure of Nadir Shah left the Mogul empire in the last stage of collapse. Bajee Rao was the first to recover from the general stupor, and hostilities were renewed with the nizam in the Deccan. His death stayed but for a moment the projects of the Mahrattas. He was succeeded by his son Balajee, who extended the chowt into Bengal, and obtained a formal cession of Malwa and Cuttack in sovereignty. On the death of Shao without issue, the peishwah adopted the not unfrequent expedient of placing a child on the throne, transfering all power to himself: from this time the raja of Sattara has been only the nominal head of the Mahratta confederacy. The Rohillas, a band of Affghan adventurers who had seized the country from Oude to the Himalayas, next rose in insurrection; and in the midst of these internal troubles the expiring empire became again the prey of foreign invasion.

Nadir Shah having fallen a victim to assassination, provoked by his intolerable cruelties, the Affghans in his service fell back upon their own country, and in 1747 placed on the throne at Kandahar the head of the Abdallee or Duranee tribe, by the title of Ahmed Shah. This monarch instantly invaded and occupied the Punjab, and soon after marched upon Delhi. The city was again taken (A.D. 1756), and nearly all the horrors of Nadir Shah's invasion were repeated.* The new invader was no sooner gone than the Mahrattas were called in by one of the factions of the empire, and Delhi opened its gates to Holcar, who became master of the emperor's person A.D. 1758. Soon after they seized the Punjab and openly talked of the conquest of Hindustan. These pretensions brought back the Affghan monarch to oppose them, and the famous plains of Panniput witnessed one more last struggle between the Mussulman and the Hindu races.

The Mahratta forces had exchanged the character of mere predatory bands for that of an army numbering ten thousand infantry, the best that had been yet seen in India, with a well-mounted cavalry and a train of artillery much superior to the Mogul's. It was commanded by the peishwah's cousin, called "the Bhao," accompanied by his son Wiswas Rao and all

* Elphinstone, vol. ii. p. 665.

the great Brahmin and Mahratta chiefs, with a considerable force of Rajpoots. Ahmed Shah being joined by all the Mohammedan princes, was at the head of forty thousand Affghans, thirteen thousand Indian horse, and thirty-eight thousand infantry, of which the Rohillas were the only very efficient portion. He had also thirty pieces of cannon, but was in the aggregate too inferior to the Mahrattas to venture on the attack.

The decisive struggle was fought on the 6th January, 1761: for a time the advantage inclined to the Mahrattas; but Ahmed Shah charging at the critical moment with his reserve, "as if by enchantment the whole Mahratta army turned their backs and fled at full speed." The pursuit was continued for fifteen or twenty miles, and the rout was complete. Both the Bhao and the heir-apparent were among the slain, whose number amounted to two hundred thousand. Scarcely a chief escaped unwounded, and the whole Mahratta people mourned as for the deathblow of the nation. The wreck of the army saved itself in the Deccan, evacuating Hindustan; but the peishwah's government never recovered its vigour. On the other hand, the Mohammedan confederation dissolved on the cessation of the common danger. Ahmed Shah returned to Affghanistan, leaving Delhi in the hands of the vizier, who had previously murdered the emperor Alumghir. The heir-apparent Shah Alum had escaped into the provinces. "The actors having now all left the stage, the history of the Mogul empire here closes of itself. Its territory is broken into separate states; the capital is deserted; the claimant to the name of emperor is an exile and a dependent, while a new race of conquerors has already commenced its career, which may again unite the empire under better auspices than before."*

It was surely time for the bloody strife to cease. For seven hundred and fifty years the Mohammedan power had been engaged in the subjugation of India. Its first conquests were made when the Danes were contending with the Saxons for the mastery of England: the sceptre fell from its grasp while England was disputing with her North American colonies, in the reign of George III. The Norman Conquest, the Wars of the Plantagenets and the Roses, the Mediæval Church, the Protestant Reformation, the Great Rebellion, the Restoration, successively stamped their character on this island while India was plunged in one monotonous series of barbarian ravages. The British constitution was born, matured, cast away, recovered, and carried towards completeness, while Hindu liberties lay struggling under the iron heel of Mussulman despotism. Literature was planted in England, and nourished up to her present stately growth; the principles of civil and religious liberty were developed from the very germ: private honour and public faith grew up as the pillars of society; and the light of compassion was thrown upon the deepest recesses of poverty and crime, in a period during which India learnt absolutely nothing from her Mohammedan rulers.† Blood had flowed enough to steep the British isles in one crimson sea. Treasure was heaped together, of which England, with her agricultural riches and inexhaustible commercial credit, never saw the

* Elphinstone, vol. ii. p. 688.

† Sixty-five Mohammedan conquerors and rulers of Hindustan are enumerated from Mahmoud of Ghizni (A.D. 1001) to the last of the Moguls (A.D. 1760). Of this number, twenty-four were assassinated, eleven deposed or abdicated, two slain in battle, one killed by a fall, and twenty-seven alleged to have died a natural death.

tithe in one place. Magnificence, which all the courts of Europe could not match, dazzled even the oriental eye. The padishas had ruled and moved as very gods among their prostrate subjects. And now that all was gone—

> "The cloud capped towers, the gorgeous palaces,
> The insubstantial pageant faded"—

not one national or social benefit remained to compensate for the awful price of the show. The empire was dissolved: Islam had achieved no victory over idolatry; and the result of the struggle was a vast diminution in numbers, wealth, and morals. The ruins of ancient cities attest, to the present hour, the desolation in which alone the Mussulman could make peace with the Hindu: and with every allowance for inaccuracy, the accounts of the Greeks testify to many qualities which are sought for in vain from the servile, but revengeful race which emerged from under the sceptre of the Mogul.

Such is the contrast between the civilization of the Gospel and that of the Koran. Such are the effects of ruling populous nations for the sole advantage of a dominant race: and similar must be the consequences at all times of trying to govern India by the sword alone.

CHAPTER VII.

EUROPEANS IN INDIA.

Concurrence of events—Baber and Luther—Discovery of America and Cape of Good Hope—Vasco de Gama—Zamorin of Calicut—Idolatry—Carries off the natives—Reception at Lisbon—Expedition under Cabral—Burns Calicut—Aggressive policy—Vasco de Gama reappointed—Cruel massacre—War with the Moors—Taking of Goa—Malacca—Ormuz—Portuguese empire—Inquisition at Goa—Decline of empire and commerce—Dutch—Their East India Company—Take Ceylon—Cochin—Negapatam—English—First East India Company—Sir Thomas Roe—Court of Shah Jehan—Surat—Fort St. George—Fort St. David—Hooghly—Accident to the emperor's daughter—Bombay—Factories attacked—Territory—Hostilities with Aurungzebe—Submission of English—Grant of Calcutta—Fort William—Second East India Company—Bribery—United Company—Opposition of subahdar of Bengal—Another medical success—New grants—War with France—State of native powers—Fort St. George capitulates to the French—Violation of treaty—Death of Asoph Jah—Hostilities between French and English—Decline of the latter—Clive—Capture and defence of Arcot—Triumph of English interests—Clive governor of Fort St. David—Suppression of Angria—Events at Calcutta—Black Hole—Clive recovers Calcutta—Truce with subahdar—Battle of Plassey—Meer Jaffier made subahdar—Advance and retreat of the Shahzada—English masters of Bengal—Presents from natives—French interests—Comte de Lally—Capture of Vizagapatam—Nizam treats with English—Defeat of French in Carnatic—Fall of Pondicherry—Extinction of French interests—Reasons of English success.

THE close of the fifteenth century was marked by a concurrence of events which, more than any other in the world's history, have affected the condition of mankind, and the natives of India in particular. The same year (A.D. 1483) witnessed the birth of Baber, the founder of the Great Mogul empire in India, and of that Augustinian friar who, from more unlikely beginnings, became the honoured instrument of erecting the far nobler and imperishable kingdom of God's written word. The discovery of America in 1492, and of Newfoundland in 1496, ushered in the colonial empire of Great Britain, upon which the natural sun never sets, and the light of Christianity has hitherto shone with increasing lustre. Only two years later the Portuguese, after several failures, succeeded in rounding the southern cape of Africa, and changing its name to that of Good Hope,* crossed the Indian Ocean, with a Hindu pilot obtained on the east coast of Africa, and arrived at Calicut in Malabar, May, 1498. This expedition was commanded by Vasco de Gama, who, however distinguished for maritime skill and daring, appears in his intercourse with the natives, both of Africa and India, to have conducted himself more like a pirate than a Christian admiral. He bombarded their ports on the most frivolous pretences, carried off the inhabitants as slaves, and scrupled not to torture the unhappy persons who fell into his hands, in order to extort information.

The throne of Delhi was occupied at this time by Secunder Lodi. In the Deccan the Bahmanee dynasty, which had extended its arms from Masulipatam to the Concan, was fast expiring under Mahmoud II., and the Mohammedan kingdoms of Beejapore and Ahmednuggur had just been erected out of its dominions. The coast where the Portuguese touched was still independent, being ruled by several petty Hindu princes, the chief of whom was styled the *zamorin* or *tamuri raja*. His capital was

* The southern cape was discovered by Bartholomew Diaz more than ten years previously, and named *Cabo Tormentoso* (Cape Tempestuous) from the storms he encountered in its neighbourhood. The sagacious foresight of the Portuguese king, John II., immediately substituted the designation, which it has since retained, of *Cabo de Bom Esperança*.

Calicut, where a considerable commerce existed, conducted principally by Mussulman traders from Arabia and Africa, who were styled by the European writers *Moors*, in contradistinction to the Moguls and Patans.

The zamorin received the new comers kindly, and admitted them to an audience, at which he appeared clothed in white calico, flowered with gold, and adorned with precious gems. His couch was placed in a hall furnished with rich carpets and tapestry, and a golden fountain poured out its waters before it. The Portuguese, unacquainted with Indian customs, had provided no *nuzzur* for the prince, who repaired the omission by demanding a golden image of the Virgin, which he had heard of in their possession. This proposal was declined on the plea that it was only of wood gilt, and moreover could not be parted with, as it preserved its votaries from the dangers of the sea.

The reply was little calculated to advance the professed object of Portuguese adventure — the conversion of idolaters. Nor was their subsequent demeanour more edifying. Some of the party in perambulating the place entered a splendid pagoda, and perceiving it to be decorated with images, which they took for the Madonna and the saints, concluded they had lighted on some of the Christian communities of the country, and began to prostrate themselves in adoration. Nothing could more distinctly attest the identity of Romish idolatry with the heathen: the Portuguese were confirmed in their mistake by the sight of priests wearing rosaries, sprinkling the people with holy water, and by the sound of bells, or gongs, pealing around. One of them, however, happening to cast a more curious eye on the objects of their worship, was startled to see the hideous forms supplied with three or four heads, and half a dozen pairs of arms a-piece; springing hastily to his feet he exclaimed, "If these be devils, it is God whom I worship!"

The Moors soon received intelligence from their correspondents in the Mozambique of the outrages committed by De Gama in his voyage out, and communicating the tidings to the zamorin, he seized upon two of the Europeans who happened to be ashore. De Gama retaliated by entrapping some twenty natives on board his vessel, demanding his men in exchange. The demand was complied with, but the admiral perfidiously refused to liberate his prisoners. The natives, exasperated by his breach of faith, were preparing a fleet of boats to attack the intruders, when they at once made sail, and after an absence of two years and two months arrived in the Tagus, August, 1499, with only fifty-five persons surviving, out of the one hundred and sixty who had originally formed the expedition.

Such was the unfavourable aspect under which European Christianity was first exhibited to the natives of India;—such was the conduct of an expedition which sailed under a banner consecrated with the authority, hitherto unquestioned, of the Roman pontiff as vicegerent of Christ, and of which the officers and men, having confessed and received absolution and the Holy Communion, were conducted from the church to their ships by a procession of ecclesiastics, bearing tapers and chanting prayers. Such, in fine, were the successes for which the most faithful king on their return publicly rewarded the survivors, and bestowed on the commander a triumphal entrance into Lisbon, after an octave of religious services in the church from which he had been sent forth.

This commencement was too certain an augury of the spirit in which the subsequent career of the Portuguese was to be conducted. A fleet of thirteen ships was fitted out under Alvarez Cabral, on board of which sailed eight Franciscan friars, with orders to carry fire and sword to every nation that should refuse their preaching. Nevertheless, a show of milder measures being judged expedient at the outset, De Gama was retained in Lisbon, while the captives he had carried off were sent back with costly presents. Being restored by Cabral, he obtained a favourable reception, with permission to establish a factory in Calicut. There a violent and unscrupulous outrage soon provoked an attack on the part of the natives, in which more than fifty of the Portuguese were slain. Cabral retaliated by first seizing all the shipping in the harbour, and then bombarding and burning the city. After this he sailed away to Cochin, where the ruler, being at enmity with the zamorin, eagerly embraced the European alliance.

On Cabral's return to Lisbon the policy of aggression was deliberately resolved upon, and supported by yet more powerful armaments, "in order to carry out," as the Portuguese historian expresses it, "what the Apostle St. Thomas had begun." Vasco de Gama returned to India at the head of the new expedition, and, presenting himself before Calicut, began by seizing on fifty unoffending natives, as hostages during the progress of his negotiations.

He then demanded compensation for the destruction of the factory, and producing an hour-glass, he declared that unless the matter were settled before its sands were run out, all the prisoners should be massacred. The atrocious menace was fulfilled to the letter: the heads, hands, and feet of the mutilated victims were cast on the shore as examples to the Hindus of the spirit which demanded an entrance among them in the name of Christianity.

It is no part of the present design to write the history of the Portuguese empire in India. They proved, as Alexander had done, how easily a small force, disciplined and commanded by European skill, triumphs over the vain-glorious and unwieldy armies of India. The war was transferred from the petty princes of Malabar to the Mohammedan sovereigns of Guzerat and Cairo, who were aided by the Venetians, enraged at the appearance of other Europeans in a commerce which had hitherto been monopolized by themselves. Great battles were fought by land and sea with alternate success; in all of them the Portuguese exhibited a determined courage, joined with the most flagitious perfidy and cruelty. Goa was captured A.D. 1510, "and not one Moor was left alive on the island." The Hindus, however, were treated with lenity, confirmed in their property, and encouraged to intermarry with the Portuguese. The next year Malacca was seized. Aden, the great commercial emporium for Hindustan, China, and the eastern islands, was attempted without success; but in 1515 Ormuz in the Gulf of Persia, a still more valuable prize, fell into the hands of Albuquerque. Their empire eventually extended, in their own boastful language, from the Cape of Good Hope to the frontiers of China—a coast of twelve hundred miles in length. The fact was that they alone of European nations had established factories on this extended coast. These were about thirty in number, but few possessed any territory beyond their walls.

In the height of their greatness the eastern dominions of Portugal included Sofala, Mozambique, Mombaz, on the coast of Africa; Ormuz and Bussora, in the Persian Gulf; fifteen or sixteen stations on the west coast of India, extending from Diu in Guzerat to Quilon, and comprehending Bassein, Bombay, Goa, Mangalore, Cannanore, Cranganore, Calicut, and Cochin; on the eastern coast, Negapatam, St. Thomé, and Masulipatam, with a large part of Ceylon. These possessions were subject to the authorities of Goa, the capital of the Indo-Portuguese empire, where an area of a thousand square miles had been conquered from the natives. From this centre a constant succession of predatory attacks were directed against the coasts of Guzerat and Malabar. By lending their assistance to the sovereign of the former country (Bahadur Shah) against the Mogul emperor, they obtained permission to erect a fort at Diu, together with the cession of Bassein.

The factory of Surat was erected by leave of the same prince, and fortified without his knowledge. A dispute arising in consequence, the Portuguese viceroy invited the monarch to a conference on board his vessel. The controversy was not adjusted when the sultan rose to depart. Being forbidden to leave the ship, he drew his sword and cut down the Portuguese who opposed his progress. Then finding himself hemmed in by the rest, he leaped into the sea and there perished, as the Mohammedans affirm, by the weapons of the Europeans. In 1556 the Portuguese arms were pushed into Sindh: they had a few commercial posts also in Bengal, but in neither of those countries was any territorial dominion ever acquired.

In the year 1560 the character of Portuguese enterprise was further developed in the arrival of the first archbishop of Goa, attended by a retinue of inquisitors for the suppression of Jews and heretics. The priests had long considered the conversion of the heathen an object of inferior moment to the inculcation of the peculiar dogmas of Rome. The Christian communities bearing the name of St. Thomas steadily rejected the papal supremacy, with many of the doctrines and ceremonies of that see. These ancient Christians were declared guilty of disturbing the new converts of Xavier and his fellow-labourers. The number of Jews also on the western coast of India called for tho tender mercies of the inquisition. After some preliminary efforts at persecution, the holy office was established in Goa, with a ferocity proportionate to the general character of Indo-Portuguese administration.

"Never did idolatrous pagan or professed devil-worshipper pollute this fair earth by any crime of so deep a dye as the hideous *auto-da-fé*, usually celebrated on the first Sundays in Advent. Dellon, a French physician, who languished two years in the dungeons of Goa, has given a life-like picture of the horrible ceremonials of which he was an eye-witness.* He

* Dellon was accused of heresy, for having spoken disparagingly of the adoration of images. He had also grievously offended by calling the inquisitors "fallible men," and the "holy office" a fearful tribunal, which France had acted wisely in rejecting.

heard every morning for six weeks the shrieks of unfortunate victims undergoing the *question*, and he judged the number of prisoners to be very large; the profound silence which reigned within the walls of the building enabling him to count the number of doors as they were opened at the hours of meals. At the appointed time the captives were assembled by their black-robed jailors, and clothed in the *san benito*, a garb of yellow cloth, with the cross of St. Andrew before and behind. The relapsed heretics were dressed in the *samarra*, a grey robe, with the portrait of the wearer painted upon it, surrounded by burning torches, flames, and demons. On their heads were placed sugar-loaf-shaped caps, called *carochas*, on which devils and flames were also depicted. The bell of the cathedral began to ring a little before sunrise, and the gloomy procession commenced—men and women indiscriminately mixed, walking with bleeding feet over the sharp stones, and eagerly gazed on by innumerable crowds assembled from all parts of India to behold the "act of faith" of a European nation. Sentence was pronounced before the altar in the church of St. Francis, the grand inquisitor and his counsellors sitting on one side, the viceroy and his court on the other. The victims received the final intimation of their doom by a slight blow upon the breast from the alcaide. Then followed the immolation; the viceroy and the court still looking on while the prisoners were bound to the stake in the midst of the fagots, and hearing, as a periodical occurrence, the shrieks and groans of these unhappy creatures. The vengeance of the inquisition ceased not even here: the day after the execution the portraits of the murdered men were carried to the church of the Dominicans, and there kept in memory of their fate; the bones of such as had died in prison were likewise preserved in small chests, painted over with flames and demons."*

While these atrocities disgraced the name of religion, the secular affairs of Goa were conducted on the maxim that no faith was due to infidels. It is little wonder that the Portuguese acquired the undying hatred of the natives, a feeling which they little cared to mollify, since the latter were long unable to cope with them in arms. The combined armies of the four Mohammedan rulers of the Deccan and the zamorin of Calicut besieged Goa for many years, but were obliged to retire unsuccessful. At last, in 1580, the crown of Portugal was united to that of Spain, and the American possessions of the latter engaging the chief attention of government, the Indian empire was neglected, and began to sink under the assaults of its enemies. European rivals also appeared on the seas and in the field, and by the end of the sixteenth century, the pompous titles of the viceroyalty at Goa covered only a nest of illicit traders and pirates. In spite of apostolic bulls and *autos-da-fé*, or perhaps in consequence of them, both its commerce and its empire were passing into other hands.

The first to confront them on the scene of their eastern dominions were the sturdy republicans, whom the new sovereign of Portugal had provoked to rebellion and defiance in the Netherlands. The Dutch, excluded by the jealousy of Philip from legitimate commerce with his possessions in Europe and in India, determined on helping themselves to a share in

* Hough's "Christianity in India," quoted in the "Indian Empire," by Montgomery Martin.

the eastern trade. They attempted first to find a passage by the North Sea to Russia and China, and thence to the Indian Ocean, but soon adopting the course of their rivals round the Cape of Good Hope, they appeared in the Indian waters, and began to contend for maritime and commercial supremacy. The ships of either nation seized and plundered those of the other, the advantage soon declaring for the Dutch.

In 1602 the States General chartered a united company of merchants, with authority to commission forces, make war, and establish settlements, to the east of the Cape. The company, which was divided under six chambers sitting in the several states of the republic, commenced its operations with a capital exceeding half a million sterling. Its fleets were chiefly sent to the islands and straits to the east and south-east of the Indian peninsula; but they early wrested from the Portuguese Ceylon, Cochin, and Negapatam, while another power, which had often aided the struggles of Holland against the great Papal monarchies of Europe, was preparing itself, all unconsciously, to occupy the remainder, and far more than the remainder, of the Portuguese empire in Asia.

The English, like the Dutch, endeavoured first to reach the Indian Ocean through the Arctic Sea; but in 1577 Drake commenced his voyage round the world, taking the route by the Straits of Magellan, and returning by the Cape of Good Hope. After this, several ships were despatched by the latter route to India. In 1599 queen Elizabeth sent an embassy to the Great Mogul, but without any apparent result; and at the close of the year 1600, a company was chartered by the name of the "Governor and Company of Merchants of London trading to the East Indies."

James I. renewed the attempt at opening a diplomatic intercourse with the court of Delhi. Sir Thomas Roe was despatched on this mission, and graciously received by Jehanjire. His letters describe the nobles as a class without principle, universally open to corruption. The treaty of commerce he was sent to negotiate was delayed for upwards of two years, till the vizier had been bribed with a valuable pearl. Accompanying the emperor on a march, he found no proper arrangement for the transport of baggage; even water was often wanting at the court. The emperor, though professedly a Mohammedan, wore the figures of Christ and the Virgin at the head of his rosary, and had even allowed two of his nephews to embrace Christianity.* In private society, the "Great Mogul," as he was universally styled in Europe, exhibited a strange contrast of external grandeur with inward littleness. He sat at table on a throne covered with diamonds, pearls, and rubies, while the board was loaded with a gorgeous display of gold plate enriched with jewels. In the midst of this magnificence the king and his courtiers drank to intoxication. The monarch intermixed his maudlin conversations with "weeping and various passions, which kept them to midnight." On another occasion, the padishah seized on a convoy, coming to the ambassador from Surat, and rummaged the contents in person, offering the meanest apologies to sir Thomas, who was justly provoked by his dishonesty.

Roe, having at last obtained his treaty of commerce, repaired to Surat, where he presided for some time with great advantage to the Company's affairs. This was then their principal factory for the continent of

* Sir T. Roe arrived at Ajmere, December 23rd, 1615. He accompanied the emperor into Guzerat, and quitted his court at the end of 1618.

India, while another at Bantam, in Java, served for the trade of the eastern islands. The first stations on the Coromandel coast were at Masulipatam and Armegum; but in 1640 the raja of Chandragiri, a descendant of the old Hindu sovereigns of Beejanuggur, invited the English to settle at Madraspatnam, where he granted a territory on the coast of five miles in length and one in breadth. The new station was called Chennapatam, after the name of the local ruler's father, an appellation still retained by the natives. Here a fort was erected, which was named Fort St. George, and appointed the first "Presidency" in India. Tegnapatam, still lower down on the same coast, was purchased from the raja of Travancore, and became for some time an important station, under the name of Fort St. David.

About the same period the Company began to establish their factories at Hooghly, a town on the river of the same name in Bengal. This town is thought to have been founded by the Portuguese A.D. 1537; after their expulsion by Shah Jehan A.D. 1632, it became the royal port of Bengal. The preçise date of the appearance of the English in this port is uncertain, as also of the providential occurrence which brought the new traders to the particular notice of the court of Delhi. Jehanara, the favourite daughter of Shah Jehan, had the misfortune to set her dress on fire, and was fearfully burned before the flames could be extinguished. The surgeons of the English ships having acquired a great reputation among the natives, an express was despatched to Surat to request that one of them would attend the princess. Mr. Gabriel Boughton was selected for this service, which he performed so much to the satisfaction of the emperor, that he was desired to name his own reward. He asked and obtained a license for the Company to trade throughout the empire, exempt from custom dues, in all places except Surat, with permission to erect factories at their several stations.*

Under this license, granted by prince Shuja then viceroy of Bengal (confirmed by Aurungzebe A.D. 1680), a factory was erected at Hooghly A.D. 1676, which was soon afterwards fortified, and provided with a guard of twenty soldiers; this was the first military establishment of the English in Bengal.†

In 1662 the island of Bombay was ceded to Charles II., as part of the marriage portion of the infanta Catherine. The "merry monarch," doubtless for a suitable compensation to his privy purse, granted the new possession to the East India Company, who soon after removed to it the establishments at Surat, and made it their principal settlement in India. The fortifications were enlarged and strengthened, and under the encouragement held out to European and native settlers, a mixed population of English, Germans, Hindus, Mohammedans, and Parsees, was rapidly located in the new acquisition.

All these "factories" were originally only houses of agencies for the sale and purchase of goods, but, containing very often large amounts of treasure and merchandise, it was found necessary to guard them, not only against the attacks of European nations with whom the English might be at war, but still more against the native chiefs and rulers, who invariably

* This incident is dated by sir John Malcolm in 1636, by col. Dow in 1643, by others in 1651.

† Thornton's Gazetteer.

plundered whatever property they could lay their hands upon. Following the examples of the Portuguese and Dutch, and indeed of every other proprietor, in a country where the constituted authorities were always the most formidable robbers, the English surrounded their factories with fortifications, and trained their servants to carry arms in their defence. These fortified factories were often the scenes of severe conflicts, in which the Company's agents defended their property with all the courage of their nation, and with the usual superiority of European over Asiatic combatants. These collisions led to alliances with the native powers for mutual self-defence; while not unfrequently claims for compensation arose, which necessitated further intercourse and negotiation at the different courts.*

While still only traders in the land, the English company clearly perceived the inevitable necessity for territorial possessions, which had forced itself on the Portuguese and Dutch. "The increase of our revenue," they wrote in 1689, "is the subject of our care as much as our trade: it is that must maintain our force when twenty accidents may interrupt the trade: *it is that must make us a nation in India.* Without that we are but a great number of interlopers, united by his majesty's royal charter, fit only to trade where nobody of power thinks it their interest to prevent us; and upon this account it is that the wise Dutch, in all their general advices which we have seen, write ten paragraphs concerning government, their civil and military policy, warfare,

* Surat was attacked and plundered by Sevajee A.D. 1664, on which occasion the English stoutly defended their factory, and afterwards insisted on compensation for their losses.

and the increase of their revenue, for one paragraph they write concerning trade."

The directors, when they gave expression to these views, were ignorant that their agents had been on the point of being expelled for ever from India, on account of a too eager manifestation of similar intentions. Sir John Child, governor at Bombay, even dared to make war on the Mogul, but Aurungzebe, in whose vigorous grasp the sceptre was not to be trifled with, issued orders for the expulsion of the English, seized their factories, and threw their agents into irons. The death of Sir John Child, and the abject submission of his colleagues, alone enabled them to purchase peace, with the restoration of their commercial privileges.

During these hostilities, the council at Hooghly had retreated down the river to Chuttanutree, where they were allowed to build a factory, while the same privilege was extended to the Dutch at Chinsurah, and to the French at Chandernagore. Hostilities having broken out between a local raja and the Mogul government, the Europeans were told by the subahdar to defend themselves; this they interpreted into leave to erect fortifications round their factories. Azim, the grandson of Aurungzebe, being appointed to the viceroyalty of Bengal, Behar, and Orissa, the English obtained from this prince a grant of Chuttanutree, and the adjoining villages of Govindpore and Calicutta, so called from a temple dedicated to Kalee. Here they were permitted to erect a fort, which, in honour of the prince who had just mounted the British throne, was called Fort William.

While these events were occurring in India, the

Company was exposed at home to the rivalry of other merchants, English and Scotch, excited by rumours of their extraordinary success. Trading licenses were purchased from the Stuart monarchs in manifest derogation of the Company's charter. A new company was even incorporated, on the allegation that the old one had failed to establish proper forts and factories for the British trade. Considerable sums were expended in bribing the ministers of the crown, and other leading members of the legislature. At last in the year that followed Aurungzebe's decease, the two companies were amalgamated under the appellation of "the United Company of Merchants of England trading to the East Indies," and prepared, with the combined experiences of previous adventure, to grasp at once the failing commerce of the Portuguese, and the now declining sceptre of the Great Mogul.

The East India Company has been often represented as sliding imperceptibly, and without intention, from the character of merchants into that of sovereigns; and it is true that, with the national reserve and dislike of ostentation, they long avoided, and with reluctance at last submitted to, the assumption of imperial titles. The king of Portugal had proclaimed himself "Lord of the navigation, conquest, and commerce of Ethiopia, Arabia, Persia, and India," and despatched his viceroys to India, before a single foot of territory was acquired in sovereignty or in property. The English, on the other hand, long sheltered their actual possession of dominion under a variety of fictions, afraid to confess even to themselves the true character of their position. Yet it is plain, from the extract already given from the Company's despatches, as well as from the attempts of their agents, and the discussions that followed them in England, that the new charter was solicited and bestowed with no indistinct intention of the English "becoming a nation"—and a principal one, in India. Their progress to territorial possession, however, was still slow; and no idea was for long entertained of aspiring to actual sovereignty.

The contests between the agents of the two companies had rendered Aurungzebe himself uncertain which was really entitled to represent the English nation:* after their union, the natives generally continued strangely ignorant of the character and extent of European resources. The more discerning, however, had imbibed Aurungzebe's jealousy against permitting the foreigners to establish themselves in the land. Of this class was Moorshed Kooli Khan (called also Jaffier Khan), who held the government of Bengal under the emperor Feroksheer, great-grandson of Aurungzebe. It was in spite of his influence, that the Company were enabled to enlarge their territory by another singular incident of medical success. Mr. Hamilton, one of their surgeons, was permitted to cure the emperor of a malady under which he had long suffered, and obtained in return a grant of new privileges to his employers. It was conceded by the imperial firman, that the "*dustuck*," or pass-

* This astute and inquiring prince is represented as reproaching his tutor with the ridiculous ignorance in which he had been educated of the state of Europe—"You taught me that the whole of Frangistan [Europe] was no more than some inconsiderable island, of which the most powerful monarch was formerly the king of Portugal, then the king of Holland, and afterwards the king of England. In regard to other sovereigns of Frangistan (such as the king of France and the king of Andalusia), you told me they resembled our petty rajas; and that the potentates of Hindustan eclipsed the glory of all other kings."—*Brock's Bernier*, vol. ii. p. 166.

port, of the president at Calcutta should exempt all goods from stoppage or examination by the Mogul officers, on any pretence; that the imperial mint at Moorshedabad should be available for the coinage of the Company's money; that all persons, whether European or native, who were accountable to the Company, should be delivered up to the presidency at Calcutta; and, lastly, that thirty-eight villages might be purchased with the same immunities as had been granted by prince Azim at Calcutta.

Some other privileges were granted at the same time; as a fixed composition for all duties levied on the trade at Surat; the grant of three villages at Madras; and an island near Masulipatam. If full effect had been given to the imperial charter, a great stride would have been taken at a step in the British career. The viceroy, however, continuing to obstruct their claims, the directors shrewdly ordered them not to be prosecuted, so as to alarm the native governments. The territory, which would have included a district of ten miles from Calcutta, on either side the river Hooghly, was only partially entered upon. The "dustucks" were limited by the subahdar to goods imported or exported by *sea*, in order to preserve the inland trade to the natives. Still the value of the concessions was great, and they were augmented, after Nadir Shah's invasion of Delhi, by permission to surround the English territory with a trench or ditch, to protect it from the incursions of the Mahrattas.*

* This entrenchment is still known as the Mahratta ditch. It was on the occasion of this invasion of the Mahrattas under Balajee Bosla, A. D. 1740, that they established their claims to the *chowt* of Bengal (for which the subahdar agreed to pay twelve lacs of rupees annually), and further obtained a cession of Cuttack, or Southern Orissa.—*Elphinstone*, vol. ii. p. 649.

The progress of empire now received a new impulse from the declaration of war between England and France, A.D. 1744, and the consequent appearance of the belligerent fleets in the Indian seas. The Mogul empire had experienced its death-blow in the invasion of Nadir Shah. The subahdar of Bengal, Behar, and Orissa, was Ali Verdi Khan, who, after putting to death the heir of his former commander, had usurped the dominion of the three provinces, and become practically independent. The vizier of the empire, who also held the subah of Oude, laid claim to what remained of Mogul authority in Hindustan. Asoph Jah was, in like manner, *de facto* king of the Deccan, though retaining only the title of subahdar or nizam; and similar pretensions were advanced, with equal justice, by the nabob of Arcot to the sovereignty of the Carnatic, though the nizam still claimed the fealty of this chief as a subordinate functionary of the empire.

On the other side of India, the raja of Sattara, the representative of Sevajee and nominal head of the Mahratta confederacy, had been induced or compelled to transfer the powers of government to his peishwah Balajee Rao, who held his court at Poonah; while the province of Malwa, wrested from the crown of Delhi, was partitioned between his dependent chiefs, Holkar and Scindia. In the south, Tanjore was in the possession of a Mahratta raja, descended from the brother of Sevajee; and Trichinopoly, to which the nabob of the Carnatic laid claim, was also in Mahratta hands.

Such was the state of the native powers at the time when the English and French factories were precipitated into hostilities on the coast of Coromandel. The French, with the connivance of the nabob, compelled Fort St. George to capitulate, and then, violating the treaty, took possession of Madras, and marched the governor and principal authorities prisoners to Pondicherry. Dupleix, the French governor, whose name is stained by this act of perfidy, almost immediately broke with the nabob, who transferred his alliance to the English, thus effectually checking the further progress of French arms.

The peace of Aix-la-Chapelle restored Madras to the English; but hostilities again broke out on the death of Asoph Jah, followed by a dispute for the succession among his family. The several competitors eagerly sought European support, and the rival merchants were not indisposed to avail themselves of the opportunity. The French espoused the cause of Mozuffar Jung, the grandson by a favourite daughter of the deceased nizam, while the English supported his second son Nazir. Success attended the former, who availing himself of his power to set up a rival nabob of Arcot, the cause of the English was every way in danger. Dupleix had himself been elevated to high native rank, and his durbar was held at Pondicherry with all the state of an oriental potentate. The English were on the point of being deprived at once of political influence and trade, when the genius of CLIVE retrieved their position, and, under Providence, laid the foundation of the magnificent empire which has since accrued to the British crown.

This distinguished soldier and statesman was the son of a country gentleman, of good lineage but moderate patrimony. He had been sent out to India as a writer in the Company's service, an appointment then nothing more than what the name denoted; but finding in the counting-house no field for his abilities or inclination, the youth obtained a commission as ensign in the few troops employed for the defence of the factories. Clive was among the prisoners of war at the capitulation of Madras to the French, and on the violation of the treaty he succeeded in making his escape to Fort St. David. He was present at an unsuccessful attack made from this settlement on Pondicherry, under admiral Boscawen. Dissatisfied with the timid, petty spirit in which the war was conducted, he sought and obtained permission to reduce Arcot (A.D. 1751), an achievement which he effected with a force of only two hundred Europeans and three hundred Sepoys.

The glory of this capture was exceeded by that of its subsequent defence against the united forces of the French and the rival nabob Chunda Sahib. For fifty days the fort was closely invested by an army of ten thousand native troops, aided by one hundred and fifty Frenchmen. The assault, when at last delivered, was repulsed at every point by the heroic little garrison, and the next day the siege was precipitately abandoned.

This memorable defence raised Clive at once to fame as a military commander. Having received reinforcements from Madras, he took the field in pursuit of the retreating foe. Chunda Sahib's cause soon became desperate, and he proposed to save his life by surrendering to the English; but being dissuaded by M. Law, who seems to have thought more of French interests than the safety of his prince, he finally yielded himself to the Tanjore general, and was assassinated in his custody. The French escaped destruction by capitulating to the English.

The reigning nabob Mohammed Ali, and with him the interests of his English defenders, were again in the ascendant, when Clive retired to England, where he was received with the greatest distinctions. The operations in the Carnatic were left to be conducted by his friend and patron, major Lawrence. Several brilliant victories were gained under his command; but the continuance of hostilities in India between the subjects of two European crowns, which were at peace at home, could no longer be tolerated. The struggle was terminated at the end of 1754 by the recall of Dupleix, and the conclusion of a treaty of peace with the English by his successor. This treaty left each party in possession of their existing advantages. The English continued to aid the nabob in establishing his authority throughout the Carnatic, while the French rendered similar assistance to the nizam in the Deccan, where their services were richly remunerated by a grant of the extensive province called the Northern Circars.

Clive returned from England in 1756, with the appointment of governor of Fort St. David, accompanied by a force intended to be employed against the French. Landing at Bombay, he found a better use for their services in co-operating with admiral Watson in an attack on the Mahratta pirate Angria, who, for many years, had seriously annoyed the trade of the western coast. Two of his strongholds, Severndroog and Bankote, had been taken by the English in 1755, and the entire destruction of the piratical fleet was now effected, along with the capture of Gheriah its principal harbour. The prize was afterwards exchanged with the peishwah, and the territories so added to the island of Bombay formed the germ of the presidency which now bears that name.

Meantime events were occurring on the Hooghly which were to issue in the establishment of a third, and more important, presidency in Bengal. They resulted, like the others, from complications with the native powers, arising out of arrangements made for the protection of English commerce.

Aliverdi Khan, the subahdar of Bengal, died in April 1756, and was succeeded by his grandson, Mirza Mahmood, or, as he styled himself on his accession, Sooraj-u-Dowlah. The new prince was actuated by a bitter animosity against the English, deepened, it is said, by the advice of his predecessor, whose last caution was directed against the growing military power of the foreigners. He despatched an order to Fort William, requiring the fortifications to be immediately stopped; and his command being demurred to, on the ground of apprehended hostilities with the French, the nabob marched in person to enforce it. The factory at Cossimbazar yielded to his arms without a struggle, and the authorities at Calcutta were inclined to follow the example. Both the Dutch and the French had refused their application for assistance. An offer of money was rejected by the incensed subahdar, and at the first sound of his guns, the governor, military commandant, and many of the residents, fled with the women and shipping down the river, leaving about one hundred and fifty of their countrymen exposed to the fury of the enemy. Mr. Holwell, one of the members of Council, having assumed the command, endeavoured for two days to delay the fall of the place, while signals were made to the fugitives to return to their assistance. A sloop with fifteen brave men might have come up and carried all away in safety; but the effort was not made, and the subahdar became master of the settlement.

On entering the fort he assured Mr. Holwell, on the word of a soldier, that no harm should befall the garrison; but the same night they were all imprisoned in the Black Hole, a cell in the barracks used for the confinement of military offenders, which measured eighteen feet by fourteen, and had only two small windows for the admission of air and light. The space, of course, soon proved too little for the numbers that were crowded into it, amounting to one hundred and forty-six persons, mostly Europeans, and many suffering from recent wounds. Suffocation became imminent; but the guards, refusing both entreaties and bribes, declared that no change could be effected without the orders of the subahdar, who was asleep and could not be disturbed. In the morning an order was sent for the release of the prisoners; but when the door had been opened, with much difficulty from the number of bodies that lay against it within, and a way was cleared for the survivors, only twenty-three persons came out of the dungeon alive, several of whom died soon after from the effects of their sufferings. One hundred and twenty-three lives fell a sacrifice in that single night to the habitual inhumanity of Mohammedan tyranny. The survivors received nothing but menaces of instant death, unless they disclosed the treasure supposed to be concealed in the fort.

The receipt of this intelligence in England, where the details were subsequently verified in person by two of the sufferers, kindled a flame of resentment and horror, which was only in some degree appeased by learning the resolution of the council at Madras, to inflict condign chastisement on the author of so atrocious a massacre. This resolution was arrived at on the urgent representations of Orme, the best historian of the period, who was then one of the Madras council, and having resided nine or ten years at Calcutta, was well acquainted with the disposition of affairs in that place.

An expedition was immediately fitted out, the military portion of which was commanded by Clive; while the fleet co-operated under admirals Watson and Pocock. The latter, with two of the ships, was missing on the arrival of the remainder in the Hooghly; but Clive, impatient to avenge his countrymen, landed with his diminished force, and advanced upon Calcutta, from which the nabob had withdrawn to Moorshedabad. The native governor with three thousand men fled at the first engagement with the British, and Clive re-occupied Fort William after the discharge of a few shots.

He was preparing to march against the nabob, when he was disconcerted by intelligence that war had been again declared between England and France. The French garrison at Chandernagore nearly equalled the whole European force at his disposal, and the possibility of their junction with the nabob, now advancing with an overwhelming army of natives, was enough to daunt even the daring spirit of Clive. On the other hand, the nabob had been thoroughly frightened by the gallantry of the British attack on Calcutta, and was further disquieted by tidings of another Affghan invasion of Delhi, which he dreaded would extend to his own dominions.

In this situation a hollow treaty was concluded,

viewed on both sides as a suspension, more than a cessation, of hostilities. The nabob immediately opened negotiations with M. Bussy in the Northern Circars (which extend to within two hundred miles of Calcutta), proposing with his assistance to extirpate the English; while Clive, fully aware of this design, was addressed from the nabob's own camp with proposals for the tyrant's overthrow. The weakness and cruelty of Sooraj-u-Dowlah's character had already, in a reign of less than fifteen months, evoked the usual remedy of a conspiracy for his dethronement. The intended successor was Meer Jaffier, a near relative of the nabob, and invested with a high command in his army. The nabob was not ignorant of the disaffection prevailing among his troops, nor even of the communications opened with his European enemy. Not exactly knowing whom to trust, he accepted a solemn oath of fidelity, which Meer Jaffier scrupled not to take on the Koran; and being, at the same time, relieved from his anxiety on account of the Affghans by their retirement from Delhi, he despatched a letter of defiance to the English commander. Clive replied by an exposure of the nabob's correspondence with the French, and other breaches of the treaty. The armies were put in motion on both sides, and in the month of June, 1757, lay encamped on the opposite banks of the Hooghly, near the village of Plassey ninety-six miles north of Calcutta.

Clive was in a position of the highest responsibility and anxiety. His disproportion to the enemy in point of numbers was enormous. On the other side of the river lay the army of a native prince, commanded by Mohammedans long inured to victory, and till very recently entertaining the profoundest contempt for the English traders. The enemy mustered fifty thousand men, of whom fifteen thousand were cavalry, with upwards of forty pieces of artillery. The British force consisted of six hundred and fifty European infantry, one hundred artillerymen, augmented by fifty sailors from the men-of-war, two thousand one hundred Sepoys, and a small number of Portuguese, making a total of little more than three thousand men, with eight field-pieces and one or two howitzers. The European soldiers were the Company's levies, recruited in the streets of London, and complained of as the refuse of the metropolis. The Sepoys were natives armed and disciplined to a certain extent on the European system, some of whom Clive had brought with him from Madras, where they had been exercised in the wars of the Carnatic, and others had been hastily raised in Bengal for the emergency. This was the whole British force in Bengal. Their commander felt, as he afterwards stated, that in the event of a defeat not a man would return to tell the tale. He was still uncertain of the course that would be pursued by Meer Jaffier, though well-nigh hopeless of success if the enemy should prove united.

In this anxious moment Clive called the only council of war that he ever summoned, and proposed the question, whether or not an attack should be hazarded, declaring his own conviction that, without the aid of some country power, it would be hopeless.* The majority, as usual, declared against the risk; but Clive almost immediately after overruled a decision which would have sealed the expulsion of the English

* See the different versions of the phraseology employed in Thornton's History of India, i. 235.

from India, and issued orders for the army to cross the river and attack the enemy. The action was fought on June 23rd, 1757; it resulted in the defeat of the nabob, who fled the same evening to Moorshedabad, leaving his army without a commander. He had no confidence in his troops, nor his troops in him, or in each other. No one knowing how far disaffection extended, none was willing to advance to the front, when the most dangerous enemy might be found in the rear.

Success having declared for the English, Meer Jaffier, with some misgiving as to his reception, joined their camp. He was immediately saluted as subahdar of Bengal, Behar, and Orissa, a dignity with which he was formally invested by Clive in the palace at Moorshedabad a few days afterwards. Sooraj-u-Dowlah, flying in search of shelter, was given up by a sufferer from his former tyranny, and being brought back a prisoner to Moorshedabad, experienced the frequent end of oriental power in being assassinated by order of Meer Jaffier's son.

The battle of Plassey is justly regarded as inaugurating the British empire in India. Our military reputation, which had always been inferior to that of the French, was prodigiously increased by so complete a success; aided, though it was, by widespread treachery in the ranks of the enemy. The political result was to elevate the English traders, in a moment, to a position among the native powers, which neither the Portuguese nor French, with all their craving for empire, had attained. The new nabob was the creature of British power, and needed its constant intervention to sustain his position. Clive was not the man to refuse the responsibility of such support, or to fail in improving it to the aggrandizement of his country.

The emperor Alumghir was now little better than a prisoner in the hands of his vizier Ghazee-u-din, who having originally placed him on the throne, after deposing and blinding his predecessor, had recently taken forcible possession of the capital. The heir-apparent had escaped to a place of safety, and on this prince the emperor or his minister conferred the subah of Bengal, on receiving intelligence of the death of Sooraj-u-Dowlah. The shahzada advancing to claim his government laid siege to Patna, at the same time endeavouring to open negotiations with the English. Clive, however, turning a deaf ear to his overtures, marched promptly to the relief of Patna, when the invaders retired into Oude. The vizier soon deserting the prince's cause, transferred the subah to his brother, and despatched an imperial edict to Meer Jaffier to confirm him in the government as lieutenant of the new subahdar, enjoining him at the same time to secure the person of the elder prince. The shahzada was thus reduced to apply to Clive for protection, who supplied him with money to make his escape; and this characteristic assistance was the commencement of British intercourse with the falling house of Timour.

The acknowledged mastery of the kingdom of Bengal was now in the hands of the English. Clive was created an ameer by the emperor, and Meer Jaffier added a jaghire of thirty thousand pounds a-year to support the dignity.* The readiness of the Company's agents to

* Clive's jaghire consisted of the crown rents from the lands occupied by the Company in and around Calcutta. It was insisted by the directors that such a grant ought to have been accepted for the Company, and not

enrich themselves at the cost of the native princes, occasioned considerable animadversion in England. It was defended on the plea that oriental custom rendered presents indispensable to all political transactions, and that the native princes were well able to afford them. Clive afterwards declared, that when he remembered his entering the nabob's treasury at Moorshedabad, and the heaps of gold and silver, crowned with jewels, that surrounded him, he was surprised at his own moderation. The treasure, however, had been exacted from the native population with no very scrupulous hand, and every "gift" of the Mohammedan ruler was sure to fall in the end with tenfold weight on the oppressed population.

Meer Jaffier himself began to complain that his English patrons claimed more from his gratitude than his exhausted resources could supply. He even secretly invited the Dutch up the Hooghly, in order to effect a counterpoise to the burden of their yoke. But Clive inflicted a signal defeat on the intruders, and their discomfiture added new force to British authority.

While the English were thus surely, though still half unconsciously, achieving empire in Bengal, the French were as rapidly losing all their magnificent prospects in the south. Entering India nearly fifty years later than the English, they had far more eagerly applied themselves to the acquisition of political power; and their dexterous management, in the disputes for the succession at Hyderabad, gave them

for the private behoof of their governor; and, after some altercation, Clive consented to compromise the dispute by limiting himself to ten years' enjoyment of the grant, and making over the perpetuity to the government.

a paramount influence in the Deccan, which was acknowledged by a grant of territory comprehending six hundred miles of sea coast. On the renewal of war between the two countries, in 1756, the Count de Lally, one of an Irish family which had followed James II. into France, was sent out with the appointment of governor-general of all the French possessions in India, backed by a force eager to enlarge them. Fort St. David and Devi Cottah were wrested from the English, and Madras itself sustained another siege for two months, but without being reduced.

Unfortunately for French interests, Lally thought fit to recall Bussy from the territories of the nizam, where his great influence was said to have excited the jealousy of his superior. No sooner was this experienced general removed, than a native raja attacked Vizagapatam, and dispossessed the French garrison. He then offered his conquest to the English, on condition of their assisting him to reduce the remainder of the territory granted by the nizam to their common foe. The Madras council being in no condition to contribute military succours, the raja transferred his overtures to Clive, by whom they were promptly accepted, and an expedition was embarked under colonel Forde for Vizagapatam.

The countries to be conquered were to belong to the raja, with the exception of the ports and mouths of rivers which the English claimed as their share, the expenses of the war being wholly borne by the raja. The nizam advancing to support the cause of his European ally, seems to have been struck by the convenience of this arrangement. The authority exercised by the French in the internal government of the country had already excited great umbrage at his court, and the English policy was further commended to his attention, by the rapid capture of Vizagapatam and Masulipatam by the troops under colonel Forde. Receiving intelligence, also, that his brother was taking advantage of his absence from Hyderabad to intrigue for the throne, the nizam hastened to conclude a treaty with the English, by which he granted them a coast of eighty miles in length, and bound himself no longer to retain the troops of their rival in his service.

This blow to French ascendancy was followed by military operations under colonel Coote, which quickly deprived them of almost every station in the Carnatic. A decisive victory was gained at Wandewash, another at Arcot, and M. Lally saw his government reduced to a narrow area round Pondicherry, which the English were rapidly circumscribing. The French capital was itself besieged; and after a close investment, and much distress gallantly endured, was under the necessity of surrendering to colonel Coote, on the 12th January, 1761. Lally was embarked as a prisoner for Madras, and, following the precedent set by himself on the capture of Fort St. David, the fortifications of Pondicherry were demolished. The place was restored at the peace, with two or three other mercantile stations, but the French power in India fell with their capital, and became extinguished.

Their commanders had been men of great genius and military talent, while the national passion for empire had shaped itself into plans which were pursued with ardour, and their disappointment was severely felt in France; but an American writer, well acquainted with India, contemplates the result with no little satisfaction. "Had the French succeeded in their object of becoming the controlling power of India, there is reason to believe they would have pursued a course of conquest in ways, and by means, at least as unscrupulous as the English have used. The French have never succeeded so well as the English in governing their foreign possessions, and there is reason to believe that the state of India has been better under the government of England than it would have been under the government of France. Had France become the governing power of India, the religion of the European population in it would have been Roman Catholic; and if we may judge from the French policy in their foreign possessions, no other form of religion would be tolerated, or if tolerated, they would allow no means to be used for propagating any other form of Christianity, and so all the inhabitants would be shut up to receive the Roman Catholic faith, or to continue in their present religious state of ignorance, superstition, bigotry, and idolatry. There is reason, therefore, in contemplating the present religious state and prospects of India, for thankfulness to Him who rules among the nations, and disposes of countries and kingdoms according to his pleasure, that this country with its vast population has come under the government of England, rather than of France, or any other European nation."*

The same impartial author assigns as the chief human cause of the result, the different treatment which the agents of the two nations in India received from the authorities at home:—"France failed to support her cause in India, and censured and punished,

* Allen's India, p. 218.

even with imprisonment and death,* the distinguished men who had done their utmost to support her cause and extend her power; while England supported her cause with great vigour, supplying money, men, and all the materials of war, and rewarding those who distinguished themselves in her service, (as Clive, Hastings, Cornwallis, and others,) with wealth and honours. And the consequences of this different course of policy were, that the French were expelled, their power annihilated, and India has long been included in the foreign possessions of England.†

When we consider, however, that during the same period in which India was won to the British crown, its North American colonies were lost by the arbitrary and injudicious policy pursued by the king's ministers, in a parliament which knew nothing of the country for which they legislated, it cannot but be concluded that the issue was greatly favoured by the happy withdrawal of Indian affairs from the vortex of European politics, to be committed to the exclusive care of the merchant princes who constituted the East India Company. By this arrangement the manly and independent judgment which distinguishes the most intelligent portion of the middle classes—the class of Washington and Clive, of Franklin and of Hastings—has been allowed to operate in the administration of Indian affairs, free from the intrigues of a court, and the intricacies of European diplomacy. If the career of empire has been retarded by the timidity, or even at times stained by the

* Dupleix was imprisoned, and Lally beheaded, on their return to France, where failure was a more unpardonable crime than the arrogance and indiscretion which neutralized the really brilliant talents of both commanders.

† Allen's India, p. 218.

cupidity, of trade, it must be acknowledged that our Indian empire has advanced quite as fast as was consistent with safety, and that no other government, conducted on the more imperial policy whether of our own or any foreign crown, can point to a history less blotted by the failings and vices of human nature.

CHAPTER VIII.

THE BRITISH EMPIRE.

Injurious change in the government—Disputes with Meer Jaffier—Cossim Ali proclaimed nabob—Bribes to the council—Invasion and defeat of the emperor—Renewal of the dispute about transit duties—Violence of the council—Restoration of Meer Jaffier—Atrocities of Cossim Ali—His flight into Oude—Victory of Buxar—Junction of the emperor with the British—Death of Meer Jaffier—Return of lord Clive—Defeat of the vizier—Restored by treaty—Grant of Dewannee to the Company—Northern Circars—Confirmation of nabob of Carnatic—British ascendancy—Final departure of lord Clive—Pecuniary corruptions—Disastrous policy at Madras—War with Hyder Ali—Carnatic ravaged—Hyder before Madras—Humiliating peace—Dissatisfaction in England—Royal commission—Dethronement of raja of Tanjore—Double government of Bengal—Warren Hastings governor—Open exercise of the Dewanny—Courts of justice—British sovereignty—Emperor goes over to the Mahrattas—Bengal independent—New treaty with the vizier—Rohilla war—Resolutions in Parliament—New form of government—Hastings governor-general—Supreme Court of Judicature—Dissensions in the council—Charges against the governor-general—Execution of Nuncomar—Excesses of Supreme Court—Renewed disputes in the council—Mr. Francis—Appointment of sir John Clavering—Refusal of Hastings to vacate—Duel with Francis—War in Bombay with the Mahrattas—Madras, dissensions in the council—Lord Pigot's arrest and death—Restoration of the raja of Tanjore—Renewal of war with the French and with Hyder Ali—Defeat of colonel Baillie—Disastrous position at Madras—Hastings suspends the governor—Arrival of sir Eyre Coote—Death of Hyder—Tippoo Sultan—Hastings's dispute with the raja of Benares—New treaty with the vizier—Resumption of jaghires—Resignation of Warren Hastings—State of the British empire—Impeachment of Hastings—His acquittal, pension, honours, and character—Want of religion in India—Progress of empire—Lord Cornwallis—Renewal of war with Tippoo—Siege of Seringapatam—Treaty of peace—Land revenue settlements—Judicial reform—Rules and regulations—Sir John Shore—Hyderabad—Oude.

On Clive's return to Europe, in 1760, a modification, previously ordered from home, was effected in the constitution of the Calcutta government. The council was augmented to ten, and the majority was invested with the decision of every question. The results were eminently injurious to the interests of justice and equity. The members of council were largely engaged in trade on their private account, and they now insisted, under the grant of the Mogul emperor, upon conveying their merchandize inland, from place to place, free of the transit duties, which formed a considerable item in the revenues of the native rulers. They even pretended to sell this right to native agents and merchants, to the manifest injury of other traders, and the great detriment of the public revenues. Meantime the directors at home, in the belief that enormous treasures lay at their disposal in Bengal, not only made no remittances to that presidency, but left the other presidencies to draw upon Calcutta for their expenditure. Money was imperatively demanded, while every day it became more impossible for the nabob to fulfil the expectations with which he had been raised to power.

Meer Jaffier, moreover, proved to be unpopular with all classes of his subjects. Indolent, voluptuous, and tyrannical, his exchequer was ever in difficulties, though the people at the same time groaned under intolerable exactions. The council soon made the discovery that no improvement could be expected while the government continued in his hands. Owing his elevation entirely to the English, and incapable of sustaining himself for a moment without their support, he yet received their remonstrances with indifference, and seemed to be careless of their good-will. The same complaint has been reiterated of almost all the native princes who have since, in greater numbers, been taken under British protection. A change was declared to be indispensable. Colonel Calliaud, indeed, who was now in command of the troops, urged that it would no doubt be "possible to find a successor as great a rogue as our nabob, and perhaps not so great a coward nor so great a fool, but in consequence much more difficult to manage. As to the injustice," continued the plain-speaking soldier, "of supporting this man on account of his cruelties and oppression, and his being detested in his government, I see so little chance in this blessed country of finding a man endowed with the opposite virtues that I think we may put up with these vices."

These sentiments were probably shared by others of the council; still it was determined to make another experiment. Without deposing the nabob, it was proposed to vest the collection and administration of his revenues in the hands of his son-in-law, Cossim Ali. The arrangement was not without precedent under the native system of government, which was divided into two principal branches—the *Dewannee*, including the collection of the revenue, with the judicial and military power requisite for that purpose; and the *Nizamut*, comprehending the other functions of sovereignty. The two departments were not unfrequently committed to separate administrators; and the council in wishing their nominee to be constituted *Dewan*, with a direct responsibility to themselves, had no intention or wish to abrogate the sovereignty of Meer Jaffier in other respects. The president was not a little shocked, therefore, when Cossim proposed to facilitate the arrangement by assassinating his father-in-law. Still intent on the scheme which alone promised to gratify their cupidity, the council opened it to Meer Jaffier, who at once resolved to spare his son-in-law further trouble and guilt, by tendering his abdication. He was well aware that the power of the exchequer was in fact the power of the kingdom; in parting with its control the princes of India always sank into mere pageants and pensioners on their Dewans, and not unfrequently finished by becoming their victims. The council eagerly accepted the proffered abdication, and Cossim was formally proclaimed nabob of Bengal, Behar, and Orissa, the Company receiving in return the districts of Burdwan, Midnapore, and Chittagong. Bribes under the name of "presents" were profusely distributed among the members of council. Mr. Vansittart the president had £50,000; Mr. Holwell £27,000; Mr. Sumner £22,400; colonel Calliaud £22,000; Mr. McGuire £26,000; Mr. Cullen Smith the secretary, and major Yorke, each £13,400.*

During the progress of this transaction the provinces were again invaded by the unfortunate Shah Alum, who, in consequence of the murder of his father Alumghir, had assumed the barren title of emperor. Some hesitation was exhibited by the native authorities in advancing against the person of the fallen Mogul, but colonel Calliaud, marching into Behar, encountered his forces on the 22nd of February, 1760, and inflicted the first regular defeat on the house of Timour, before which the foreign merchants had but lately cowered in alarm, and whose name still commanded admiration throughout Europe.

Being subsequently reinforced by M. Law with the remnant of the French troops, the emperor laid siege to Patna, but after sustaining a repulse from the garrison he was again thoroughly routed by major Carnac on the 1st of January, 1761. In this

* Thornton's History of India, vol. i. p. 402.

engagement Law and his followers were taken prisoners.

This success in the field was followed up by offers of negotiation, which were eagerly welcomed by the emperor, who had always evinced his desire for an alliance with the English. He readily agreed to confirm Cossim Ali in the subah, on condition of receiving the imperial tribute of £240,000 per annum. This arrangement effected, the emperor retired into Oude, after narrowly escaping with life from an insurrection in his own camp.

Cossim Ali was now invested with a sanction which his predecessor had never enjoyed; but colonel Calliaud's predictions were speedily verified, and the council were no better pleased with their new nominee than with the old one. The dispute about the transit duties continued. The president came to an arrangement with the nabob, which the majority at Calcutta disallowed. The exorbitant demands of the latter were in turn angrily rejected by the nabob. Throughout the dispute, the president seems to have advocated a fair and moderate compromise, but he was supported only by the single vote of Warren Hastings: the majority of the council, led by a Mr. Ellis, insisted on their demands at all hazards. The nabob tried to cut the Gordian knot by abolishing the transit duties altogether, in order to place his native subjects on an equal footing with the foreigners; but this the council, now regardless of every consideration but those of self-interest, declared to be a violation of English rights. Acts of hostility followed between the agents of the two parties, and the council determined on once more restoring Meer Jaffier to the authority of which they had deprived him but three years before. A proclamation to that effect was issued under the Company's seal (A.D. 1763), and the English forces were put in motion to support it.

In the brief war which ensued, Cossim Ali, abandoning all appearance of moderation, indulged in acts of detestable atrocity. Large numbers of natives were seized and put to death without cause. He surprised Patna, where Mr. Ellis was chief of the factory, and having received the surrender of the English residents as prisoners of war, caused them all to be barbarously murdered, with the single exception of the surgeon. Similar atrocities were perpetrated in other places, till as many as two hundred English lives had fallen a sacrifice to his inhuman revenge.

These acts, which were paralleled with the massacre of the Black Hole, roused a similar resentment in the minds of the English both in India and at home. Cossim Ali was quickly expelled from the three provinces, and fled into Oude, where he was protected by the emperor and the vizier. The English advanced to the frontier with a demand for his immediate surrender; but a mutiny among the troops, fomented by some French and German soldiers, who had been imprudently admitted into the army, compelled them to withdraw, till discipline had been restored by the summary execution of a number of the ringleaders. Major, afterwards sir Hector Munro, then taking the field, inflicted a memorable defeat on the combined forces of the enemy, at Buxar on the Ganges. This victory immediately produced overtures from Shah Alum, who declared himself a prisoner in the hands of the vizier. These were followed by the emperor's escape to the British camp, and the continuance of the war, under his auspices, against the vizier and

Cossim Ali. The latter soon shared the fate of the helpless in India. His ally, though refusing to purchase peace by surrendering him to the English, felt no scruple in plundering him himself. He was glad to escape by flight, and finally ended his days in exile on the banks of the Indus.

Meantime the British advanced to Allahabad, which they occupied in the emperor's name. The remainder of the vizier's dominions were freely offered them by their imperial ally, on the condition of subduing his rebellious vassal; but the temptation was resisted. The vizier having retired to Lucknow effected an alliance with Holkar the Mahratta prince; while the attention of the English authorities was recalled to Bengal by the death of Meer Jaffier.

The succession was disputed between the infant child of his eldest son (who had died before his father) and his second but eldest surviving son Noojum-u-Dowlah. The former being excluded by the rules of Mohammedan law, the council, after some hesitation, recognised the latter as nabob; not forgetting to exact a treaty allowing all their objectionable demands in respect of transit duties,* with a further consideration in the way of bribes.† At the same time to provide against the new nabob's admitted incompetency to govern, a Mussulman of rank and character, named

* The Court of Directors justly characterized this act as "done in express breach and violation of their orders, and as evincing a determined resolution to sacrifice the interests of the Company and the peace of the country to lucrative and selfish views." They add, that "this unaccountable behaviour puts an end to all confidence in those who made this treaty."—*Thornton's History*, i. 471.

† Mr. Spencer, who had succeeded Mr. Vansittart in the chair, received £20,000, Mr. Johnstone £23,700, Mr. Senior and Mr. Middleton £12,250 each, Mr. Leycester £11,250, Messrs. Pleydell, Burdett, and Gray, £10,000 each.—*Ibid.* p. 473.

Mohammed Reza Khan, was appointed *naib*, or chief manager.

Such was the situation of affairs when Clive, who had been elevated to the Irish peerage, and re-appointed to the government at Calcutta, arrived with instructions to supersede the corrupt majority of the council, by a select committee nominated from home. These powers were immediately put in exercise; the Company's civil and military servants were required to execute covenants not to accept of any present whatever without the court's permission. Mohammed Reza Khan, having used his sole authority to abet the improper designs of the majority, was compelled to share his powers with two other native commissioners. A further arrangement was made with the nabob, by which he agreed to accept an annual allowance of £53,000 for the support of his dignity, and leave the remainder of his revenues to be disbursed under the direction of the English. Clive then proceeded to the camp, where overtures for an accommodation had been received from the vizier, in consequence of another and final defeat, experienced on the same day that Clive landed at Calcutta—3rd of May, 1765.

A treaty was concluded between the English, the emperor, and the vizier, by which the latter was restored to the greater part of his dominions, greatly to the disappointment of the emperor, who, after the refusal of his offer to bestow them on the Company, had expected to secure them for himself. He received only the districts of Allahabad and Korah, and was further obliged to remit a large arrear of tribute due from Bengal, in consequence of the utter exhaustion of the nabob's treasury. A far more beneficial and permanent arrangement was also effected on this occasion.

The emperor had formerly proposed that the Company should itself accept the *dewannee* of the three provinces; an arrangement which, doubtless, promised a better security for his tribute than could be found in any native administration. The offer then declined was now recurred to, and carried into effect. The *nizamut* was at the same time confirmed to the young nabob, the Company agreeing to pay him out of the revenues £53,000 per annum for the support of his dignity, in addition to the imperial tribute of £240,000.

The opportunity was further taken to obtain the emperor's sanction to the Company's possession of the Northern Circars, and the confirmation of their ally Mohammed Ali, as the rightful nabob of the Carnatic. British ascendancy was thus consolidated in both presidencies, under the sanction of the only native prince who had any pretensions to legitimacy in India. From that moment, if not from an earlier one, it became, in the language of lord Clive, a "necessity to go forward; to retract was impossible." It was not the policy of the Company, whose instructions had been invariably pacific, nor the ambition of their agents, who seemed intent only on amassing private wealth, which brought power and dominion to the feet of a mercantile corporation. The foundations of that empire were laid by its enemies more than its defenders. The hostility of the French, with the treachery and internecine strife of the native powers, forced upon England a sovereignty which she had neither sought nor desired: and in this result of the warring passions of men, the Christian cannot fail to recognise the overruling hand of that Judge who "putteth down one and setteth up another," and who, after centuries of oppression and bloodshed, was at last about to visit India with the blessings of civilization and peace.

Lord Clive finally quitted India and returned to England in 1767. He was received with the highest honours, and yet retains the reputation of a consummate military commander. Still his character is clouded by too many instances of the pecuniary corruption which prevailed in India, and which, towards the close of his administration, he struggled earnestly to reform. The evil, however, was not to be extirpated without a greater change in opinion and practice than was yet contemplated at home or abroad. The official salaries of the Company's servants were small; their recognised position, while disposing of the thrones and treasures of the East, was only that of mercantile agents. The invariable custom of native society accompanied the transaction of all affairs, public or private, with an interchange of presents, and office was deemed valuable in proportion only to its opportunities for emolument. The strangeness of the position, the remoteness of the scene, and the associations of the country, engendered a thirst for riches which no attempt had been made to regulate. It is not surprising that individual rectitude should be unable to supply the want of law and authority in India, in an age when the first ministers of the British crown, and the leading members of the legislature, were neither ashamed nor afraid to dip their hands into the Company's coffers at home.

While matters proceeded thus prosperously in Bengal, a very different result attended the government policy in Madras. Notwithstanding the imperial grant obtained by lord Clive, Nizam Ali, now subahdar of the Deccan, resolutely claimed the Northern Circars as a portion of his dominions, and the council of Fort St. George weakly agreed to pay him tribute for their occupation. They further covenanted to assist him against all his enemies; this condition involved immediate hostilities with Mysore, a powerful Hindu state, never permanently reduced under the yoke of the Mogul empire, where the chief authority had been recently acquired by a Mussulman adventurer, named Hyder Ali Khan.

This man had raised himself from the command of a body of freebooters to the head of the Mysore army, and the practical administration of the state, the raja being little better than a prisoner in the hands of his general. Nizam Ali, in conjunction with the peishwah, had determined to attack Mysore; but no sooner had the English become involved in the war, than it assumed an aspect more conformable with oriental than European precedent. Hyder first bought off the Mahrattas, and then induced the nizam to turn his arms against the British, and enter the Carnatic in conjunction with himself. The English authorities proved wholly unequal to cope with this anomalous and perilous position. Their troops, indeed, amply sustained the national credit in the field, defeating the combined enemy at a prodigious disadvantage in point of numbers, and so alarming the nizam that he hastened to make overtures for peace. But the valour of the army was neutralized by the folly and want of principle which marked the conduct of government. It was again weak enough to enter into an alliance with the perfidious nizam, on the terms of paying tribute for possessions already their own, and again criminal enough to undertake the reduction of Mysore to his obedience, on condition of the dewannee of that kingdom being conferred on the Company.

The war which followed this unprincipled conspiracy was deservedly disastrous. The British forces had occupied the passes, captured several forts and places in the Mysore, and were pursuing their wonted progress to victory, when the tide was suddenly turned. Hyder, descending a pass of which they had no knowledge, burst into the Carnatic with fire and sword. The plain was scoured by his horse, and the council, alarmed for the presidency itself, commenced negotiations of which their enemy determined to make them feel the full humiliation. Hyder appeared before Madras on March 29th, 1769, and there, compelling the chief members of government to attend him in his camp, dictated the terms of a dishonourable peace.

The dissatisfaction justly produced by such intelligence in England was augmented by complaints against the Company's officers, addressed from the nabob of the Carnatic, through a private agent, to the ministers of the crown. A cry was raised for the interference of the supreme authority, and a royal commission was actually despatched to control or supersede the Company's government in its transactions with the native rulers. The first commissioner was the admiral in the Indian Seas; the next that same sir Robert Fletcher whom a court-martial had dismissed from the Bengal army for mutiny.

Nothing but discord could be expected from the presence of two conflicting authorities at the seat of government. The royal commission was soon withdrawn; but Fletcher, in the face of his dismissal from Bengal, was appointed to the command in chief of the Madras army, with a seat in the council. Here he vindicated the justice of his former sentence by again flagrantly disobeying the orders of government; but having continued to hold the seat in the House of Commons, to which he was indebted for his promotion, he escaped from punishment by claiming to return to his duties in parliament.

Meantime the nabob had not only made up his quarrel with the Madras government, but induced them to assist in the reduction of Tanjore. The legitimacy of Mohammedan rule in India seems to have been taken for granted by the English officers, who looked upon the rajas and polygars who refused to submit to it as rebels and traitors. This was Koran doctrine, no doubt; and its too ready adoption by the English enabled the revolted feudatories of a decaying empire to enforce claims which the Great Mogul, in the plenitude of his power, had failed to establish. In truth, however, both Hindu and Mohammedan princes were equally destitute of genuine legitimacy. There was not a ruler in the country possessed of a higher title than forcible possession; in most cases of very recent origin, in all without a shadow of national sanction. The sword was the arbiter acknowledged at once by people and prince, and it would be idle now to inquire into the merits of rival claimants to power, when all power was in the hands either of actual usurpers, or of men but one degree removed from usurpation.

The Company's government was fast becoming disengaged from such questions by the growth of its own sovereignty. In obtaining the dewannee, Clive had not contemplated, or not thought it prudent, to employ European agency in the collection of the revenue, and in the contingent judicial process. The only department of government administered by the Company's servants was the military; the remainder was confided to a native minister, under whom all the old machinery was continued. The same minister acted also as the deputy (naib) of the nabob, thus in fact combining in his person both the ancient functions of the subahdar, though under responsibility to two different masters. This double system of government could only be transitional. The sovereignty of which Clive had laid the foundations was soon to be openly wielded by the GREAT CIVILIAN who had shared his counsels, and was possessed of a genius still more daring and sagacious.

Warren Hastings, after being successively resident at the court of the nabob of Bengal, and member of council at Calcutta and Madras, was placed at the head of the former presidency in April, 1772. The idea of British sovereignty in India had long been realized in his lofty mind; no man was more thoroughly impregnated with the conviction expressed in Clive's memorable dictum, that where it was too late to draw back the path of safety lay in pressing forward.

The nabob, dying shortly before, had been succeeded by an infant brother, under whom Mohammed Reza Khan continued to act as naib. His administration, however, had been accused to the Court of Directors, through the machinations of a Brahmin named raja Nuncomar, who had stood high in Meer Jaffier's favour, but, being a man of infamous character, had been rejected by Clive in his pretensions to the naibship. The court resolved to discontinue the native agency, which had hitherto masked their authority in Bengal, and openly to exercise the dewannee by European servants. They further ordered the governor to arrest Mohammed Reza, and bring him to trial on the charges of Nuncomar.

In carrying these orders into effect, Hastings assigned the guardianship of the young nabob's person to Munny Begum, the favourite wife of his father, but whose principal recommendation was, that being connected with neither of the native factions, she was wholly dependent on the English governor. In the end Mohammed Reza was fully exonerated from the charges of Nuncomar, who was not only baulked of his revenge, but doomed to see the office, for which he had been scheming so long and so unscrupulously, abolished by the very proceeding which he had hoped would transfer it to himself. From this moment Hastings became an object of the most intense hatred to the vindictive Brahmin, and the consequences were such as neither could then anticipate.*

* "What the Italian is to the Englishman, what the Hindu is to the Italian, what the Bengalee is to other Hindus, that was Nuncomar to other Bengalees. The physical organization of the Bengalee is feeble even to effeminacy. He lives in a constant vapour bath. His pursuits are sedentary, his limbs delicate, his movements languid. During many ages he has been trampled upon by men of bolder and more hardy breeds. Courage, independence, veracity, are qualities to which his constitution and his situation are equally unfavourable. His mind bears a singular analogy to his body. It is weak even to helplessness for purposes of manly resistance; but its suppleness and its tact move the children of sterner climes to admiration, not unmingled with contempt. All those arts which are the natural defence of the weak are more familiar to this subtle race than to the Ionian of the time of Juvenal, or to the Jew of the dark ages. What the horns are to the buffalo, what the paw is to the tiger, what the sting is to the bee, what beauty, according to the old Greek song, is to the woman, deceit is to the Bengalee. Large promises, smooth excuses, elaborate tissues of circumstantial falsehood, chicanery, perjury, forgery, are the weapons, offensive and defensive, of the people of the Lower Ganges. All those millions do not furnish one Sepoy to the armies of the Company. But as usurers, as moneychangers, as sharp legal practitioners,

In assuming the dewannee, one of Hastings's first acts was to constitute courts of justice throughout the three provinces in subordination to the government at Calcutta, for the administration of the civil and exchequer jurisdiction by judges appointed from the Company's European servants. At the same time he erected criminal courts ostensibly in the name of the nabob, to whom that jurisdiction pertained as nizam; but these were, equally with the others, under the supervision of the Company's servants, and were in fact established without consultation with the native authority. This act of supremacy was subsequently adduced by Hastings himself, and accepted by the highest court of justice in India, as evidence that the nabob was now become the pageant which had been foreseen, and that the

no class of human beings can bear a comparison with them. With all his softness, the Bengalee is by no means placable in his enmities or prone to pity. The pertinacity with which he adheres to his purposes yields only to the immediate pressure of fear. Nor does he lack a certain kind of courage, which is often wanting to his masters. To inevitable evils he is sometimes found to oppose a passive fortitude, such as the Stoics attributed to their ideal sage. A European warrior, who rushes on a battery of cannon with a loud hurrah, will sometimes shriek under the surgeon's knife, and fall into an agony of despair at the sentence of death. But the Bengalee, who would see his country overrun, his house laid in ashes, his children murdered or dishonoured, without having the spirit to strike one blow, has yet been known to endure torture with the firmness of Mucius, and to mount the scaffold with the steady step and even pulse of Algernon Sidney. In Nuncomar the national character was strongly, and with exaggeration, personified. The Company's servants had repeatedly detected him in the most criminal intrigues. On one occasion he brought a false charge against another Hindu, and tried to substantiate it by producing forged documents. On another occasion it was discovered that while professing the strongest attachment to the English, he was engaged in several conspiracies against them, and in particular that he was the medium of a correspondence between the court of Delhi and the French authorities in the Carnatic. For these and similar practices he had been long detained in confinement. But his talents and influence had not only procured his liberation, but had obtained for him a certain degree of consideration even among the British rulers of his country."—*Macaulay's Essay on Warren Hastings.*

sovereignty of the country was *de facto* vested in the Company.*

It was speedily disembarrassed of another, and more inconvenient fiction. Shah Alum was ever scheming to recover the palace and power of his ancestors at Delhi. Being invariably denied the assistance of the English, he placed himself in the hands of Scindia, by whom he was conducted to the imperial city. The Mahratta chief received in return a grant of the districts of Corah and Allahabad, which the British had compelled the vizier to restore to the emperor. The transfer was made without reference to the Calcutta government, and to the aggrandizement of a power which was regarded in that quarter with well-founded jealousy and alarm. Hastings pronounced the districts to be forfeited, and further resolved to discontinue the payment of all tribute from Bengal while the emperor should continue allied with the Mahrattas. The dewannee was thus finally converted into an independent sovereignty, for the payments were never resumed. Their discontinuance had in fact been previously discussed between the Court of Directors and their agents in Calcutta, and it was disingenuous to seize upon this pretext for the execution of a "foregone conclusion," if, as it is stated, the emperor was encouraged by British officers to undertake the expedition to Delhi, and assured of an honourable reception again in case of its failure.

The governor and council justified the act by the stronger plea of absolute necessity; their revenues could no longer bear so ruinous a drain for an

* Mr. Hastings's affidavit in the Supreme Court of Judicature, July 31, 1775.—See his impeachment.—*Burke's Works*, xvi. 202.

authority purely nominal. The forfeited districts were restored to the vizier in consideration of half a million of money paid into the Company's treasury, and the alliance with Oude was henceforth regarded as the chief native support in the impending conflict with the Mahrattas.

In pursuance of the new policy, Hastings agreed to assist his ally in the reduction of the Rohilla Sirdars, a band of Affghan free-lances who had served under the standard of the Moguls, and, on the break up of the empire, had quartered themselves on the districts between Delhi and Oude, where they constituted a number of independent chiefs. The vizier claimed their allegiance as chief officer of the empire; he had further pretensions in right of certain stipulations made with the Rohillas themselves, as the condition of defending them against the Mahrattas. His cause of war would probably not have endured the scrutiny of European jurists, but it was as good as most others in India, and Mr. Hastings felt justified in assisting to strengthen the frontier of the Company's "only useful ally." The real owners of the country, the Hindu population, were little regarded by either of the belligerents; nor were *theirs* the wrongs which afterwards engaged the sympathies of politicians in England, by whom the Rohilla Sirdars were held up as examples of bravery and patriotism, and their subjugation denounced as lawless and inhuman. Yet their enforced subjection to the arms of the vizier was certainly a measure of stricter justice than their own recent appropriation of the country; while in the interests of freedom and patriotism, it would be difficult to appreciate the gain of the Hindu population in being subject to the rule of the Sirdars, or their loss in receiving one Mussulman tyrant in exchange for many.

Hastings agreed for a sum of four hundred thousand pounds to accommodate the vizier with a large portion of the Company's army, to be subsisted out of his revenues; an arrangement highly convenient in the exhausted condition of the Bengal treasury. By this force the Rohillas were attacked and defeated with prodigious slaughter, and the territory annexed, or restored, to the vizier's dominions. The campaign being conducted under the direction of that prince, could not fail to be stained by the savage and inhuman practices of native warfare, though the presence of British officers must in some degree have mitigated their severity. In England, however, the public mind was justly shocked by the accounts which came home, and the Indian government began to receive the serious attention of parliament.

In 1772 the House of Commons resolved:—

1. That all acquisitions made under the military force, or treaty with foreign princes, do of right belong to the state.

2. That to appropriate acquisitions so made to the private emolument of persons intrusted with any civil or military power of the state, is illegal.

3. That very great sums of money and other valuable property have been acquired in Bengal, from princes and others of that country, by persons intrusted with the civil and military powers of the state, by means of such powers, which sums of money and valuable property have been appropriated to the private use of such persons.

The East India Company were as ready as the parliament to censure the malversation of their servants. But when the argument was pressed against themselves, as no less servants of the British crown, and their possessions in India were claimed as the property of the state, they strenuously demurred. The directors still clung to the fictions which had so long masked the real situation of affairs. They contended that the Indian sovereignty was still in the emperor of Delhi, as whose minister the Company was acting in Bengal. They considered their territorial acquisitions, equally with their commercial assets, the private property of the corporation; and in this claim they were supported by no less an authority than the lord chief justice Mansfield. The legislature, nevertheless, overruled the argument by passing an act to limit the Company's dividends, and appropriating a share in the profits of the dewannee to the national exchequer.

Parliament determined at the same time, in the exercise of its new-found responsibility, to provide a better system of government for the Indian dependencies of the British crown. A constitution was framed for five years, by which Bengal was declared the chief presidency. Mr. Hastings was appointed governor-general, with a council of four, three of whom were sent out from England in order to counteract the corruption prevailing among the Company's servants in India. A Supreme Court of Judicature was also established at Calcutta in the king's name, consisting of a chief justice and three puisne judges, armed with all the powers of the superior courts of law and equity in England

The new government came into operation at Calcutta in 1773, and was almost immediately paralysed by internal dissensions. Its English members, arriving with the most exaggerated impressions of the corruption and rapacity supposed to be inseparable from the

Company's service, plunged at once into open hostilities with its most distinguished member, the governor-general. They even considered it their duty to search for matters of accusation against him, and charges of the grossest nature were advanced and retorted. The governor-general was accused of bribery by Mr. Francis, on the authority of the Brahmin Nuncomar, who eagerly seized the opportunity to gratify his long-treasured animosity. With oriental instinct he imagined the governor-general must be already fallen when councillors were sent out from England to correct and share his authority. The new members were credulous enough to receive his unsupported accusations, and malicious enough to produce them at the board, with Hastings himself in the chair. The governor-general asserted the dignity of his office by adjourning the council and withdrawing. The majority proceeding to the investigation in his absence, soon declared their president guilty of corruptly receiving above thirty thousand pounds.

Nuncomar, the only witness, became a willing agent for the reception of new charges, and his daily levée was crowded by native sycophants, who flocked to share the favours of the new authorities by proving accusations on the fallen governor. The triumph of the Brahmin was suddenly interrupted by a charge of forgery preferred against himself by a native in the Supreme Court, on which he was arrested and lodged in the common gaol. Being brought to trial and convicted by a jury of Englishmen, the chief justice, in accordance with the English law, passed sentence of *death*, to the amazement of the Hindus, who refused to believe that one whose person was inviolate by their law and religion for any crime whatever, could suffer the last penalty for an offence as common and as venial in their eyes as lying.

The power of mercy was vested in the chief justice, sir Elijah Impey, who had been the schoolfellow, and was still the familiar friend, of Hastings. Whether any private feeling influenced the decision, no one can know, though many have taken on themselves to affirm it. The chief justice did not exercise his prerogative, and the sentence of the law was carried into effect, to the astonishment and consternation of the assembled populace. The culprit ascended the gallows with the calmness, or rather apathy, which is so common among orientals, as not to afford even a probable presumption of innocence; but the spectators are described as agitated by a panic equal to what is caused by an earthquake. A cry of horror rose from the multitude as they saw a member of their most sacred castes ignominiously deprived of life. Dispersing on the instant, they fled with loud wailings towards the Hooghly, and plunged into the holy waters as if to purify themselves from the guilt of having looked on such a crime.

The death of Nuncomar, though charged upon Hastings by his opponents, appears to have had no further connexion with him than as removing an accuser who might be troublesome, but whose character for falsehood and perfidy was too notorious for a governor-general to have seriously dreaded his testimony. The sentence, however severe, was that of the English law, pronounced by the court which parliament had established to correct the alleged malversation of the Company's servants. Hastings was in no way responsible for the penalty or its execution, nor was any shadow of proof ever adduced that he attempted to influence the decision of the chief justice. That Nuncomar was a villain of the deepest dye has never been questioned, and it is somewhat to the credit of the authorities in those early days that the course of justice was not allowed to be defeated by the claims of an idolatrous caste.

The natives, however, had still to learn the nature and extent of the judicial powers created by the British parliament, to guard against local oppression and injustice. The Supreme Court of Judicature, though primarily intended for the administration of justice among Europeans, (the native population being regarded as subjects of the nabob,) proceeded, in the spirit of all English tribunals, to enlarge the sphere of its authority by *construction*. The judges interfered in questions of revenue, reviewed the proceedings between natives in the Company's courts, and called for the records of government, in order to adjudicate on the dismissal and appointment of its officers. Collusive arrests by process from Calcutta, and writs of *habeas corpus*, spread the new jurisdiction among all classes of natives; by whom it was so little relished, that renters of land applied to throw up their leases, and the zemindars were afraid to act in the collection of the revenue.

"No Mahratta invasion had ever spread through the province such dismay as this inroad of English lawyers. All the injustice of former oppressors, Asiatic and European, appeared as a blessing when compared with the justice of the Supreme Court."* The government was unanimous in resisting these outrages. It determined, on the advice of the law officers, to withhold the power of the state from

* Macaulay's Essay.

the execution of writs issued against the zemindars. The Supreme Court proceeded to levy by the sheriffs' officers, and the native defendant prepared to resist by force. A fight ensued: the bailiffs' men were arrested by the military, acting under the orders of government, and the court in turn granted rules to attach the officers employed. The governor-general himself was threatened with a similar process, and many great words had passed from the irate, but impotent, judges, when the contest suddenly ceased by the abandonment of the prosecution on the part of the native who had originally set the court in motion.

It has been surmised that Mr. Hastings prudently extricated the court by buying off the prosecutor: it is more certain that he sought to provide against a recurrence of the collision, in appointing sir Elijah Impey to the office of chief judge in the Company's Court of Exchequer, (called the Sudder Dewannee Adawlut,) with a salary of six thousand pounds per annum, in addition to the chief justiceship of the Supreme Court of Judicature, conferred on him by his majesty. This arrangement, though indefensible in theory, was perhaps the only means at the time of preserving the country from the intemperance of judges established by a well-meaning but ill-informed legislature.

An act was subsequently passed (21 Geo. III. c. 70) to indemnify the government for their resistance, and providing that the court should have no jurisdiction over the acts of government or the officers employed under their orders, nor over any native employed in the collection of the revenue. Still it is attested by one who lately held the highest legal position in India, that "the lapse of sixty years, and the virtue and wisdom of many eminent magistrates who have during that time administered justice in the Supreme Court, have not effaced from the minds of the people of Bengal the recollection of those evil days."

The termination of the judicial conflict was followed by a revival of the intestine strife, introduced at the council board by the same crude and ill-considered piece of legislation which had launched the Supreme Court. No provision had been made, beyond the traditional casting vote of the chair, for the not improbable contingency of a difference between the governor-general and his council; while in appointing councillors from England, with the avowed purpose of correcting the policy of the Indian servants, parliament had done its best to secure the immediate occurrence of such a collision. All the members, as well as the governor-general, being named in the act, felt in consequence a separate individual responsibility, which would acknowledge no superior.

Mr. Francis, the reputed author of Junius, exhibited from the first all the bitterness and personality which characterize those celebrated letters, and being supported by two of the other three councillors, he was able for some time to thwart every proceeding of the governor-general. When the death of one of his opponents had reduced the parties to an equality, Hastings availed himself of the casting vote to retaliate upon Francis, by overruling all his proposals, and governing at his own discretion.

Powerless in India, Francis had many supporters in England. The court of directors, uniformly adverse to war, disapproved so strongly of the hostilities in Rohilcund as to pass an address to the crown for the removal of the governor-general. This was overruled by a contrary vote in the court of proprietors, with whom, as with the public in general, Hastings enjoyed the favour always extended by the British nation to brilliant and successful services.

The ministers of the crown, however, who were the political friends of his rival, sided with the directors; and Hastings, fearing a recall, desired his friends at home to save him from that humiliation by tendering his resignation. This expedient was eagerly caught at, and a successor precipitately appointed in the person of general Clavering, the commander-in-chief at Calcutta, and one of Hastings's opponents in the council. The general was further honoured with the order of the Bath, a mark of royal favour which was viewed as a censure on the governor-general.

Indignant at this slight, Hastings denied having resigned, and refused to vacate the chair. The other attempted to seize it by force; and the spectacle was exhibited of two rival governments meeting in Calcutta, and fulminating resolutions against each other, till the judges of the Supreme Court ended the indecent strife by delivering their opinion in favour of Hastings, as having never actually resigned nor been removed from the government. The strife in the council continued so high that a duel was at last fought between Hastings and Francis, in which the latter received a wound, and departing soon after to England, the governor-general was left master of the field of action, while his rival proceeded to exert all the malice and ability of an ill-regulated mind to effect his condemnation at home.

Hastings was now at liberty to concentrate his

powerful genius on the affairs of the great empire which had been submitted to his supreme authority. In each of the minor presidencies transactions of immense importance demanded his attention.

In Bombay the English had always claimed the islands of Salsette and Karanja, as included in the dotation of the infanta of Portugal, but the authorities of that nation had refused to transfer them. They were now in the possession of the Mahrattas, with whom negotiations had been set on foot for their cession. Disappointed with the progress of the negotiations, the Bombay government took forcible possession of the two islands, and then availed itself of a disputed succession in the court of Poona to obtain a confirmation of their claims. The peishwah had died without offspring, and his brother Ragoba or Ragonath Rao was in the exercise of power, when the widow of the deceased prince gave birth to a son, whose legitimacy was denied by the uncle. The Bombay government entered into engagements with the latter to assist him with troops in return for a grant of Bassein and the other places of which they desired possession. Meantime the supreme government had decided on favouring the claims of the infant, and concluded a treaty accordingly. Much mischief ensued from this division of councils. The military operations, also, were marked at the outset by incapacity and disaster. A Bombay force stooped to capitulate to the Mahrattas, on condition of restoring the places seized. The government, however, refused to ratify the treaty, and Hastings despatched a force from Bengal, which partially retrieved the disgrace. It was finally arranged that Ragoba should act as regent during the minority of his nephew, who was acknowledged as peishwah; and the war closed after being extended to the territories of Scindia and Holkar, without any territorial advantage to the English. The terms of peace included a mutual restoration of conquests; Baroach, also, which the British had conquered from the local nabob, was made over to Scindia in reward for his services in effecting the pacification.

At Madras a similar conflict of authority was raging to that which had so long paralysed the arm of government in Calcutta. The court of directors had sent out orders for the restoration of the raja of Tanjore, dethroned to gratify the nabob of the Carnatic. The nabob's numerous creditors, European and native, seeing in this act of restitution the destruction of their questionable claims on his exchequer, combined to resist it. An enormous bribe was offered to lord Pigot, the governor, to delay the court's orders, and his virtue being found proof against the temptation, an opposition was organized in the council to overthrow his authority. The governor hastily suspended two of the councillors on a charge of conspiring for this purpose, and ordered the commander-in-chief into arrest for combining with the suspended members to form a new government. This officer was not famed for obedience to orders, being no other than the notorious sir Robert Fletcher, whose parliamentary interest had again raised him to command, in spite of two former dismissals. The mutinous general was so far from submitting to superior authority, that in conjunction with the members of council he arrested and imprisoned the governor. The admiral commanding in the roads interfered in the king's name for his release, but was told the crown had not empowered him to require the removal of a Company's servant from the authority of the Company's governments, and lord Pigot actually died in confinement before any measures for his release could be enforced.

During these extraordinary proceedings the governor-general forbore to interfere, perhaps from a well-founded conviction that neither party was free from blame. Such at least was the opinion expressed by the authorities in England. The Court of Directors severely censured lord Pigot's assumption of the power to suspend his council, while on the other hand the House of Commons, after some hesitation, ordered three of the refractory councillors to be prosecuted for the arrest of the governor, and they were fined in one thousand pounds each.

A new government was formed at Madras, under sir Thomas Rumbold, which, on the breaking out of another war with the French, sent an expedition against Pondicherry, and captured it after a short resistance. Proceeding to take Mahè also, the British awakened the displeasure of their old enemy Hyder Ali, which was augmented by their passing through a portion of his territories to the assistance of Basalat Jung, the brother of the nizam, on whose possessions Hyder was supposed to have formed a design.

The Madras government, about the same time, making the discovery that the tribute paid to the nizam for the Northern Circars was unnecessary and disgraceful, avowed their determination to hold those districts as the free gift of the emperor. Hastings's superior intelligence was alarmed at the prospect of uniting the two great powers of the Deccan against the Company. He hastened to overrule this determination, and pacify the nizam.

Hyder, meantime, had collected his forces unobserved, and in 1780 once more broke into the Carnatic, ravaging the country to within fifty miles of Madras.

All was again confusion and alarm in that presidency. A force under colonel Baillie, which marched from Guntoor to effect a junction with sir Hector Munro at Conjeveram, was defeated and made prisoners, with the loss of thirty-six officers killed and thirty-four wounded. The remainder, surrendering to the Mysore tyrant, were loaded with chains, and marched to the dungeons of Bangalore and Seringapatam, where they endured the most infamous ill usage during a lengthened imprisonment, which few of them survived. Sir Hector Munro fell back powerless on Madras, and the authorities in the utmost alarm invoked aid from Calcutta.

With the Mahratta war still pending at Bombay, and the raja of Berar manifesting designs on Bengal, Hastings was called upon to save the government of Madras from annihilation. No man was ever more full of resources, and his spirit always rose with the emergency. He suspended the governor of Madras, (who was soon after dismissed the service by the court of directors, for a long course of shameful corruption,) and sent sir Eyre Coote to take command of the army. When he arrived Arcot had fallen to Hyder. The nabob was without money, men, or influence ; the British general found that he had to create an army before he could command it. Yet within a short time Coote, who was ever the idol of the Sepoys, contrived twice or thrice to defeat Hyder in person, and recover possession of the chief holds on the Carnatic. Lord Macartney arriving from England as governor, the general returned to Bengal, and the next year the war received a check in the death of Hyder. He was succeeded by his son Tippoo, who, exceeding his father in literary attainments and Mussulman zeal, was in every military quality, save an intense hatred of his enemy, immeasurably his inferior.

The French alliance was lost to him in consequence of the re-establishment of peace in Europe; but Tippoo continued the war, and conducted it in the true spirit of his barbarous religion. The garrisons which capitulated to his arms were subjected to the most shameful treatment in violation of his plighted faith. European and Christian prisoners were thrown into irons, and suffered the most cruel indignities, torture, and death.

Meantime the government of Madras was a prey to the corruption of some members, and the untimely dissensions of others. Commissioners were despatched to negotiate for peace, who were received by Tippoo with every mark of insolence and scorn. A treaty was, notwithstanding, concluded on May 11th, 1784, on the basis of a restitution of conquests, but no compensation was either obtained or demanded for the atrocious treatment of the English prisoners. General Mathews, captain Rumby, and many others, had perished in captivity, under their inhuman sufferings, but the Madras government was too eager to terminate a war which they knew not how to prolong, to institute an inquiry into their fate.

Hastings disapproved the treaty, and on other matters also differed from lord Macartney, but the influence of the latter was superior to his own with the authorities at home. The career of the great civilian was now approaching its close. Before it ended he was engaged in transactions in Bengal which aggravated the censures heaped upon him in England. Cheyt Singh, the raja of Benares, held the zemindary of that district under the vizier of Oude, and subsequently under the Company's government, to whom the vizier by treaty had transferred the sovereignty. Necessities, occasioned by the war, induced Hastings to call upon his vassal for further assistance beyond the ordinary tribute. The justice of an extraordinary levy in time of war was not denied, but the raja of course disputed the amount, and procrastinated in the payment. The demands of government increasing, Hastings, who believed the raja to have concealed enormous wealth in his fortresses, resorted to extremities in order to enforce the required contribution. The raja was arrested by his order at Benares: his retainers rose to the rescue, and Hastings himself escaped with difficulty from their fury. Having ordered up the troops, he deprived Cheyt Singh of the zemindary, and transferred it to another member of his family at an increased rate of tribute.

At Benares the governor-general was met by the vizier, who came to represent the impoverished condition of Oude. He was unequal to meet his engagements with the British government unless some relief were afforded, and Hastings proceeded accordingly to review his liabilities. It was agreed to reduce the subsidiary force maintained at his cost for the defence of his dominions; but as this relief was inadequate, the vizier proposed to resume some of the jaghires, granted with too liberal a hand by his predecessor and himself. Mohammedan sovereigns seldom scrupled to exercise this privilege whenever they had the power, but the Company were in some cases parties to the grant, and Hastings therefore stipulated that the holders of such fiefs should be paid the net income through the British resident. A third article in the treaty referred to Fyzoola Khan, one of the Rohilla chiefs, who had obtained an extensive district on condition of assisting the vizier with troops, and was now required to augment his contingent.

Among the persons affected by the article for the resumption of jaghires were the mother and grandmother of the vizier, who had been endowed by his predecessors with domains from which they were supposed to have realized enormous wealth. It was principally, indeed, from the resources of these *begums* that the needy prince expected to recruit his finances; but the ladies were far from quietly submitting to his demands. The interference of the military was found requisite to obtain possession of their treasures; their servants were imprisoned, and the ladies themselves, either by the insolence of the vizier's officers, or by their own desperate resistance, were exposed to a publicity which is thought indecorous by Mohammedan women.* These transactions had little effect on the progress of the British empire, and their character is, therefore, beyond the province of these pages. They are noted only as prominent incidents in the eventful career of the first governor-general.

In February, 1784, Warren Hastings closed his administration and embarked for England. He had held the reins of power in India, not without censure, yet still by the common consent of all who knew his talents, and the necessity for their employment, during the period of England's severest struggle at home and

* A portion of the jaghires of which the begums were deprived was afterwards restored to them by the personal mediation of Hastings.

abroad. He had been consolidating a noble empire in the East, while the ministers of the crown were losing one in the West, by the revolt of the American colonies. Britain came out of the great European war with glory, but still not without the loss of many prizes that had previously fallen to her arms. "The only quarter of the world in which she lost nothing was the quarter in which her interests had been committed to the care of Hastings." His was the mind which prompted, directed, and sustained the whole administration of India at a crisis of unexampled confusion and peril. He received little assistance from home, and found less at the council-boards of the three presidencies. "Out of a frightful anarchy he educed at least a rude and imperfect order. The whole organization by which justice was dispensed, revenue collected, peace maintained, throughout a territory not inferior in population to the dominions of Louis XVI. or of the emperor Joseph, was formed and superintended by him. He boasted that every public office, without exception, which existed when he left Bengal was his creation. It is quite true that this system, after all the improvements suggested by the experience of sixty years, still needs improvement, and that it was at first far more defective than it now is. But whoever seriously considers what it is to construct, from the beginning, the whole of a machine so vast and complex as a government, will allow that what Hastings effected deserves high admiration."

Lord Macaulay, whose words are here employed, rates his abilities as a statesman above those of the most celebrated European ministers. He adds, that "in the great art of inspiring large masses of human beings with confidence and attachment, no ruler ever surpassed Hastings. The affection felt for him by the civil service was singularly ardent and constant. The army, at the same time, loved him as armies have seldom loved any but the greatest chiefs who have led them to victory." With the natives of all classes his popularity has never been equalled by any other governor. The bronze faces of the Sepoys blazed with delight as he passed down their lines, his slight figure clad in the civilian's blue coat, and with uncovered head thanked them for their bravery and fidelity. "Even now, after the lapse of more than fifty years, the natives of India still talk of him as the greatest of the English, and nurses sing children to sleep with a jingling ballad about the fleet horses and richly-caparisoned elephants of sahib Warren Hostein."

Services so unexampled justified the expectation of the highest honours, with which Hastings returned to his native land. His heart beat high with the anticipation of raising a decayed but ancient family to the dignity of the peerage. The king received him with marked distinction. The court of directors, who had so often censured his proceedings, taking a just review of his long and splendid administration, welcomed him with demonstrations of respect and gratitude. With the larger court of proprietors, and the public generally, his merits had always found a due appreciation. But the powerful Whig party had been inflamed against him by the representations of Francis. Mr. Pitt, who had but newly succeeded to power, was carried away by the torrent of eloquence in which Burke and Sheridan denounced the iniquity and rapacity of the Indian pro-consul. The whole of his administration was subjected to a searching ordeal. The Rohilla war, the deprivation of Cheyt Singh, and the treatment of the begums of Oude, were painted in the most revolting colours. At the bar of that House in which he had expected to receive a well-earned seat, Hastings found himself impeached of high crimes and misdemeanours by the Commons of England. The trial was protracted over a period of seven years, during which the founder of his country's empire in the East was held up to the execration of Europe, as one of the most detestable monsters that ever disgraced humanity. Burke, in the frantic zeal of a heated imagination, lavished expressions upon this aged public servant which could dishonour none but the speaker. The East India Company and its directors stood manfully forth in his defence, and the voice of the country was uttered throughout on his side.

The impeachment terminated on the 23rd of April, 1795, in the acquittal of the accused on every one of the articles laid to his charge. The expenses of the defence, which would have crushed a far larger fortune than Hastings ever amassed, were defrayed by the East India Company, who further voted him a pension of four thousand pounds a-year, and erected his statue in the general court-room. At a later period the dignity of a privy councillor graced his declining years: and before he sank into the grave the House of Commons atoned for a persecution conceived and carried forward in the worst spirit of party faction, by rising in a body and uncovering as the veteran statesman appeared to give evidence on their inquiries into Indian affairs.

Warren Hastings was not free from the faults of his age and class. Highly accomplished in classical and oriental literature, he was devoid of an influential sense of religion, lax in morals, self-confident, and ambitious. But his lofty and sagacious mind was animated more by a passion for his country's glory than for personal advantage. His defects were common to his accusers and the whole state of society in which they lived. It was the age of the French revolution, when religion and morals were at their lowest ebb throughout Europe. In India the natives were in reasonable doubt whether their conquerors owned any religion at all. There were but few clergymen, fewer churches, and no Christian missions. Such was the absence even of the externals of Christianity, that horse-races were publicly run in Calcutta on the Lord's day. It is vain to expect that human nature will be restrained by its own sense of honour or honesty, where God is denied, and the heart not illumined from above.

Public opinion was now earnest against any extension of a dominion, the acquisition of which was regarded with an uneasy conscience. Governors were henceforth selected of a pacific temperament, and charged with the most stringent injunctions to abstain from hostilities. But war was not a matter of discretion, in a country where the alternative lay between conquest and submission. Till British influence became paramount in India, no governors proved so little successful in maintaining peace as those who assumed office with that single intention.

The statute by which Hastings was appointed governor-general was enacted for a period of five years, at the expiry of which it was more than once renewed, whilst a more permanent plan of government was being hotly disputed in England. Mr. Fox proposed to transfer the powers of the East India Company to a board of directors appointed by the crown. The opposition of the king and the majority of the nation defeated this design, and overthrew the Whig administration. Mr. Pitt was called to power, and in 1784 succeeded in passing an act, of which the leading provisions have continued in operation to the present time.

By this act the East India Company were retained in the government of the British possessions in India, as well as in the enjoyment of their commercial monopoly to the eastward of the Cape of Good Hope. At the same time a board of commissioners was established from the chief ministers of the crown, to control the directors in the exercise of their political functions. All the despatches from India were to be communicated to this board, and no letter or order could be sent out by the directors until the draft had been approved by the board. The board was empowered not only to alter drafts so submitted, but to substitute other paragraphs, which the court of directors were bound to transmit to India under their own signature. In cases demanding secresy the president of the board was further authorized to require his orders to be sent out by a secret committee, composed of the chairman, deputy-chairman, and one other director, without being communicated to the remainder of the court.

The governor-general, and governors of Madras and Bombay, with the commanders-in-chief at each presidency, were to be appointed by the Company, with the approval of the crown, which practically amounted to a transfer of those high appointments to the king's ministers. The other members of council at each presidency continued in the appointment of the Company. But in order to remedy the inconvenience which had been experienced from their opposition to the governor, another act (26 Geo. III. cap. 16) provided that in case of a difference of opinion at the council-board, the members should severally record their opinions in writing, after which the governor-general (or governor) was empowered to act as he might see fit, though in opposition to the majority.

With these augmented powers, earl Cornwallis, a nobleman of distinguished reputation, was sent out to fill the chair which had hitherto been occupied by a Company's servant. He was immediately, in spite of himself, involved in hostilities with Mysore. Tippoo Sultan burned with the fiercest hatred against the British power. The walls of his capital were covered with insulting caricatures, and numerous English prisoners with whom he had observed neither faith nor humanity, were known to be still languishing in his dungeons. The government which made no inquiry after their fate, from a fear of provoking war, was yet rash enough to renew their treaty with the nizam, recognizing his claim to the sovereignty of Mysore, and omitting Tippoo from the number of princes in alliance with the Company. The sultan retaliated by attacking Travancore in defiance of a notification that the raja was a British ally.

War being now inevitable, lord Cornwallis proceeded to Madras and took the command of the army in person. After taking Bangalore (20th March, 1791), he defeated Tippoo's army before Seringapatam on the 14th May. The victory was rendered indecisive by the treachery and imbecility of the nizam's auxiliary horse, but after effecting a junction with the Mahrattas, and prosecuting the campaign with success in various parts of the territory, lord Cornwallis returned at the head of the combined forces, and commenced the siege of Seringapatam on the 5th February, 1792. Tippoo, now seriously alarmed, released some of his prisoners in order to carry overtures of peace, while many others were barbarously murdered to prevent their bearing testimony to his inhumanity. His conduct was alternately insolent and deceitful, but the siege being steadily pressed, he was compelled to accept the terms dictated, and to give up two of his sons as hostages for the completion of the treaty. By these conditions one-half of Tippoo's territories were ceded to the allied powers, and a sum of three hundred and thirty thousand pounds was exacted for the expenses of the war.

The English obtained the districts of Malabar, Dindigul, and Barahmal, adding considerably to the strength and compactness of their empire. Coorg, also, which Tippoo had treacherously subjugated, was rescued from his clutches, and placed under British protection. To the latter demand the usurper furiously objected, as not being included in the preliminaries, which were confined to territories adjacent to those of the besiegers. The raja of Coorg, however, had assisted the allies in the war, and to leave him in the tyrant's power would be to abandon him to destruction. Hostilities had almost recommenced on this point, and the young princes had been sent to the rear, under orders for their removal, when Tippoo yielded to forego his meditated revenge, and ratified the treaty as prepared by lord Cornwallis.

The terms after all were too favourable, and eventually necessitated another war for the annihilation of an enemy who was left only the more exasperated by his deserved humiliation. Seringapatam at least should have been taken and retained, as sir Thomas Munro desired, for a barrier to our own dominion; but everything, remarked that sagacious officer, was now done by moderation and conciliation. "I am still (he adds) of the old doctrine, that the best method of making all princes keep the peace, not excepting even Tippoo, is to make it dangerous for them to disturb your quiet."* It was still more unpardonable that the governor-general's anxiety for peace should have induced him to abstain from inquiring into the cruelties inflicted on Tippoo's prisoners, and while stipulating for their release, to leave the execution of the article so much to the tyrant's discretion, that many it is believed never escaped from their prisons.

War having again broken out in Europe in consequence of the French revolution, Pondicherry and its minor dependencies once more surrendered to the English. After this lord Cornwallis engaged with ardour in the internal reform of Anglo-Indian administration. The celebrated *Permanent Land Revenue Settlement* was introduced in the provinces of Bengal, Behar, and Orissa, and this reform was accompanied by the abolition of the judicial powers exercised in India by the collectors of the revenue, and the erection of distinct courts of justice for the entire civil jurisdiction. At the same time the criminal courts, which had hitherto recognised no law but the Koran, were subjected to "Regulations," which, without abrogating the Mohammedan code, mitigated those parts of it which were inconsistent with humanity and justice. The barbarous penalty of mutilation was exchanged for imprisonment; the heir of a murdered person was no longer permitted to accept compensation for the crime; and the evidence of "unbelievers"

* Life, vol. i. p. 131.

was placed on a par with that of the arrogant Mussulman.

The "Rules and Regulations" commenced by lord Cornwallis have been augmented under succeeding administrations, with the same benevolent design of extending to the natives the blessings of British justice and liberty. Unfortunately, however, they were conceived in the spirit of European rather than of native institutions, and the multiplicity and intricacy of their provisions, coupled with the nature of the process by which they are enforced, have become so odious to the natives, that many Hindus openly prefer Mussulman government, with all its tyranny and oppression, to British administration encumbered with the misplaced formalities of British law.

Lord Cornwallis was succeeded by sir John Shore, whose administration still further evidenced the difficulty of maintaining a pacific policy among the ever aggressive powers of India. In the combination formed against Tippoo by the British, the nizam, and the Mahrattas, each party had bound itself to aid the others against their respective enemies. The Mahrattas now attacking the nizam, the British declined to interfere between belligerents equally entitled to their alliance. But the case became more difficult when the common enemy, Tippoo, threw himself into the scale of the Mahrattas. The nizam demanded the support of the British, and failing to obtain it, was compelled to purchase peace from his adversaries. He immediately requested to be relieved from the burden of a subsidiary force, which consumed his revenues without fighting his battles. The governor-general could not object to a demand so reasonable;

upon which the nizam, unable to stand without European assistance, threw himself into the arms of the French, who eagerly seized the position abandoned by the English.

In Oude the governor-general had no scruple in exercising authority in the affairs of state. The last of the Rohilla chiefs dying in 1795, sir John Shore sanctioned the absorption of his jaghire into the vizier's dominions. Two years after, on the demise of the vizier, he authoritatively intervened in the settlement of the succession, first recognising his reputed son Vizier Ali, and subsequently, on proof of his illegitimacy, transferring the musnud to Saadut Ali, brother of the deceased prince.

By the treaty concluded on this occasion, the fortress of Allahabad was ceded to the English. The vizier agreed to pay an annual subsidy of seven hundred and sixty thousand pounds; in return for which the Company were to maintain a force of ten thousand men within the state of Oude. Saadut Ali further stipulated to hold no communication with any foreign power, nor suffer Europeans to settle in his dominions, without the consent of the governor-general. So unmistakably was British power now advancing to the paramount position which had been vacated in the decay of the Mogul empire, and the restoration of which, under a more beneficent administration, was indispensable to the peace of India.

CHAPTER IX.

THE BRITISH EMPIRE (*continued*).

Lord Wellesley's administration—State of the Deccan—Revival of British influence at Hyderabad—Expulsion of the French—War with Tippoo—Capture of Seringapatam—Death of the usurper—Partition of Mysore—Restoration of the raja—Tanjore—Transfer of the administration—State of the Carnatic—Treachery of the nabob—Transfer to the Company—Surat—Oude, new treaty—Furuckabad—Pensions to native princes—The Mahrattas—Raja of Sattara, peishwah, Scindia, Holkar, Guicowar raja of Nagpore—Defeat of the peishwah by Holkar—Treaty with the British—His restoration—War with Scindia and Nagpore—French state—Capture of Delhi—The emperor Shah Alum—Defeat of Scindia, and of raja of Nagpore—New treaties—Bundelcund—Treaties with Rajpoot States—War with Holkar—Siege of Bhurtpore—Intrigues and defection of Scindia—Return of sir Arthur Wellesley to Europe—Resignation of Marquess Wellesley—Re-appointment of lord Cornwallis—His death—Succession of sir George Barlow—Concessions to Scindia and Holkar—Mutiny at Vellore—Parallel with recent mutiny in Bengal—Peace in India—Conquest of French and Dutch settlements—Treaty with Persia, etc.—Marquess of Hastings's administration—State of affairs—War with Nepal—The Pindarries—Renewal of general alliance—Treaty with Scindia—Difference with the peishwah—New treaty—Its violation—Attack on the residency—Capture of Poona, and flight of the peishwah—Nagpore—Appa Sahib—Attack on the residency—Capture of the raja and city—New treaty—Dethronement of Appa Sahib—Defeat of the peishwah at Ashtee and Soonde—His submission and deposition—Enormous pension—His subsequent death—The Nana Sahib—Defeat of Holkar—Treaty of subsidiary alliance—Capture of Asseerghur—Close of the war—Extirpation of the Pindarries—Final extinction of Mogul and Mahratta empires—British power paramount.

THE next governor-general was the earl of Mornington, afterwards created marquess Wellesley for his distinguished services in India. He found the British empire threatened with the most formidable dangers in the Deccan. Tippoo, smarting under his recent humiliation, was meditating a general combination of native powers, which he ardently anticipated would drive the hated English into the sea. The Mahrattas, ever ready for hostilities which promised to lead to plunder, listened willingly to his overtures. The nizam, now wholly under French influence, was tempted by the prospect of co-operation from the Mauritius and from France itself, whither Tippoo had despatched his ambassadors. The sovereigns of Constantinople, Persia, Kabul, and Arabia, were addressed for the same purpose by this malignant and indefatigable enemy. The only ally left us in the Deccan was the nabob of the Carnatic, and he was helpless, insolvent, and treacherous.

Anticipating immediate hostilities with Mysore, lord Mornington was anxious to recover the ascendancy in the councils of Hyderabad which had been lost through the timid policy of his predecessor. The nizam, tired of his French auxiliaries, was already anxious for a restoration of the British alliance. A treaty was concluded, by which a British subsidiary force of six thousand men was to be maintained by the nizam, the Company undertaking to mediate in his differences with the Mahrattas. Similar stipulations were included to those adopted in Oude, against the settlement of other Europeans in the territories of Hyderabad. The French troops in the service of the nizam, on being required to disperse, broke out into a mutiny which only facilitated their expulsion. The officers surrendered themselves to the English, and were forwarded to their native country; while the Sepoys, to the number of eleven thousand, were compelled by force to lay down their arms.

The governor-general was less successful in his endeavour to restore the former triple alliance, by effecting a similar treaty with the peishwah. Scindia, who then possessed the chief influence at Poona, was little favourable to English interests, and their proposals were rejected.

Lord Mornington resolved, notwithstanding, no longer to delay hostilities against Tippoo, who had actually obtained assistance, though not equal to his hopes,* from the government of the Mauritius. He was called upon for explanations, which of course were unsatisfactory. An attempt was made to shake his confidence in the French, by forwarding intelligence of lord Nelson's victory in Egypt, together with a letter from the Grand Signior of Constantinople, complaining of their invasion of his dominions. Obtaining no satisfaction, lord Mornington determined not to wait the attack of his enemy. General Harris received instructions to advance at the head of a Madras army, numbering twenty-one thousand men, of whom only one thousand were Europeans, at the same time that general Stuart appeared on the coast of Malabar, with a force from Bombay six thousand strong.

Hostilities commenced on the 6th March, 1799, with an attack on the Bombay troops, conducted by Tippoo in person. This was repulsed with considerable loss. General Harris crossed the Cauvery below Seringapatam, and by the end of the month Tippoo found himself once more besieged in the fortress and island of Seringapatam. On the 20th April he asked for terms, and was required to dismiss all foreigners from his service, to cede half his dominions to the

* They consisted only of native volunteers, enlisted under a proclamation by the French governor of the island. Lord Mornington estimated the whole force at less than two hundred; and colonel Wilkes, from the records of Mysore, states the number at exactly ninety-nine.

allies, and pay two hundred thousand pounds for the expenses of the war. If these conditions were not accepted in forty-eight hours, general Harris intimated that the demand would be extended to the surrender of Seringapatam. At the expiration of the time the siege was recommenced, and on the 26th April colonel Arthur Wellesley, the governor-general's brother, opened the long and glorious career, which ended in an English dukedom and the highest military honours from all the powers in Europe, by carrying the enemy's last exterior entrenchment. This success brought another overture from Tippoo, on the rejection of which the caged and baffled tyrant sank into a stupor, from which he could with difficulty be aroused.

At one o'clock on the 4th May, 1799, major-general David Baird, to whom the command of the assault had been confided, advanced from the trenches into the river, which he forded under a heavy fire of musketry. In seven minutes the British flag was planted on the rampart at the head of the breach. The assailants here dividing to the right and left, swept the summit of the walls, and met in an hour after on the eastern rampart in full possession of the fortress. The sultan having disappeared, the killadar surrendered the palace, with the children of Tippoo, on a promise of protection. His eldest son, who was outside the fortress, surrendered the next day.

The body of Tippoo was found in a gateway, where he had fallen, fighting like a common soldier. It was interred, with all Mussulman honours, in a splendid mausoleum erected by himself for the remains of his father; and the graves of these two remorseless enemies of the British name are still tended by a numerous establishment, maintained at the cost of their government. England never met with a foe in India more implacable or more barbarous. During the siege of Seringapatam Tippoo gratified his animosity by murdering a number of English prisoners, whom he had long detained and tortured in his dungeons, in violation of the treaty formerly made for their liberation. It was, doubtless, the consciousness of this crowning atrocity which restrained the wounded tyrant in his extremity from attempting to save his life by discovering himself to the English soldiers.

The capture of Seringapatam was the greatest military exploit the English had yet performed in India. The place contained 929 pieces of ordnance, 100,000 muskets and carbines, with a considerable number of swords and accoutrements, a vast amount of powder and shot, with specie and jewels to the value of £1,100,000. Among the articles of Mussulman *virtu* which graced the tyrant's palace was a figure, still preserved at the East India House, of an English officer prostrate beneath a tiger (the emblem of Tippoo), which, by a clumsy piece of mechanism, was made to wave the arms and emit cries of agony, mingled at intervals with the growl of the devouring beast.

The fall of this usurper released the natives of Mysore from a yoke which the governor-general was happily not inclined to reimpose by continuing a Mohammedan dynasty in the persons of his children. It would have been well for the oppressed and exhausted population had it been at once transferred to the only government in India capable of exercising the functions of sovereignty with vigour and humanity. In England, however, there prevailed a morbid aversion to every extension of dominion in the East. Lord

Mornington, though his brilliant services were acknowledged by a step in the peerage, was obliged to defer to this feeling by affecting a misplaced moderation in the disposal of his conquests, and concealing under injurious disguises the power which it was indispensable to retain. He determined to restore the Hindu kingdom of Mysore, with a limited territory, under British protection. For this purpose the heir of the last raja was sought out in his obscurity, and the throne of his ancestors (found at Seringapatam) being reconveyed to the ancient city of Mysore, an infant of five years old was placed on it, under a royal salute, by general Harris and the commander-in-chief of the nizam's army.

After defining the limits of the new state, there remained, for partition among the conquerors, more than it was considered safe to divide with the nizam alone. It was determined, therefore, to admit the peishwah, whose co-operation had been invited at the commencement of the war, to a share, on his acceding to the treaty and giving satisfaction for his absence from the siege. Finally, the maritime districts of Canara, Coimbatore, and Wynaad, were specially assigned to the Company in consideration of its undertaking the support of Tippoo's family; and the island of Seringapatam, with some other military posts, were reserved to the same power for the preservation of the general peace. The peishwah failed, as was probably foreseen, to qualify himself for his share of the conquest, which, in accordance with an article in the treaty, thereupon fell back again to the nizam and the Company. The nizam's share, however, was again ceded to the English in extinction of his annual payments for the Hyderabad subsidiary force.

The result of the whole arrangement to the British

was, first, the acquisition of the chief places of strength; secondly, a direct increase of territory, valuable in itself, and still more so as tending to complete the coast line by which they were fast encircling India; thirdly, the establishment of a barrier state in Mysore, designed to be British all but in name; fourthly, the gratification of the nizam, without such an increase of power as might convert a humble friend into a dangerous neighbour; and, lastly, the riveting of British ascendancy in the Deccan by providing for the subsidiary force at Hyderabad in perpetuity, instead of by an annual subsidy.

By a separate treaty with the raja of Mysore, the Company undertook the defence of the new state in consideration of an annual subsidy of twenty-eight thousand pounds. Warned, however, by the difficulties already making themselves felt in other states under the double government of British and native authority, the governor-general inserted a clause distinctly authorizing his assumption of the whole administration, whenever it might be deemed necessary, a liberal pension being guaranteed to the raja.

From Mysore the governor-general turned his attention to the affairs of Tanjore and the Carnatic. In the former state the raja had been restored under orders from the court of directors, much to the discontent of the nabob. Dying without issue, he left his throne to an infant adopted according to Hindu custom; but the brother of the deceased prince disputing the succession, the British government, having assembled a council of pundits to investigate the validity of the rite, set aside the adoption and recognised the brother as raja. At a later period the youth, escaping to Madras, proved the pundits to have been bribed, and after consulting the Brahmins of Benares, his claim was declared valid, and the reigning prince in turn was obliged to give place to his rival.

Under each raja the state of the country had been such as to elicit the gravest expostulations on the part of the protecting power; but the abuses proving incurable by native administration, the young raja and his advisers were brought to agree that the whole civil and military administration should be transferred to the British, an adequate provision being reserved for the support of their royal dignity.

The settlement of the Carnatic was a more difficult achievement. The Company's ancient ally, Mohammed Ali, dying during the administration of sir John Shore, was succeeded by his son Omdut-ul-Omrah. Both princes had become deeply involved in debt, for which assignments had been granted with a reckless hand to a legion of unconscionable creditors, European and native. These financial difficulties were increased by the rescue of Tanjore from the usurpation of the needy nabob; and when the war with Tippoo commenced, Omdut-ul-Omrah was unable, or unwilling, to afford the supplies for which he was liable by the treaty of alliance. This failure did not prevent him from claiming a share in the conquered territory, at the same time that he indignantly rejected the interference of the British on behalf of the oppressed population already under his government. He was answered by a letter from the governor-general, transmitting evidences that had been found in the state papers at Seringapatam, of the complicity of both nabobs in the hostile designs of Tippoo, and insisting on a transfer of the revenues of the Carnatic to the Company, to whom they were largely indebted, and who had already by treaty the right to assume them in time of war. The nabob died before this letter could be delivered, leaving an adopted son, with whom, after some negotiation, a treaty was concluded on the basis dictated by lord Mornington, and the Carnatic became included in British India.

A further accession of territory was effected about the same time on the western coast. Surat was the chief port on that side of India, where the Company had established one of its earliest factories, and successfully defended it by arms against the Mahrattas. At a later period the command of the castle was transferred to the British by the inhabitants, and confirmed by a firman from the Great Mogul. Reversing the distribution of functions prevailing in Bengal, the nabob of Surat retained the civil and financial authority, while the Company undertook the military defence, a portion of the revenue being assigned them for the purpose. Disputes ensued on the amount of this provision; an increase was reluctantly conceded by the nabob; and the frequent occasion now arising of a disputed succession, the governor-general seized the opportunity to assume the entire administration, reducing the nabob, who had long been appointed by the British authorities, to the condition of a pensioner.

With all these arrangements in progress, lord Wellesley was under the necessity of maintaining a strict watch upon Oude, where the most fearful disorders prevailed under the rule of the nabob vizier. While the Company's territories contiguous were rapidly increasing in opulence, population, and prosperity, this native state, enjoying perfect tranquillity under British protection, had lamentably retrograded in every particular. Its disorderly battalions, ragged and mutinous for want of the pay which the vizier's ill-regulated finances could not supply, were a source of weakness rather than strength. The revenues were anticipated; the collections could only be made by force of arms; the people had become practically outlaws, and life and property were everywhere insecure. It was impossible for a civilized power to maintain by its arms a prince who thus failed in every function of government; and the governor-general insisted, either on a transfer of the administration to the Company, or at least a permanent subsistence for the subsidiary force, by a cession of territory adequate to its support.

After negotiations which every oriental artifice was employed to protract and defeat, the vizier submitted to the latter alternative. He strove in vain to exempt the government which remained to him from the remonstrance and advice of the British, alleging that as the Company was to govern without check the territory ceded to its possession, so he also should be sole and supreme in his own. He was reminded that a subsidized state stands on a different footing from an independent one. The British could not maintain him in power without insisting on his responsibilities. In coercing the population to his allegiance, they were bound to secure to them protection and justice.

Among the districts ceded under the new treaty with Oude, was the province of Furruckabad, where a Patan nabob governed as tributary to the vizier. It had been the system of the Mogul emperors to retain in power such local chiefs as accepted their yoke, whether Affghan or Hindu, permitting them to administer the government and collect the revenues on payment of a certain proportion to the imperial exchequer. Such nabobs and rajas, though in England often confounded with sovereign princes, were in fact only a higher kind of zemindars, and had been dispossessed as occasion offered, with very little ceremony, by the Mogul rulers. Lord Wellesley's invariable policy was to reduce all such anomalous and disturbing influences into the general system of government, so bringing the entire revenues levied from the population to contribute to the defence and good order of the realm. In furtherance of this policy, the nabob of Furruckabad shared the fate of more exalted potentates, by exchanging powers which he was incapable of wielding for a liberal pension on the revenues which he resigned to the Company.

The principal evil of these commutations lay in the excessive liberality of the terms conceded to the princes set aside. Representing no nationalities, usurpers, or at best the children of usurpers, who had used the people for their own advantage, and were deprived of power as unfit to retain it, it should have sufficed to grant them a decent maintenance for life, and leave their families to return as fast as possible into the general community. By assigning pensions in perpetuity, and permitting a succession of empty titles and honours, British generosity burdened the resources of the state with two civil lists, one for the defunct, and another for the existing, government. The large sums withdrawn from the public revenue for the maintenance of these withered branches of an evil stock, were expended, not in securing, but in disturbing, the public order. The pensioned families harboured a perpetual hatred against the hand that fed them, and their "courts" had no occupation but either to hatch conspiracies against the government, or to disgrace humanity by wallowing in the most sensual and criminal excesses.

Lord Wellesley, however, was far from being censured at home for undue lenity in his treatment of the native powers. During the impeachment of Warren Hastings, the public mind had been trained to consider every military operation in India as a war of aggression, every freebooter who assumed a title as a sacred monarch, and every transfer of a long vexed and burdened state to the protection of the British government as a covetous and unrighteous appropriation. The court of directors were alarmed at the cost and magnitude of the empire which began to rise upon their startled vision. Their remonstrances were so distasteful to the governor-general that he intimated his intention of resigning; but he was reserved to commence the extension of British supremacy over the only native power which still continued independent and formidable.

The rise and progress of the Mahrattas, with their share in the subversion of the Mogul empire, have already been traced. Their nominal head, the raja of Sattara, had long sunk into the condition of the fallen padishah, his authority being wielded by the peishwah who held his court at Poona. Two other chieftains of very humble origin had risen to the rank of rulers in Hindustan; Scindia, whose dynasty reigned at Oojein, one of the seven sacred cities of the Hindus, and Holkar, whose capital was Indore. These princes, though using the style of maharajah, still recognised the supremacy of the peishwah. Each, however, had formed the design of possessing himself, first of the confidence, and then of the person, of his chief, in order to transfer the virtual supremacy to himself. A fourth Mahratta state existed in Guzerat, whose ruler, called the *guicowar*, dwelt at Baroda; and a fifth had been founded by the Bhoonsla family at Nagpore, comprising the province of Berar, still largely populated by the aboriginal Goonds.

The Mahratta states being never without a standing army of differences with their neighbours and with each other, the pacification of India was impossible until they should be included in the general defensive alliance which lord Wellesley was labouring to establish. With this object in view, treaties and subsidiary forces had been offered in succession to the raja of Sattara, to the peishwah, and to Scindia, but hitherto without success. The object was now advanced by the exigencies produced by the internecine struggles of the Mahrattas themselves.

Holkar, resenting the ascendancy which his rival Scindia was fast obtaining over the peishwah, levied his forces, and advancing upon Poona inflicted a total defeat on the combined armies of his adversaries on the 25th October, 1802. The peishwah, alarmed by his approach, had signified before the battle his acceptance of lord Wellesley's proposals, and throwing himself after his defeat on British protection, he was conveyed from Bombay to Bassein, where a treaty of alliance was concluded on the 31st December, 1802. The forces of the Company and its allies were then put in motion for his restoration to his capital. General Wellesley marched from Mysore, and, effecting a junction with the Hyderabad subsidiary force, drove the detachments of Holkar before him, till finally making a forced march of sixty miles in thirty-two hours, he surprised and mastered the city before the enemy had time to execute his purpose of consigning it to the flames. The peishwah being conducted back was replaced on the musnud by the British resident on the 13th May, 1803. The change thus effected in the peishwah's relations was fatal to the hopes of Scindia, who thereupon entered into negotiations with the raja of Berar with a view to the recommencement of hostilities. Holkar was soon included in the combination, and war ensued between the British, aided by a small contingent from the peishwah, and the whole strength of the Mahratta confederation.

Scindia retained in his service a French *corps*, originally raised by De Boigne (at one time a subaltern in the Company's army), and since enlarged to three brigades, of which two were commanded by Frenchmen named Perron and Pedrons, and the other by an Englishman called Sutherland. Perron, who arrived in India as a common sailor, was a man of extraordinary ability and ingenuity. He had succeeded, by means of his personal influence, in founding a French state in the district of Allyghur, which had been assigned for the support of his auxiliary force. This state lying on the banks of the Jumna, on the most vulnerable part of the Company's frontier, was selected by lord Wellesley as the primary object of attack. The fortress was taken by general Lake, 4th September, 1803, and Perron surrendering himself soon after, the French principality was extinguished. The remainder of their forces were defeated by Lake in a battle fought a few days after before the city of Delhi.

The result of this victory was to throw again into British power the unfortunate heir of Timour, together with the imperial city for the possession of which he had exchanged their protection at Allahabad. Shah Alum had entered Delhi only to find himself the prisoner of his Mahratta auxiliaries. In the troubled state of the country a ruffian Rohilla chief having made himself master of the city, plundered the palace, violated the zenana, and struck out both the eyes of the fallen sovereign with his dagger. Scindia avenged the crime and restored the padishah, after the true Mahratta fashion. The fugitive Rohilla was seized and confined in an iron cage, in which, after being deprived of eyes, ears, nose, hands, and feet, he was sent back to perish at Delhi. The emperor, however, was little benefited. He was made to nominate the peishwah his prime minister, an office in which Scindia then appointed himself deputy, and continued the title to his successors. The Mahratta prince had committed the charge of the imperial city to Perron, and his overthrow now transferred it to the Company.

The British general hastened to pay his respects to the decayed representative of the imperial house. Under a scanty ragged canopy, mocking rather than imitating the royal state of his ancestors, a blind decrepid old man of eighty-three, whose prolonged life had been one unbroken scene of calamity and humiliation, received the congratulations of the strangers who came to offer again an honourable asylum for its brief remainder. "Poor, dependent, aged, infirm, and sightless, the head of the empire illustrated in his person the wide-spread ruin which had overwhelmed the empire itself." It should be added, that this ruin was the natural result of the detestable principles on which his family had obtained and exercised power. It would have been happy for both countries if the decayed and

* Thornton iii. 326.

polluted dynasty had been allowed to disappear in the sepulchre to which a righteous Providence had now conducted it, instead of being prolonged by a succession of pageant emperors to become again, in the person of another hoary Mussulman—the grandson of Shah Alum—the means of renewing India's miseries, in a last bloody outbreak against the religion and civilization of England.

The war with the Mahrattas was not long in being brought to a conclusion. Agra followed the fate of Delhi. The battle of Laswaree (fought in 1803) destroyed the flower of Scindia's army, and completely exterminated the battalions which he had termed his Deccan Invincibles. Meantime general Wellesley defeated the combined forces of Scindia and the Nagpore raja at Assaye; and colonel Harcourt, after occupying Juggernauth and Cuttack, prepared to overrun the dominions of the latter prince. The enemy began to treat with the usual duplicity of Mahratta diplomacy, but general Wellesley was not to be deceived; after another decisive victory at Argaum, and the capture of the important fortress of Gawilghur, the raja of Berar was brought to terms, and his submission necessitated that of Scindia.

The British were confirmed by the former in their conquest of Cuttack, while the cessions of Scindia comprehended his territories north of Jeypore, Joudpore, and Gohud, with the forts of Baroach, Ahmednuggur, and their dependent districts. Both princes renounced all claim on the Company's allies, the nizam, the peishwah, and the guicowar. Scindia further stipulated to abstain from interference in the affairs of the emperor, agreed to hold no communication with the French or other European powers, and finally accepted a subsidiary force from the Company, to be sustained without additional charge from the resources ceded by the treaty.

A further important acquisition of territory was made at the close of this war by the occupation of Bundelcund. This province had been bequeathed by a Hindoo raja to the peishwah in return for his assistance against the Rajpoots. At a later period an offer from the *de facto* possessor was declined by the English, in consideration of the peishwah's claims. It was now taken possession of in his name, and by him transferred to the Company in exchange for equivalent territory in the Carnatic and Guzerat. British influence was further extended in Hindustan by separate treaties concluded by general Lake after the battle of Laswaree with the rajas of Bhurtpore, Jodepore, Jeypore, and some others in the region of the Jumna. The fort of Gwalior—supposed to be impregnable—with its dependent district, was made over to the English by the rana of Gohud.

Lord Wellesley's administration, though censured by shortsighted persons as warlike and aggressive, was really directed to secure tranquillity to India by putting down the various disturbers of its peace. It remained but to reduce Holkar within the sphere of his defensive alliance, and a lasting pacification might have ensued. This wily and perfidious chief, after entering into the conspiracy against the British, had retired from the field at the commencement of hostilities, and preserving his forces unbroken stood prepared to profit by the result. A general peace was the last thing to prove acceptable to a state whose existence was devoted to predatory operations, directed without much discrimination against friend and foe. He was required to confine himself within his own territories, and replying with a menace, hostilities ensued, in the conduct of which the British forces were not handled with the prudence and courage which had formerly ensured success.

The army had suffered severely from the climate, and general Lake, falling into the error of despising his enemy, withdrew the main body into quarters, leaving the active operations to a detachment. The latter was imprudently led still further from its supports, and in returning suffered severely from Holkar, who invariably disappearing from the British front with a celerity which no exertions could overtake, never failed to harass the retreat in every possible way. The prestige of British arms seemed to be rapidly vanishing, when it was revived by colonel Burns' gallant defence of Delhi against seventy thousand Mahrattas, with a garrison so inadequate that the commander-in-chief had ordered the city to be abandoned. General Lake returning to the field succeeded in surprising the camp of Holkar, and inflicted a loss of three thousand, the remainder including Holkar himself escaping as usual by flight.

The advantage of this victory was lost by the subsequent unsuccessful siege of Bhurtpore, the raja of which had gone over to the Mahrattas. After four assaults, two of them in the presence of the commander-in-chief, and a loss of three thousand men, Lake was obliged to raise the siege, leaving his batteries to be burned by the garrison. Peace indeed was made on terms not dishonourable to the British, but the failure was deeply prejudicial to their influence. Scindia, taking heart again, demanded the restoration of Gwalior and Gohud, as having been ceded without his authority. In the course of the long and tortuous negotiations which ensued, the British resident was led from place to place in the Mahratta camp, insulted by the most barefaced falsehoods, plundered of his baggage, and finally reduced to the condition of a prisoner, while Scindia's arrangements, notoriously in progress, with Holkar and the raja of Nagpore were being brought to completion. The government were at last convinced of the defection of their ally by his open junction with Holkar, followed by an insolent offer of his mediation to adjust the difference. It was plain that the British councils were no longer under the influence of the lofty minds which had lately directed them. Sir Arthur Wellesley had returned to Europe, there to prosecute the career of glory so brilliantly opened in India. The marquess was preparing to follow, and his government already yielded to those theories of non-intervention which English politicians insisted on transferring to the widely different circumstances of India.

Lord Cornwallis came out a second time to establish the pacific policy, but dying in three months after his arrival, was succeeded by sir G. Barlow, who had sat in council with both his predecessors, and was quite prepared to undo with lord Cornwallis what he had assisted in doing under lord Wellesley. Peace at any price was the maxim now enforced. Gwalior and Gohud were surrendered to Scindia on the pretence, which had been repeatedly discussed and rejected, that the rana was subject to his authority, and had no right to transfer them without his consent. This concession was made without any satisfaction for the insults offered to the resident, and in fact while he was still detained against his will in Scindia's camp. A pension and a jaghire in the Company's territories were submissively added to meet the Mahratta's demands. The defensive alliance so earnestly prosecuted by lord Wellesley was abandoned. The Mahratta princes were left to settle their differences as they pleased. Holkar, who had fled to the Punjab on the verge of destruction, was reinstated in all his territories to the south of the Chumbul; and in order that nothing might be wanting to Mahratta triumph, the several alliances effected by the British with the Rajpoot chiefs were abandoned, and government pledged itself to make no engagements with them in future. Lord Lake, who had himself concluded many of these treaties, remonstrated against their abandonment as inconsistent with the national honour and the safety of the Company's frontier; but his remonstrances were disregarded, and he returned to England.

A transaction occurred under sir G. Barlow's administration which, though long consigned to oblivion, has been paralleled in so many points during the recent mutiny in Bengal that it has again become important to recall the particulars. From the time of lord Clive the Company's forces had mainly consisted of native battalions officered by Europeans, and disciplined, more or less perfectly, on the model of the British line. The native soldiers, or *Sepoys*, (from the Persian *sipâhi*,) were at first formed into companies under their own commanders (called *subahdars*), bearing each his peculiar ensign, such as a dagger, a crescent, or the like. An English officer commanded the battalion, assisted by an adjutant and one or two other European officers. The dress and accoutrements were a compound of the native and European fashions, with no very rigid uniformity; the whole, however, being armed with musket and bayonet, and practised in the manual and platoon exercise, according to the regulation of the king's army. The commandants of battalions exercised the entire control of the internal discipline, together with the promotion of the native officers, and so strong was the confidence reposed in some of these veteran commanders, that battalions were distinguished by their surnames, and the Sepoys gloried in the designation long after the officer from whom it was borrowed had descended to the grave.

These native battalions, however, like all mercenary troops, had always been prone to mutiny. Severe examples of military discipline had often been requisite to restore order, and the tendency to insubordination was not diminished by the improved organization, under which the native army was gradually assimilated to the European. As the companies were more closely organized in regiments, and the regiments into brigades and divisions, the authority reposed in the battalion officers became centralized at head-quarters. The colonels enjoyed less power in the promotion of native officers, and the subahdars sank, in like manner, by the appointment of a European officer to every company.

These changes were accompanied by a desire for a stricter uniformity of costume; and certain alterations, introduced with this object in view, became the occasion of a serious outbreak in the presidency of Madras. A new turban, lighter and more military in appearance, was ordered to supersede the various patterns previously worn; at the same time the rules obtaining in some regiments, and neglected in others, for trimming the beard, and prohibiting caste marks on the face whilst on duty, were directed to be uniformly observed throughout the native army. The sensitive and unreasoning jealousy of *caste* was instantly aroused. The turban was objected to by the

Mohammedans, as resembling the European *topee* (or hat), so degrading the wearer by an approximation to the *Feringhees*. The order against the marks of caste was not less offensive to the Hindus, and both classes equally resented the attack on their beards.

Symptoms of insubordination appeared early in 1806; but the authorities thinking lightly of such grievances, deemed the explanations offered to the troops sufficient, and pronounced the dissatisfaction to be at an end. In June information was given of a plot to rise and murder the Europeans, but the information was treated with the contempt which often characterizes English officers in the presence of danger, and the informant was thought mad or drunk. On the 10th of July the conspiracy took effect. The native troops at Vellore suddenly rose upon the Europeans, consisting of two companies of her Majesty's 69th regiment, and massacred one hundred and thirteen persons, including the commandant with thirteen other officers. The progress of the revolt was happily arrested by the vigour and promptitude of colonel Gillespie, the officer in command at Arcot, sixteen miles distant from Vellore. Hastening to the spot, at the head of the 19th dragoons and some native cavalry, he joined the remnant of the 69th, charged the rebels in the fort, and completely dispersed them. Three hundred and fifty were killed, and above five hundred more taken prisoners as they fled. The commandants at other stations, on the receipt of the intelligence, promptly disarmed their Sepoys, and the flame was extinguished.

It was discovered on investigation that the mutiny had been fomented by the Mussulman retainers of Tippoo Sultan's children, who were lodged in great splendour in the fort of Vellore. They were attended by no fewer than eighteen hundred servants and personal adherents, while as many as three thousand Mysoreans had settled in the place since it became the abode of the princes. The government took care to transfer the youths to safer keeping in Bengal, at the same time diminishing the revenue at their disposal for the corruption of the native soldiery. But the extraordinary similarity of recent incidents shows how little is ever learned by governments through experience.

The mutiny which broke out at Meerut on the 10th May, 1857, followed, to the minutest particular, the precedent of the 10th July, 1806, at Vellore. In both a dethroned Mohammedan family was in dangerous proximity, furnished with the means of mischief, and at liberty to apply them without check or observation. Both occasions exhibited the same ignorance on the part of the European officers of the disposition of their native troops; with the same infatuated refusal of information when proffered. The pretext for both mutinies was found in an alleged affront to the native religion and caste, and in both the oldest officers had unknowingly, or carelessly, suffered a pretext to be supplied equally offensive to Mussulman and Hindu. Both conspiracies were based on the suspicion of an organized plan to enforce Christianity, first on the troops, and then on the population. Both were fomented by extravagant rumours, industriously propagated by religious mendicants and other emissaries;* and in both the predictions of astrology

* Among other extravagancies it was currently reported that the Europeans were about to make a human sacrifice in the person of a native; that a hundred bodies, without heads, were lying on the banks of the Moose river; that the Europeans had built a church which it required a sacrifice of human heads to sanctify; and that they designed to massacre all the natives except those who should erect the sign of the cross on their dwellings."—*Thornton's India*, vol. iv. p. 73.

were called in to anticipate the downfall of British power.

In two points the parallel fails. The government of 1806 were without warning or example in the calamity which overtook them; that of 1857, with precedent of 1806 before their eyes, permitted it to be repeated on a larger and a more destructive scale.

In 1806, again, the local authorities proved equal to an emergency totally unexpected. Colonel Gillespie, sixteen miles distant from the scene, destroyed the rebels, and suppressed the mutiny in twelve hours from its outbreak. The general in command at Meerut, with three times the number of Europeans on the spot, suffered a smaller body of mutineers (of whose temper ample warning had been given in previous courts-martial) to complete their bloody work without interruption, and then making good their retreat to Delhi, set the whole army in a blaze.

The treatment of the Vellore conspirators was the subject of much difference of opinion between the governor and the commander-in-chief at Madras. The contest ran so high that both were removed from their appointments. The conciliatory policy of the former (lord W. Bentinck) was adopted; the regulations which had occasioned the revolt were rescinded, and the mutineers escaped with little punishment.

The general peace of India was preserved unbroken from the close of the Mahratta war in 1805 to the end of lord Minto's administration in 1813. This result, unparalleled in the previous history of the country, flowed unquestionably from the "war policy" so unthinkingly censured in lord Wellesley. The country enjoyed tranquillity only as long as the lovers of war were afraid to exercise their vocation.

This period was distinguished also by the conquest of the French and Dutch settlements in the Indian Ocean, leaving England without a European rival in the East.* British influence was further extended by the conclusion of treaties with the shahs of Persia and Kabul, the ameers of Sindh, and some other minor states; indicating a return from the non-intervention theory to the more decided policy of lord Wellesley.

It was reserved, however, to the earl of Moira, created marquess of Hastings, to revise and realize the imperial idea. This nobleman, who united the office of governor-general with that of commander-in-chief, found the finances exhausted, the army inefficient and discontented through the consequent retrenchments, and the external relations unsatisfactory and precarious. The government was engaged in unfriendly discussions with no less than *six* native powers; whilst India was overrun with hordes of a new description of marauders, termed Pindarries. Such were the results of insisting on peace while its inveterate disturbers were left in full possession of the powers of war.

The first to come into collision with the British arms were the Goorkhas, a tribe of Hindu race who had risen to dominion in the mountains of Nepal, and after a series of encroachments, dating from the departure of lord Wellesley, had taken forcible possession of British territory. The campaign opened, as English campaigns often do, with a series of disasters. The country was difficult; the

* The islands of Mauritius, Bourbon, and Rodriguez were captured by an expedition from home. Amboyna, Batavia, Java, and the other Dutch settlements yielded to armaments despatched from India. Of these the most valuable were weakly (it is believed ignorantly) restored by the ministers of the crown at the termination of the war.

roads impracticable; the native method of warfare novel and harassing. Lord Moira was greatly dissatisfied with the results; but in a second campaign sir David Ouchterlony succeeded in effecting the submission of the court of Nepal. The English gained nothing from the contest beyond the security of their frontier, and the conversion of these hardy mountaineers into valuable allies; a change which is only effected in India by establishing a decided superiority in arms.

Released from these harassing hostilities, the governor-general turned his attention to the suppression of the Pindarries. The origin of this name is involved in some obscurity; the persons denoted by it were a mounted banditti of the most sanguinary kind. Making their first appearance about the beginning of the eighteenth century, they had erected themselves into a permanent power, whose services were often hired by the native princes to ravage the territories of their adversaries. The task was performed with such effect that twenty years were not enough for a district to recover from the visitation. In return the Pindarries were themselves attacked and plundered without ceremony, by any ruler who felt himself sufficiently strong at the moment.

These banditti avoided fighting, their profession being confined to plunder. Their chiefs were mostly of Patan extraction, but all creeds, classes, and tribes were freely admitted into their fraternities. Discharged soldiers, fugitives from justice, with every vagabond that could command a sword and a horse, hastened to enrol themselves in the Pindarrie *durrahs.* Their operations were conducted with the utmost despatch. They appeared suddenly on the devoted spot; burned all that could not be carried away; drove the inhabitants houseless from the blazing villages; and in a few hours were gone beyond the reach of pursuit. In these forays torture was unmercifully resorted to, in order to discover concealed treasures: red-hot irons were applied to the soles of the feet; heavy stones placed on the head or chest; the clothes set on fire; or any other atrocity perpetrated that could be executed with despatch. Women were cruelly abused, and the hands of little children often cut off, as the shortest method of getting possession of their bracelets.

These atrocious marauders had gathered so much strength during the non-intervention policy of the British government, that their chiefs aspired to the dignity of princes; making treaties with the different states to exempt their territories from plunder. A course so entirely congenial with Mahratta views and institutions secured to the Pindarries the especial favour of the princes of that race. Holkar and Scindia were seldom without some of their bands in their service; and it was manifestly impossible to deliver India from this destructive scourge without recurring to a general alliance of its native powers, under the direction and guarantee of the government of Calcutta.

Such a general alliance was once more adopted as the grand object of British policy. Taking the field with a powerful army, lord Hastings addressed himself to Scindia, through whose territories it was proposed to advance, inviting his co-operation in the suppression of the Pindarries. The Mahratta entered willingly into a design which promised no little immediate plunder, with the prospect of an extension of his dominions at the expense of any state that should protect the Pindarries. A treaty was concluded, in which the opportunity was taken to abrogate the restrictions so injuriously agreed to by sir George Barlow, and the British again formed engagements with the Rajpoot states tributary to Scindia.

The negotiations opened for the same purpose with the peishwah became complicated with another question, and resulted in a general Mahratta war, combined with the operations against the Pindarries. The peishwah was involved in an old dispute with the guicowar respecting territory in Guzerat, on which the British government was bound by treaty to arbitrate. The questions being intricate and important, the guicowar's principal minister proceeded to Poona, at the instance of the British resident, to discuss them at that court, and was there barbarously assassinated. The crime was charged on Trimbuckjee Dainglia, the peishwah's prime minister, whose arrest was demanded by the resident, and long refused. He was surrendered at last, on a private understanding that no inquiry was to take place which might inculpate the peishwah himself. The criminal was confined in the fort of Tannah, whence effecting his escape, he found harbour again with the peishwah, who in the meantime had been secretly preparing for war.

The resident, finding his remonstrances disregarded, summoned a division of light troops to their support, and the peishwah was forced to yield to a new treaty, which not only provided for the extradition of the assassin, and the adjustment of the difference with the guicowar, but further bound the peishwah not to engage in negotiations with any other state without the knowledge and consent of the British. This provision in effect dissolved the Mahratta confederacy; the peishwah thereby relinquishing his supremacy and interest in the other states, and descending to the position of an ordinary ally of the Company. Bajee Rao did not find this position the more tolerable from being the result of his own perfidy and cruelty. He continued to levy troops under pretence of assisting in the reduction of the Pindarries; and his preparations being completed, on the 5th of November, 1817, he declared war by suddenly attacking and burning the British residency. Its distinguished occupant, the hon. Mount Stuart Elphinstone, was not taken unprepared. The enemy was repulsed by the division at his disposal, and reinforcements being in readiness, Poona was promptly invested, the peishwah fled, and the city fell without a blow.

While peace was thus suddenly broken in Western India, a similar act of treacherous hostility had been concerted at Nagpore. That court had long resisted the offer of a subsidiary alliance, but on the accession of a prince who was imbecile, a treaty had been effected with the regent Appa Sahib. This person being now himself the raja (not without suspicion of having made away with his predecessor) began to exhibit a less friendly disposition to the British. Affecting to doubt the sincerity of their demonstration against the Pindarries, (whose services he had occasionally employed in plundering his neighbours,) he augmented his troops at the same time with the preparations of the peishwah, and at last avowing his combination with that chief, suddenly fell upon the resident's escort, simultaneously with the like movement at Poona. His attack was repulsed with equal success. Troops were at hand, and promptly advanced: the raja was compelled to surrender, and a capitulation being granted to his Arab soldiery, the city was taken possession of by the British.

Before their prisoner was permitted to re-assume the government, the British authorities determined to deprive him effectually of the power of repeating his treachery. A new treaty was agreed upon, providing for a cession of territory in commutation of the subsidy. The hill of Seetabuldee adjoining Nagpore was ceded for a British military station, and the raja engaged to reside in the palace under the protection of the Company's troops. Any other forts in his territory that might be demanded were also to be given up, and the government was to be conducted in future by the advice of the resident. Appa Sahib accepted the terms, and in the same moment concerted measures to evade them. He was detected in correspondence with the peishwah, and arrested by the resident; further investigation established his guilt in the murder of his predecessor, and the criminal was thereupon dethroned, and confined in the fortress of Allahabad. From this place he managed to escape and return into Berar, where he maintained for some time a desultory warfare by the aid of the Pindarries; but being at last expelled, he took refuge in Asseerghur; and on the capture of that place, fled to Lahore, where he obtained a trifling pension from Runjeet Sing.

Meantime the peishwah, who had fled from Poona to the south, where he was joined by Trimbuckjee Dainglia and all his forces, experienced a total defeat at Ashtee, the raja of Sattara falling into the hands of the victors. After this rout the peishwah wandered in various directions till he was again defeated at Soondee, soon after which his army dispersed, leaving their leader a helpless fugitive. He finally made overtures of submission to sir John Malcolm, and, through the misplaced generosity of that distinguished officer, was guaranteed a pension for his life to the amount of eighty thousand pounds per annum. Deprived of sovereignty, he was also removed from the scene of his power and perfidy. A jaghire was granted him at Bithoor, a place of great sanctity on the banks of the Ganges, containing one of the few temples erected to Brahma. Here Bajee Rao ended his days, in the enjoyment of the grossest sensualities, varied by the careful performance of the rites of his caste, for he was a pure and orthodox Brahmin. Having no children, he adopted shortly before his death the sons of a wandering Brahmin from the Deccan, one of whom is Dhoonda Punt, styled the *Nana Sahib*, who in the recent mutiny in Bengal has shown himself a genuine specimen of his remorseless caste.

In the course of the Mahratta war the British forces came into collision with those of young Holkar, son of their former enemy. After opening a negotiation with the British, his army had compelled him to declare for the peishwah. The single battle of Mahidpore, fought on the 21st of December, 1817, sufficed to effect their submission. A treaty was concluded ceding all his claims upon the Rajpoot princes to the British. His possessions in the province of Candeish and some other districts were also transferred to the Company, who undertook in return to maintain an adequate field force for the defence of his remaining territories. The greater portion of his own troops were disbanded, and no European or American was to be employed in his service without the consent of the British. The treaty further released him from his subjection to the peishwah, and engaged the British to resist any attempt on the part of the latter to recover his supremacy.

The war ended in the complete dissolution of the Mahratta confederacy. The fall of the peishwah extinguished the head of this once formidable league, the members of which had been effectually severed by their separate treaties with the British. Holkar and Scindia were now in subsidiary alliance with the Company. At Nagpore the infant heir of the murdered raja was placed on the musnud, bound by stipulations of more direct subordination. Of the territories subject to the peishwah's own rule the larger part was annexed to the British possessions. The remainder, in imitation of the precedent set in the partition of Mysore, was assigned to the raja of Sattara. The captive descendant of Sevajee was released from confinement, to receive from the hands of a European superior some poor semblance of the sovereignty of which his house had long been stripped by its native dependents.

In the course of these operations the Pindarries had been everywhere hunted out and destroyed. Their organization and existence as a permanent body were annihilated. India once more enjoyed the blessings of peace, and this time under an ascendancy capable of maintaining it. The era was marked by a significant incident. The style and title of king was assumed by the nabob vizier of Oude, by the advice and authority of the British governor-general. The extinction of the rival empires which had so long desolated India was complete. Mogul and Mahratta had passed away together from the field they had so long polluted with rapine and blood. The British government, assuming the place to which a beneficent Providence had conducted it, stood forth as the paramount power, and proclaimed itself henceforth the sole arbiter of peace and war to the exhausted states of India.

CHAPTER X.

THE BRITISH EMPIRE (*continued.*)

Government of lord Amherst—War with Burmah—Capture of Rangoon—Stockades—Sufferings of the troops—Conquest of Assam and Arracan—Occupation of Prome—March on Ava—Submission of the Burmese—Treaty of peace—Tenasserim provinces—Capture of Bhurtpore—Tranquillity in India—Lord William Bentinck—Incorporation of Coorg—Assumption of government in Mysore — Retrenchments and abolition of corporal punishment in native army—Suppression of Suttee—Annexation of Sattara—Affghan war—Kingdom of Kabul—Shah Shuja—Kamran—Dost Mohammed—Russian influence—Recent conquests in Persia—Agents in Affghanistan—Restoration of Shah Shuja—Capture of Ghiznee—Entry into Kabul—Surrender of Dost Mohammed—Breaking up of the army—Disaffection of Affghans—Insurrection at Kabul—General Elphinstone—Akbar Khan—Assassination of sir W. Macnaghten—Retreat of the army—Confusion, flight, and destruction — Kandahar preserved by general Nott—Surrender of Ghiznee—General Pollock at Peshawur—Defeat of lord Auckland's policy—Succeeded by lord Ellenborough—Advance of Pollock and Nott—Recapture of Kabul—Recovery of prisoners—Close of the war—Sindh—Treaty with Ameers—Seizure of Kurrachee—Occupation of the country—Hostilities—Sir C. Napier—Battle of Meeanee—Annexation — Results — Gwalior — Battle of Maharajpoor — New treaty — Recall of lord Ellenborough—Sir Henry Hardinge—War in the Punjab—Sikhs—Runjeet Singh's death—Hostilities—Peace dictated in Lahore—Dhuleep Singh — Renewed aggressions — Chillianwallah — Re-occupation of Lahore — Annexation — Results — Boundary of Indus — Burmese violate the frontier—War—Pegu annexed—Oude—Mal-administration—Accession of Wajid Ali—Character—Enormities—Dissolution of British alliance—Annexation—Latest acquisition—East India Company—Trade—Political powers—Court of Directors—Board of Control—Double government—Secret committee—Supreme government in India—Legislative council—Governments of Madras and Bombay—Civil service, covenanted and uncovenanted—"Regulation" provinces—Judicial department — Company's courts — Abuses—Taxation — Land revenue — Zemindars — Permanent settlement — Ryotwar settlement — Village system — Advantages — Retirement of lord Dalhousie — State of the empire — Causes for apprehension — Want of European troops — Bengal native army—Sepoys in Oude—Alarm of zemindars—Brahmin predictions—New rifle and cartridge—Objection of caste—Mutiny at Barrackpoor—Massacre

at Meerut and Delhi—Proclamation of Mussulman king—Outrages—Resistance of English—Christian courage—Exertions of government—Siege of Delhi—Capture—Massacre at Cawnpore—The Nana Sahib—General Havelock—Capture of Lucknow.

On the return of the marquess of Hastings to Europe in 1823, Mr. Canning was appointed his successor; but that distinguished statesman being almost immediately offered the seals of the foreign department, the government of India was transferred to lord Amherst. Though not, like his predecessor, a military man, the new governor-general found himself quickly precipitated into war. Beyond the mountains usually considered to be the eastern boundary of India, a branch of the Hindu race retaining the tenets of Buddhism had settled in a number of petty states, which, like those of their Brahminical kinsmen, were at perpetual war with each other. Two of these, Pegu and Ava, had alternately conquered each other, when, towards the close of the eighteenth century, the ruler of Ava obtaining the ascendancy laid the foundation of a great power, which was subsequently enlarged by the subjugation of Arracan, Manipur, and Assam, once independent states, and the acquisition of the Tenasserim coast from the kingdom of Siam. Such was the origin of the Burman empire, which after the manner of such powers conducted itself with invariable arrogance towards every other whose superiority in arms had not been experienced.

The British frontier was continually violated by these barbarians, and two missions despatched to the court of Ava returned without redress or security. The Burmese sovereign next demanded the extradition of some natives of Arracan, who on his conquest of their country had taken refuge in Chittagong. This was followed by a requisition for the surrender of Chittagong, Moorshedabad, and Dacca, on pretence of their being dependencies of Arracan. The Burmese began to cross the boundary and make prisoners of British subjects. A guard was attacked, and some of the Sepoys killed. Cachar, a native state on the frontier, was then invaded, and the British, on the request of the raja, determined to assist by arms in the common cause.

Hostilities commenced in Cachar on the 17th of January, 1824, and a declaration of war with Burmah was issued by the governor-general in the following month. An expedition despatched from Calcutta and Madras by sea arrived off Rangoon on the 9th of May, and ascending the river, captured the town with little or no opposition, the enemy retiring into the jungle. The war which ensued is still fresh in recollection. The enemy fought with a courage and perseverance not experienced from the feebler races of India. Their mode of warfare resembled that of the Goorkhas, in erecting stockades, from which they were dislodged with the greatest difficulty. The troops, European and Sepoy, suffered severely from the climate, and were more than once obliged to be withdrawn. Still the campaign was pushed under sir Archibald Campbell, till Prome was occupied and the whole province of Pegu in the power of the British. Meantime the Burmese had been driven out of Assam and Arracan by a land force from Bengal, designed to co-operate with the expedition under sir Archibald Campbell, but it was found impracticable to effect a junction of the two armies, from the difficulties of the road and the prevalence of disease.

Sir Archibald Campbell advanced nevertheless upon Ava, when the Burman monarch, alarmed for the safety of his capital, came to terms, and peace was concluded on the 26th of February, 1826. By the conditions of the treaty the British retained possession of Assam and Arracan, so advancing their boundary to the Youmatoung mountains. The conquered provinces of Ye, Tavoy, Mergui, and Tenasserim, with their dependent islands, were also added to British India, and a crore of rupees (one hundred thousand pounds) was paid by the Burmese for the expenses of the war.

During the progress of the Burmese war the honour of the British arms was elevated throughout India by the capture of Bhurtpore. On the decease of the raja, leaving an infant successor, an uncle had obtained possession of the youthful prince in the capacity of regent, and then as usual aspired to the royal title himself. The interference of the British was invoked, but the usurper confided in the possession of a fortress believed to be impregnable, and which had successfully resisted four assaults from the army of lord Lake. It was contended by some that England having clearly nothing to gain by taking part in such a contest, the natives should be left to fight it out among themselves. Such a policy, however, was inconsistent with the position of the paramount state, and might have endangered the peace of all India, where such forbearance could only be attributed to the dread of a second failure. Bolder and wiser counsels prevailed. Lord Combermere having collected a sufficient force opened his batteries on the 28th of December, 1825, and delivering the assault on the 18th of January, carried the impregnable fortress in eight hours.

This transaction can hardly be considered as breaking the tranquillity that reigned throughout India after the complete establishment of British ascendancy. From the close of the Mahratta war to the invasion of Affghanistan, a period of more than twenty years, the native states remained at peace with the British and with each other, under the strong arm of a government which allowed neither itself nor others to draw the sword except in a just and necessary cause. It was a spectacle which India had never seen before, and contrasting it with the ceaseless succession of battle, plunder, and pillage which stains the annals of its previous history, it must be felt in every Christian heart that whatever of earth had mingled in the views of those who established it, that ascendancy was the happy instrument by which God had graciously determined to give rest to the land.

The general repose was scarcely more interrupted by the events which led to the incorporation of Coorg, under lord W. Bentinck's administration in 1834. The raja, son and successor of the faithful ally whom lord Cornwallis rescued from the clutches of Tippoo Sultan in the first partition of Mysore, had been guilty of acts of mingled folly and wickedness, which seemed to indicate aberration of intellect. His sister having fled with her husband to the British residency in Mysore, to escape his guilty passion, he demanded their delivery, and being refused, resorted to violence. An expedition was despatched against him, which penetrated to Mercara, and seized the capital without resistance. The occupation of the country disclosed a scene of tyranny, murder, lust, and robbery, perpetrated by the raja, which rendered it a duty to his subjects to remove him from power so atrociously abused. He was dethroned, and having himself caused every male of his family to perish by the hand of the assassin, the territory in default of heirs was incorporated with British India.

Some little time previous, the vices of native administration had induced the governor-general to put in force that clause in the treaty with Mysore, which provided for the assumption of the government by British officers. During the infancy of the raja the finances had been confided to Purneah, a Brahmin who had managed the revenues for Tippoo, and was selected by lord Wellesley to continue in the trust. His good management increased the annual revenue from six hundred and nineteen thousand one hundred and sixty-two pounds, to seven hundred and forty-two thousand one hundred and ninety-five pounds, and when the raja came of age, and was put in possession of the government, there was an accumulation of two million eight hundred and twelve thousand five hundred pounds in the treasury. In a few years the whole of this large sum had disappeared, though there had been neither war nor public improvements to absorb it. The annual revenues were further so burdened and anticipated that the country was full of confusion and insubordination. The people abandoned their villages, threw their lands out of culture, and drove away the revenue officers. They did not resort to arms, but assembled in the jungles, obtaining food by night from their stores. The troops of the raja declined to act against their oppressed countrymen, and the cry of the people was loudly raised for British administration.

This cry could not be neglected by the paramount power, itself the author of the government which inflicted so much oppression. The raja was moreover in arrear with his subsidiary tribute. The treaty was put in force. The raja received a liberal provision, on which he still resides in his palace, attended by guards and the outward usages of native royalty. The country was not annexed, but its administration was assumed, and is still conducted, in the raja's name and upon native principles and usage, modified by European supervision. The "assumption," however, will probably endure for the life of the prince, and as he has no heir, Mysore will lapse at his death into British India. The British commissioner on taking possession found the revenue reduced to four hundred thousand pounds per annum, while the population was burdened with no less than eight hundred and six items of taxation, direct and indirect. Of these items, seven hundred and sixty-nine have been since abolished, yielding a sum of one hundred thousand pounds, but the total revenue has nevertheless increased to eight hundred and twenty thousand pounds per annum. Meantime above a million sterling has been paid in the liquidation of debt and subsidy, and the country throughout is in a most flourishing condition. These are some of the results of British empire in India.

Lord William Bentinck was authorized by the home government to effect a similar beneficial transfer of administration in the state of Oude, whose misgovernment had been the subject of constant anxiety to every governor-general from Warren Hastings downwards. But the measure was deferred. The governor-general was occupied with those measures of retrenchment and reform which are thought appropriate to seasons of tranquillity. Orders from home, which had been twice withheld by previous governors-general, were now enforced for the reduction of an allowance to the army called *batta*. The allowances of the civil officers also were retrenched, and great discontent ensued in both services. The complaints of the army amounted in some cases to insubordination; and lord Combermere, the commander-in-chief, resented the orders so deeply as to resign his command.

To lord William Bentinck the Sepoy is indebted for the abolition of corporal punishment in the native army. But as the governor-general had no power over the king's regulations, the singular anomaly ensued of the European soldiers—the superior race—remaining subject to a punishment from which the Mussulman and Hindu were exempted as degrading. The penalty of discharge (inapplicable to the European) was deemed sufficient to secure discipline among the Sepoys, to whom the service offers too many advantages to be lightly relinquished. Still it was far from sustaining the moral dignity of the English soldier, and not very respectful to his religion or descent, to induce a comparison between himself and the native so little favourable to the former.

In another reform, lord W. Bentinck secured the concurrence of all good men, and covered his administration with its distinguishing glory. He abolished the rite of *suttee*. It had been made apparent, through increased acquaintance with the acknowledged standards of Hindu faith, that the destruction of living widows on the funeral piles of their deceased husbands was not a matter of religious obligation. It might be called (in the language of another creed) a "counsel of perfection;" but the Brahmins themselves admitted there was no divine command; and this point being cleared, the act could only be regarded as one of murder or suicide. As such it was forbidden to be practised throughout the British territories; and the influence of successive governments has almost abolished it in the native states.

In re-establishing the raja of Sattara the marquess of Hastings had been influenced by reasons analogous to those which induced a similar relinquishment of the rights of conquest in Mysore. A like failure attended both pieces of generosity. The descendant of Sevajee was unable to divest himself of the traditions of his race. He began to intrigue for the re-establishment of the Mahratta empire, and even made overtures to the Portuguese to assist him against the British, to whom he owed at once his existence and his throne. The conspiracy being detected, the raja was removed from power, and his brother proclaimed in his stead. The death of both princes subsequently left the throne without an heir, and Sattara was incorporated with the British dominions.

Hitherto the English empire in India had grown out of local circumstances, and been carried forward under what was felt by the Indian government as the pressure of immediate necessity. It had been involved in many wars, but they were at least conducted with Indian objects in view; they had experienced only discouragement and rebuke from England. During the administration of lord Auckland, war was for the first time ordered by the home authorities, and upon views at least as much connected with European as with Indian politics.*

The Affghans were at this time divided into several

* The paternity of the Affghan war has been disputed. The president of the Board of Control, sir John Hobhouse, afterwards lord Broughton, claimed the whole proceeding as his own spontaneous act; but the secretary to government in Calcutta has no less positively affirmed that the conception originated with the governor-general in India. The contradiction disappears if we suppose that lord Auckland privately suggested the expedition, and sir John Hobhouse adopting and enforcing his views, considered himself, as in fact he was, the legal and responsible author. It is certain that the East India Company were not consulted. The orders were issued by sir John Hobhouse in the secret department, and earnestly protested against as soon as they became known to the directors.

petty principalities. On the death of Nadir Shah, and the consequent dismemberment of his extensive empire, Ahmed Shah, the head of the Dooranee tribe, erected a monarchy at Kandahar which was powerful enough to invade India, and play an important part in the struggle between the Moguls and the Mahrattas. He was succeeded by his son Timour, who removed the seat of government to Kabul. The next king, Zemaun Shah, more than once threatened India with invasion, and excited some apprehension in the mind of lord Wellesley. Zemaun Shah, however, was removed from the throne by a younger brother, blinded, and imprisoned,—a fate which he had himself inflicted on his elder brother. Mahmood, the successful usurper, was in turn dethroned by another brother, Shuja, though without suffering the loss of sight. Regaining his liberty, he appeared again in arms, and compelled Shuja to take refuge in the court of Runjeet Singh at Lahore. Here he was at first hospitably received; but being afterwards plundered, and apprehending further mischief, Shuja fled into the British territory, where he received an asylum and a maintenance. In the meantime Mahmood having cruelly put to death his vizier Futteh Khan, to whom he owed his success, the brothers of that personage headed a new revolution, and Mahmood was driven to Herat, where he died, transmitting his limited dominion to his son Kamran. Kabool and the surrounding country was seized by Dost Mohammed Khan, the elder brother of the murdered vizier; three other brothers held Kandahar and its district in joint sovereignty; and Runjeet Singh made himself master of Peshawur.

These revolutions were beheld with indifference by

the British authorities till a new influence began to be apprehended in Affghanistan. The care of British interests in Persia had been early confided to an envoy appointed by the crown, and in immediate relations with the king's ministers. This mission has been generally unfortunate in its diplomacy; at the present juncture its influence was reduced to the lowest possible pitch, while the rising ascendancy of Russian counsels was regarded with considerable uneasiness in India. Russia had but lately conquered from Persia a territory equal in extent to the whole of England. Since the accession of Peter the Great, she had advanced her frontier one thousand miles in the direction of India. Her garrisons on the western shore of the Caspian were observed with alarm to be as near to the Indus as to Moscow, and actually further from St. Petersburgh than Lahore. In invading Persia her armies had advanced more than half the way from her own capital to Delhi, while by the treaty adopted at the conclusion of the war, Persia was left defenceless against her formidable neighbour, and virtually subject to Russian ascendancy.

Now, Persia had claims upon Herat, the present ruler of which had actually paid tribute to the shah, which might be extended, in right of the conquests of Nadir Shah, to the whole of Affghanistan. If Russia should instigate and abet such pretensions, she would advance herself, by the means of an impotent ally, to the very banks of the Indus. Alarmed at this prospect, lord Auckland despatched agents into Affghanistan to concert an alliance with its rulers, and so interpose a barrier to Russian progress. They found themselves everywhere anticipated by Russian emissaries, already tempting the

Affghan chiefs with gold and promises of military assistance. The court of St. Petersburgh, when applied to for explanation, disowned the agents and denied the designs; but they were not the less confidently believed in India, and the governor-general determined on another course to counteract them.

Finding the existing rulers of Affghanistan indisposed to his alliance, he turned to the exiled monarch Shah Shuja, by whom it was, of course, eagerly accepted. Runjeet Singh, the powerful ruler of the Punjab, entered warmly into the scheme, and a joint expedition was resolved upon, to replace Shah Shuja on the throne of his ancestors in alliance with the governments of Calcutta and Lahore. A British force of twenty-eight thousand men entered Affghanistan under the command of sir John Keane. They were aided by six thousand Sikhs and four thousand troops, raised under British influence in the name of Shah Shuja. The march was attended by dreadful privations and sufferings, from the nature of the country and climate, but no enemy appeared in serious encounter. On the 8th May, 1839, Shah Shuja was enthroned in great state at Kandahar.

Advancing towards Kabul the first check was experienced at Ghiznee, a fortress which proved much more formidable than had been anticipated. It was carried without breaching or escalade by the daring expedient of blowing open a gate with gunpowder. On the 7th August, the Shah, under the protection of the British force, made his public entry into Kabul, signalizing his return to the capital of his ancestral kingdom by instituting an Order of Knighthood, on the model of the Bath, with which the officers of the army of the Indus were liberally decorated. The battle of Purwan, on the 7th November, seemed to crush the last remnants of opposition. Dost Mohammed flying from the field, attended by a single horseman, repaired to Kabul and surrendered himself to the British envoy, by whom he was forwarded with all honourable treatment to Calcutta. The war was now at an end. The army was broken up, and honours showered with open hand on its leaders. The governor-general was created an earl, the commander-in-chief received a peerage (lord Keane) and a pension; Mr. Macnaghten (the envoy) and colonel Pottinger were created baronets, and the honours of knighthood were largely distributed.

A portion of the British troops, however, were left in Affghanistan for the defence of the throne on which they had seated their new ally, and it soon appeared that no easy task had been undertaken. The reports which had found credence with lord Auckland in respect to the disposition of the Affghans proved to be wholly unfounded. In place of welcoming back their king, they regarded him with a hatred and contempt sufficiently justified by his own character and conduct, and deepened by the presence of foreign bayonets. The Mussulman hatred of Feringhees is said to have been exasperated by the licentious demeanour of some of the English officers and soldiers. The most inveterate hostility was displayed by the wild tribes who held the mountain passes, and the convoys were continually harassed or intercepted. With these abundant proofs of being still in an enemy's country, the arrangements of the British were made with peculiar want of military precaution. All eyes seem to have been closed to the danger; no feelings but those of security and enjoyment crossed the minds of men who were already on the brink of destruction.

The outbreak began at Kabul on the 2nd of November, 1841. Colonel sir Alexander Burnes and his brother were assassinated in the city, where an infuriated mob obtained the mastery in consequence of an erroneous disposition of the troops. The shah became a prisoner in the hands of his subjects, unless in truth he was (as many suspected) an accomplice in the treacherous assault. The bulk of the British army was quartered in cantonments about three miles from the city, under the command of general Elphinstone, an officer of considerable attainments and irreproachable character, and one of a family to which India is under many obligations, but whose age and failing health would have better suited a quiet function in England than the command of an Indian division. The plain around the cantonment swarmed with Affghans, among whom Akbar Khan, a son of Dost Mohammed, was conspicuous. Vigorous measures were demanded by sir William Macnaghten the envoy, but all was indecision and supineness on the part of the military.

The cantonments became in a state of siege, and after losing his commissariat by a piece of gross carelessness, the general declared his inability to resist any longer. The envoy, with a desperate courage, ventured to meet Akbar Khan in the plain, to treat of an honourable arrangement. He was assassinated by that chief's own hand, under the eyes of the military, without an effort being made to avert or to avenge his fate.* General

* "The murder of a British envoy was perpetrated in the face and within musket-shot of a British army, and not only was no effort made to avenge the dastardly deed, but the body was left lying on the plain to be mangled and insulted, and finally carried off to be paraded in the public market by a ruffianly mob of fanatical barbarians." — *Lieut. Eyre's Military Operations*, p. 199.

Elphinstone then capitulated to the enemy on the condition of being allowed to evacuate Affghanistan, abandoning Shah Shuja to his fate. He consented also to leave behind his guns and treasure, together with the sick, to pay a ransom of one hundred and forty thousand pounds in bills on the government, and to pledge its services to restore Dost Mohammed to the kingdom. Hostages were given for the performance of these conditions. The Affghans demanded the wives and children of the officers, and the feeble commander was disposed to oblige them, but their husbands and fathers could not be induced to consent.

The army quitted the cantonments on the 6th of January, 1842, and began its retreat through mountains white with snow, and thronged by an enemy yet more relentless. Four thousand five hundred fighting men still constituted the force; a number more than twice as large as under other commanders had sufficed to win an empire in the East. Twelve thousand followers, besides women and children, encumbered its steps. The army had no sooner cleared the cantonments than the Affghans opened fire upon its rear, and plundered the baggage. All order was immediately lost. The force presented to an eye-witness the appearance of "a mingled mob of soldiers, camp-followers, and baggage-cattle, preserving not even the faintest resemblance of that regularity and discipline, on which depended its only chance of escape from the dangers which threatened it."* The retreat became a flight. The Affghans crowned the defiles through which the fugitives had to pass, firing on them without intermission. Lady Sale received a ball in her arm; a girl and a boy, children of officers, were made

* Eyre's Military Operations.

prisoners. It was again proposed by Akbar Khan, who accompanied the force with an escort and affected to lament the attacks of his countrymen, that the ladies and children should be delivered into his charge, in order to protect them from further injury. The general, impotent and despairing, consented and resumed his flight. The sepoys soon became powerless through frost, and the European soldiers, who alone retained physical efficiency, were utterly cowed by the novelty and despair of the situation. No resistance was offered to the murderous assaults of the Affghans; numbers deserted to their side; others lay down and perished by hundreds on the road. General Elphinstone at last resigned himself, with his second in command, to the tender mercies of Akbar Khan, and the remnant of the army proceeded without its chief. The enemy redoubled their exertions for its entire extermination, as the end of the pass was at hand. At last *one man*, Dr. Brydon, rode into Jellalabad, which sir Robert Sale still held gallantly against all the power of the Affghans, and reported of the army of Kabul that he alone was escaped to tell its fate. Every other individual was either slain or in the hands of the enemy.

A similar fate had been prepared for the force at Kandahar. Akbar Khan, in company with a son of Shah Shuja, approached that city in the hope of effecting an arrangement like that concluded at Kabul: but general Nott, who commanded in Kandahar, was a man of a different calibre. Marching instantly out with all his disposable force, he gave battle to the Affghans, and easily routed their undisciplined hordes. The treaty of Kabul had provided for the entire withdrawal of British troops from Affghanistan, and Nott received orders from general Elphinstone accordingly; but under the circumstances he bravely and prudently determined to postpone obedience.

The same precaution was not exhibited at Ghizni. The fort was given up on a solemn engagement of protection, sworn to on the Koran; but its guns were instantly turned on the retiring garrison. The sepoys attempting to escape were cut to pieces, and the officers became prisoners to the Affghans. Kandahar, Jellalabad, and Peshawur, where general Pollock maintained his ground, were the only positions left to the British in Affghanistan. The policy devised by the ministers of the crown, and rewarded with the highest honours in England, was utterly and irretrievably defeated. In place of a friendly state occupying the passes into India, Affghanistan was swarming with inveterate and intractable enemies, while all India was agitated by military reverses such as had never before tarnished the British arms, and seemed to presage the overthrow of their power.

The intelligence was received at home with indignation and dismay. Lord Auckland was replaced by lord Ellenborough, who had succeeded sir John Hobhouse as president of the Board of Control, and was, of all English statesmen, the best acquainted with Indian affairs. Impressed with the impolicy of the Affghan expedition from the first, the new governor-general issued instant orders for the entire evacuation of the country, but against this course the generals commanding beyond the Indus remonstrated as precipitate and unsafe. Sir Robert Sale had continued to hold Jellalabad in the face of the most formidable difficulties, till relieved by general Pollock from Peshawur. General England was less fortunate in an attempt to relieve Kandahar from Sindh; but a second effort proving successful, general Nott found himself strong enough to join with Pollock in urging an advance upon Kabul, as a step indispensably necessary to retrieve British honour, to recover the prisoners and hostages, and to render the final evacuation safe and honourable. Their views prevailing, the two generals had the honour of thoroughly accomplishing the achievement so courageously recommended. General Pollock, advancing through the passes lined with the bones of the unhappy fugitives from Kabul, drove the enemy before him wherever they appeared, and on the 16th September, 1842, once more planted the British colours on the Bala Hissar in Kabul, amid the shouts of his victorious army. He was joined the next day by general Nott, whose advance from Kandahar had been marked with no less success, and included the recovery of Ghizni.

Meantime, Shah Shuja had been murdered by a party of his subjects. It remained, therefore, but to recover the prisoners, and the British might retire with honour from a country into which all now regretted they had ever entered. This also was happily accomplished, through the able negotiations of major Eldred Pottinger with the chief to whom Akbar Khan had confided their custody. On September 20th the emancipated captives entered the camp of sir R. Sale, whose wife and widowed daughter were among their number.

The Affghan war was now indeed over. The troops were withdrawn. Dost Mohammed was released and allowed to return to his mountains. Nothing remained of this great expedition, ordered by the ministers of the crown in contravention of the ancient policy and the earnest remonstrances of the Company, but the memory of a bitter humiliation, the graves of the many dead, and a sum of fifteen millions sterling added to the Indian debt.

The Affghan war had entailed complications with a neighbouring country, which resulted in a further extension of the British empire. The long tract of sandy and alluvial soil through which the Indus approaches the Arabian Gulf, called from the river *Sindh*, was at an ancient period, according to native annals, the seat of a great Hindu kingdom. Famed for the beauty of its women, it was ravaged by the early Arabs in quest of inmates for the harem of the caliph. It was also one of the earliest provinces subdued by the sultans of Ghizni. Sindh was incorporated with the Mogul empire under Akbar, transferred to Persia by Nadir Shah, and subsequently became an appendage of Kabul. Towards the end of the eighteenth century, the Talpoor tribe of Belochees, ejecting the reigning prince, succeeded in rendering it an independent state, governed by nine ameers in sovereign co-partnership. These rulers, with a considerable proportion of the population, professed the Mohammedan religion; the bulk however were of the Hindu race, descended from persons who were forcibly converted to Islam under the Mussulman emperors.

No very amicable relations had ever subsisted between these warlike tribes and the British government. Treaties of commerce had been concluded which led to frequent disputes. The relations became a little more friendly in 1836, when Runjeet Singh was prevailed on by government to lay aside his intention of subjugating Sindh, and in 1838 a British resident was admitted at Hyderabad. This officer was instructed to invite the co-operation of the ameers in the design of restoring Shah Shuja to the throne of Affghanistan. They were assured at the same time of British mediation, in adjusting the claims which the restored sovereign might advance upon Sindh, as an ancient dependency of the Dooranee throne. Such an invitation was not likely to be cordially received. The ameers produced a document from Shah Shúja himself, expressly releasing them from any such claim. The reply of the governor-general was to demand a passage through Sindh for a portion of the forces advancing into Affghanistan. This demand was contrary to the express stipulations of an existing treaty, nevertheless it was reluctantly submitted to. The fortress of Bukkur was also surrendered to the British for the purposes of the war. These concessions were requited by an order of the governor-general stationing a British force in Sindh itself, and by the seizure of Kurrachee, the only safe port in the territory. A new treaty was then forcibly imposed on the ameers, by which Sindh was reduced from a state of independence to one of vassalage to the British government. Thus, on the tyrant's plea of necessity, a state which had offered neither insult nor injury was deprived of liberties, which, however unfavourable to the development of commerce or the internal resources of the country, were not likely to be surrendered by its high-spirited chieftains without a struggle.

On the occurrence of the disasters in Affghanistan, the ameers exhibited proofs of hostility which occasioned a demand from lord Ellenborough for further securities, and sir Charles Napier was despatched at the head of an army to conduct the negotiation. A new and more stringent treaty was dictated to the ameers. With undisguised reluctance they affixed their seals, but their infuriated subjects at once repudiated the transaction. The British general promptly resorted to arms, and the battle of Meanee, fought on the 17th February, 1843, at a prodigious disadvantage in point of numbers, quashed all resistance. The victory resulted in the complete subjugation of the country. The ameers were deposed, and removed to Calcutta, and Sindh was incorporated with British India.

This is undoubtedly one of the least defensible acquisitions in the whole empire. It may be granted that the government of the ameers was uncivilized and oppressive, that their conduct was inconsistent with the terms of a treaty which lord Ellenborough found in existence, and might consider it his duty to uphold. But that treaty was itself a recent usurpation, forcibly imposed on the rights of the native government, and destitute of any moral obligation. The conquest and annexation of Sindh seem to have been determined upon as a counterpoise to the British losses in Affghanistan. They were effected, equally with that unhappy expedition, in contravention of the usual policy and the earnest remonstrances of the East India Company. The value of the acquisition also was long in question. Nevertheless the result has not failed, as in all similar instances, to be productive of indubitable benefits both to the province and the empire. The ameers were Belochee chieftains, with no other title than the sword, and whose government was polluted by all the inherent vices of Mohammedan misrule. A marked improvement is already discernible in the face of the country. Lands have been brought under cultivation which had lain waste for half a century;

canals long stopped have been re-opened, and new ones are in course of construction. New villages are springing up. A railway has been commenced to traverse the province from the now flourishing port of Kurrachee; and as the direct result of a settled government, the population have laid aside their arms and live in tranquillity and confidence.

The administration of lord Ellenborough was marked by hostilities in another part of India, of which the object and origin are not very clear; but as they resulted in no accession of territory, they are of less importance to the present sketch. The heir of the line of Scindia was an infant, the adopted son of a widowed ranee, herself only thirteen years of age. A regent had been appointed with the sanction of the British government, who was afterwards expelled by one of the intrigues so common in native courts. The British resident quitted Gwalior in displeasure, and retired to the neighbouring state of Dholpore. After some further complications a war-like attitude was assumed by the governor-general. He crossed the Chumbul at the head of an army, disguising this act of hostility on the Mahratta territory under the pretence of advancing to the assistance of its infant ruler.*

The army had, in fact, usurped all real power in Gwalior. Since the death of Dowlut Rao Scindia a mass of forty thousand troops had been concentrated at the

* The Mahratta chiefs declared, before this step was taken, that for a British army to cross the river without waiting for the infant prince would be a breach of all precedent, and eternally disgrace the maharajah and the government of Scindia. They warned him that the troops of Gwalior would regard the passage as a hostile step, and implored him, with joined hands, to await the coming of the maharajah on the British bank."—*Thornton's India*, vi. 502.

capital, often in a state of mutiny, always in a state of disorder bordering upon mutiny. The British forces under sir Hugh Gough came unexpectedly into collision with these troops at Maharajpoor on the 29th December, 1843, and gained a complete victory, though not without the heavy loss of nearly eight hundred killed and wounded. Two other defeats at Chonda and Puniaur disposed of the Gwalior soldiery. The governor-general entered the capital, where a treaty was concluded by which the somewhat loose arrangements previously subsisting were reduced to the usual terms of a subsidiary alliance. The mutinous soldiery were dispersed, and a contingent organized under British officers for the defence of the maharajah and his dominions. The revenue of certain specified districts, estimated at eighteen lacs, (£180,000,) was assigned for the support of this contingent, and the civil administration of these districts was transferred to British officers. Twenty-six lacs (£260,000) were paid in discharge of the claims on the British government on the state of Gwalior, and the resident was invested with the control of the regency during the minority of the maharajah.

Lord Ellenborough's career was cut short by an unexampled act of vigour on the part of the Court of Directors. Uniformly upholding the authority of their governors-general, this body so resented the insubordinate tone of their nominal servant, that by a unanimous vote they exerted the one independent power reserved to the Company's representatives, and recalled the governor-general. The ministers of the crown not only refused to concur in the act, but promoted the object of the Court's censure to an earldom.

Sir Henry Hardinge, a distinguished general, succeeded to the government, the command of the army continuing with sir Hugh Gough. The new governor-general was quickly plunged into a war which his predecessor must have clearly foreseen. In the alliance for the restoration of Shah Shuja, a prominent station had been occupied by Runjeet Singh, the ruler of the Punjab. He was one of the *Sikh* people, whose rise as a religious sect, and subsequent persecutions by the Mogul emperors, have already been noticed. Runjeet, by birth a Jat, one of the most numerous but humblest of the Rajpoot families, had obtained a grant of Lahore from Zemaun Shah, to whom the sovereignty of the Punjab pertained in right of its cession by the Mogul emperor to his ancestor Ahmed. In the decay of the Dooranee monarchy Runjeet Singh asserted his independence, and extended his arms over the greater part of the Punjab. Mooltan fell to him in 1818: the same year he crossed the Indus, and seized Peshawur: Cashmere, with portions of Thibet, followed in a few years.

These conquests were not effected without some uneasiness on the part of the British, with whom, however, the "Lion of Lahore" uniformly cultivated amicable relations. Runjeet Singh died in 1839, and as usual in such tribes, the loss of the leader was the signal for revolution among his followers. His two immediate successors perished by assassination in a few months. A competition for the throne ensued, and the successful candidate was again disposed of by assassination. The Sikhs then relapsed into a general and sanguinary anarchy, which speedily gave rise to aggressive movements upon British India. Their incursions were repelled and chastised in the hard-won fights of Ferozeshah, Aliwal, and Sobraon, the last of which was fought on the 10th of April, 1846. Peace was dictated in Lahore, where a new treaty was formed with Dhuleep Singh, the youthful heir to the throne.

Peace, however, could only subsist with a people so turbulent and aggressive under the curb of a strong and resolute hand. The young maharajah proved wholly unequal to a task which had tested the iron energies of Runjeet Singh. Again the frontier was violated; and the earl of Dalhousie, appointed governor-general 4th of March, 1847, resumed the war with a determination to conduct it with vigour, and ultimately to occupy the country. The Sikhs, who are possessed of far more physical strength than other Hindus, fought with all the courage and fanaticism of their race. A great battle at Chillianwallah resulted so little to the satisfaction of the English that apprehensions prevailed for the final issue of the struggle. These were quickly dispelled by a complete victory at Guzerat on the 29th of March, 1849. Lahore fell again into the occupation of a British army, the dynasty of Runjeet Singh was finally set aside, and the Punjab was incorporated into the dominions of its conquerors.

The acquisition was hailed in England with a satisfaction commensurate with the splendour of the prize. The governor-general was created a marquess; and the dignity of the peerage was accorded to the long and honourable career, in Europe, China, and India, of the veteran commander-in-chief sir Hugh Gough. The approval of the home authorities has been justified by the moral and material progress of the newly acquired territory. The population, hitherto so lawless and turbulent, began immediately to settle down to peaceful and industrious pursuits. In a few years, safety and tranquillity reigned throughout a province which had never known peace from the days of Alexander the Great. Crime was reduced to the ratio of the best administered portions of the Anglo-Indian empire. A mass of oppressive taxation was remitted, and a settlement of the land revenue was effected on the basis of the old village system, which promises to avoid the evil experienced under both the zemindaree and the ryotwar plans, and to confer immense advantages on the agricultural population. Notwithstanding the sacrifice of income occasioned by these arrangements, the surplus revenue of the Punjab amounted to £520,000 in the first year, and to £645,000 in the second year of its incorporation with the British empire.

Reversing in all respects the order of antiquity, under which India was uniformly entered by military invaders from the north-west, the English landing as simple traders on the eastern shore had now advanced their dominion to the banks of the Indus. From the Suleiman mountains to the Youmadoung, and from the Himalayas to Cape Comorin, the long vexed land was at rest under their sway, while from Kurrachee to the Irrawaddy its unbroken line of coast invited the approach of commerce with her attendant blessings. Still the progress of empire was not yet arrested. From the Punjab lord Dalhousie's attention was directed to the opposite frontier of the empire. The Burmese had again exhibited an unfriendly disposition, since the accession of a monarch who cherished a dislike amounting to enmity against the British nation. By his desire the residency was withdrawn from Ava, and all political intercourse ceased. The commanders of two British vessels being subjected to outrage by the authorities at Rangoon, reparation was applied for and insultingly denied. War was declared by lord Dalhousie in 1852. Martaban, Rangoon, Pegu, and Prome, fell in rapid succession to his arms. The ancient kingdom of Pegu being once more in possession, it was determined not to repeat the mistake of delivering it again into the bondage of the Burmese, who had severely revenged on its inhabitants the kindness shown to the British during their former occupation. A proclamation was issued, incorporating Pegu with the British dominions, and the war terminated. No treaty was concluded with the court of Ava, but it submitted in silence to a penalty it was unable to avert, and has since abstained from hostilities.

The substantial benefits uniformly accruing to every population under British rule had now been repeatedly contrasted with the effects of native administration, under every modification of which it seemed susceptible. The result was undeniably in favour of the policy of "annexation," and in 1856 attention was once more imperatively demanded to the affairs of Oude. The lamentable condition of this state under every governor-general from Warren Hastings downward has been noticed. With all the efforts of British influence and advice, the country continued to present the same melancholy contrast with the adjacent territories, which had been dwelt upon by lord Wellesley. The evils were plainly traceable to vices of administration, which, often pointed out, continued under every reign, and, in spite of repeated engagements, unreformed. The court was licentious, venal, and tyrannical; the exchequer was anticipated, plundered, insolvent. The army, inordinate in numbers, mutinous and unpaid, helped itself at the expense of the people. Justice, when not sold to the highest bidder, was administered only after the barbarous and intolerant dogmas of the Koran. Property was at the mercy of the robber chiefs, and each man looked to his own arm alone for protection. The peasant in Oude still went to his field with sword and buckler at his back.

This is the general picture of a native state, and foremost among the misgoverned states of India was Oude. Nasseer-ood-Deen, who succeeded to the musnud in 1827, displayed a mixture of intelligence and profligacy only to be accounted for on the suspicion of insanity. His freaks of power, often ridiculous, were often also atrociously cruel. The British resident, though all-powerful with respect to Europeans, was not entitled to interfere, even by remonstrance, between the despot and his native subjects. A word or a sign from the prince sentenced noble and peasant alike to beggary or death, for any or for no offence that moved the royal caprice. On the accession of another prince in 1842, the reforms required for the tranquillity of the state were again pressed on his notice, and a time assigned by lord Hardinge within which they were to be completed. Nothing was either effected or attempted. Wajid Ali Shah succeeded in 1847, and again the demands of justice were urged, with an intimation that, if neglected, the country would be placed under British administration. This prince proved more weak, profligate, and worthless than his predecessors. The functions of sovereignty were abdicated, while the monarch spent his time with fiddlers, songsters, and eunuchs. The most revolting enormities were perpetrated throughout the country with impunity. Lord Dalhousie sent the British resident on a tour through the kingdom to judge of its condition; and the cry of an oppressed people rose up at every step. So complete was the alienation between the court and its subjects, that sir William Sleeman reported, that if British protection were withdrawn the population would rise in a mass and sweep away the government in a moment.

To persevere in complicity with crimes which no remonstrance could avert was impossible; and not less so to withdraw from all concern with a country which lay in the heart of our own territory, and supplied the larger part of the recruits for the Bengal native army. Instructions were issued from home to assume the administration of the country in the name of the king. The latter, however, refusing to sign the treaty prepared in conformity with these directions, lord Dalhousie declared the alliance dissolved, and annexed the long harassed territory to the Company's dominions.

Oude was the last important acquisition to the British empire in India,* the progress of which has now been summarily sketched, from the first grant to a mercantile company of a few factories in the forts which continue to be the seats of government at the present day. The political powers confirmed to the East India Company by the act of 1784, were substantially re-enacted for periods of twenty years in

* The following minor acquisitions were made in the years specified:—

1852. Ali Morad's territory in Sindh resumed.

1853. Part of Cachar resumed—the remainder having lapsed in default of heirs in 1830.

1853. Odeipore, a small state on the south-west frontier of Bengal—lapsed in default of heirs.

1854. Jhansi in Bundlecund—Ditto.

1855. Boodawul in Kandeish—Ditto.

1858. Dhar in Malwa: annexation disapproved by the home government.

1793, 1813, and 1833. Its commercial privileges, the original object of the incorporation, underwent considerable modification at each renewal. In 1793 the Company was required to provide a limited amount of tonnage in their ships, for private adventure. In 1813 the trade with India was thrown open, the monopoly with China continuing undisturbed; and in 1833 the Company was called upon to place its commercial charter in abeyance, transferring its assets to the crown, and accepting in lieu an annuity of £632,000 in payment of a dividend at ten and a half per cent. on its capital stock.

The political functions of the Company were continued in 1853, after a searching examination into the manner in which the trust had been discharged. The powers of the crown, however, were augmented. The directors were reduced in number from twenty-four to eighteen, one-third of whom were to be nominated by the crown, and the other twelve to be elected, as before, by the proprietors of East India stock. The appointment of members of council in India, hitherto in the absolute patronage of the court, was made subject to the royal veto, like that of governors and commanders-in-chief, so virtually transferring them to the ministers of the crown; and the commander-in-chief of the queen's forces in India was declared to be *ex-officio* the commander-in-chief of the Company's army. The entire direction of the Indian governments in every department had, in fact, long been in the hands of the Board of Control, or rather of the cabinet minister who bears the title of president, the Board itself being seldom or never assembled.

Since the year 1833, therefore, the phrase "East India

Company" has ceased to designate a commercial corporation at all; nor did it require that extinction of its mercantile character to divest the Company of a pecuniary interest in the trade acquired by its exertions. The dividend which the directors were at liberty to declare had long been limited to ten and a half per cent. on the Company's capital, giving, in fact, only the usual interest of money on the market price of its stock. The remainder of the commercial profits were applied to the expenses of the government of India, which derived from this quarter a sum of nearly five millions during the fifteen years commencing 1814–15.*

The East India Company is, in fact, a department of the public service for the government of India; its office is to supply a body of intelligent advisers acquainted with the country, and taking a special interest in its welfare, but independent of the political parties which determine the constitution of the queen's cabinet. A parliament, which is the best security for the rights and liberties of the people it represents, may be wholly disqualified to govern millions of another race who have no voice in its constitution. The ministers of the crown, therefore, being necessarily the creatures of parliament, it is indispensable that some adequate representation of the special interests of India should be associated on an independent footing

* The loss of this advantage to the Indian territories ought to have been compensated by some indisputable benefit to the English merchant, whose interests have been uniformly more considered in parliament than those of the native cultivator or carrier. It may be questioned, however, if such proportionate results have been realized from the Indian trade, while the opening of China to indiscriminate adventure has been followed by two hostile collisions with the authorities of Canton, and must be allowed to have hitherto disappointed the expectations of British influence, so fondly cherished by the mercantile classes.

in their counsels. Public opinion has often inculpated the East India Company for transactions to which its authority was given, sometimes without the knowledge, often without the sanction, and not unfrequently in defiance of the earnest remonstrances, of the directors who constituted its governing body.

In India itself the entire direction of this vast empire is confided to a governor-general, whose salary is twenty-five thousand pounds a year, having Governors under him at Madras and Bombay, with lieutenant-governors at Calcutta and Agra. The governor-general is assisted by a "Council of India," consisting of the commander-in-chief, three members selected from the civil or military service of the Company, and one appointed from the legal profession in England. This last appointment was created by the act of 1833, its first occupant being the present lord Macaulay. It was designed to result in a code of laws, the want of which is the greatest defect in the British administration of India; but the task has hitherto proved too difficult to be accomplished.

The supreme government was invested with legislative powers in 1833, which were revised and regulated in 1853. In exercising these powers, the council is enlarged by the addition of the chief justice and one other judge of the supreme court at Calcutta, by four members specially selected for this purpose from the civil service in either presidency, and by two other members nominated by the governor-general. The legislative council, thus consisting of twelve persons including the governor-general—of whom seven are a quorum—is invested with full authority to make laws for India, and its acts are binding both on European and native subjects. The governor-general possesses a veto on every act of the legislative council.

At the subordinate presidencies of Madras and Bombay there are also councils of government, composed of the commander-in-chief and two members of the civil service.

The civil service is a body of gentlemen who proceed to India at an early age, with the designation of "*writers*," and are there promoted by seniority and ability to the several offices of government. They are called covenanted servants, from being protected in their situations and pensions by covenants executed by the Company. The minor offices are filled by large numbers of uncovenanted servants, European, Indo-Briton, and native. The functions of government, political, financial, and judicial, are administered by the civil servants, except when for particular reasons officers of the army are sometimes selected for civil employ. Admission to the civil service was formerly in the gift of the directors, and formed their most valuable patronage; but by the act of 1853, the "writerships" were thrown open to public competition.

The British territories in India are divided into two classes, the "regulation" and the "non-regulation" provinces; the former comprehends all the older territories, which are subject to a system of administration embodied in the published "regulations" and acts of the Indian governments. The latter consists of more recently acquired districts, in which the regulations have never been introduced, but the government is administered by special and varying instructions issued to the functionaries in charge. It is in these latter territories that military officers have been mostly selected for political authority. The regulation provinces are administered through established offices filled exclusively from the civil service: they contain about two-thirds of the native population.

The two great departments of civil government are the collection of the revenue and the administration of justice; departments which the native system combined in the same functionaries, and the British still entrusts to members of one service. Except in the queen's courts at Calcutta, Madras, and Bombay, the judges are not of the legal profession; a want which is little to be regretted, when it is remembered that justice in India is to be administered to natives who neither understand nor appreciate the intricacies of English law. It is the custom of the country, the religious law, or the social obligation, that has to be decided upon; and on these an educated English gentleman, well acquainted with the people, is better qualified to collect and weigh the evidence than a lawyer from Westminster Hall. The judicial department of the Company's civil service is in effect a profession of itself; the mischief is, that the "Regulations" which form its statute law are so numerous, cumbrous, and intricate, as to reproduce many of the worst parts of English jurisprudence in an aggravated shape. The Company's courts swarm with native *vakeels* or advocates, who fatten on the litigation they engender. The parties are bewildered, the witnesses perjured, the judge hampered, and impotent. Many families have been deprived of their estates through the dexterous management of adversaries better versed in the Regulations; and so great is the terror they inspire, that a body of Hindu cultivators declared to the British resident in Oude, that they would rather suffer all the outrage and extortion of that atrocious government than live under these Regulations. "Your courts of justice are the things we most dread, sir, and we are glad to escape from them as soon as we can, in spite of all the evils we are exposed to on our return to the place of our birth."*

The collection of the revenue also is governed by the Regulations. Taxation in India, as a whole, is not excessive. The total revenue levied in the year 1856 was £29,864,090. Under Aurungzebe, whose territory was nothing near so extensive, the sum amounted to £37,724,615. The present levy is in fact only four shillings and four-pence a head on the population of British India, while in England, in the year 1852, the average taxation was one pound nineteen shillings and four-pence a head.

More than half the Indian revenue, moreover, is derived from the land, and partakes of the character of rent. The ancient village tenure of the Hindus has already been described. During the Mohammedan usurpation its features were in many parts obliterated, and when lord Cornwallis came to settle the revenue of Bengal, he found a class in possession, termed *zemindars*, or landholders. These were in some cases the representatives of old Hindu proprietors or princes, who had been continued as collectors of the revenue under the Mussulman government. In others they were simply middlemen, farming the government dues. Lord Cornwallis, with the natural leaning of an English nobleman, was induced to regard all the zemindars as proprietors of large estates, and the cultivators (though often the

* Sir W. Sleeman's Diary of a Journey in Oude.

actual owners) as merely tenants or labourers. A permanent settlement of the revenue was effected on this hypothesis. The zemindar were rated at a fixed annual payment, and obtained all the powers of sale and ejectment usual to owners. This is what is termed the *zemindary* system.

At a later period it was discovered that rights, which lord Cornwallis had never suspected, existed in the cultivators of the soil. Sir Thomas Munro taking up the inquiry in the south, where Mussulman misrule had not so extensively obliterated the ancient institutions, arrived at exactly the opposite conclusion from that obtaining in Bengal. He considered the strict fee of the land to be in the sovereign, and the ryot, or actual cultivator, to be tenant of the state, but with a customary right of continuance so long as he discharged his rent. For that rent, accordingly, he proceeded to treat immediately with the peasant, and hence the system denominated *ryotwarree*, which acknowledges no real property save in the government: it is now generally allowed that the assessment on the cultivator was set too high under this system.

Further research has since brought to light the traces of the old village system still subsisting in various parts of India, and once, perhaps, universal. This discovery has initiated a third plan of collection, distinguishing the village proprietary, or little band of freeholders, alike from the tax-gatherer and from the hired labourer. This is the system now most commonly pursued in the non-regulation provinces. The civil and military officers employed in those districts administer them in conformity with local usage and opinion, aided without being superseded by European intelligence, under the immediate direction of government, and with the inexpressible advantage of popular support. It is by thus preserving an elasticity and simplicity of administration that the resources of Mysore, the Punjab, Pegu, and some of the north-western provinces, have been so happily developed. None but active, intelligent, and zealous functionaries can find place in such a system of administration; and it is to the credit of the East India directors, and the middle classes among whom their patronage has been distributed, that the Indian services have ever yielded men of the highest stamp to discharge with unparalleled ability duties which in no other department of the British empire are surpassed or perhaps equalled in importance.

Such was the government from which lord Dalhousie retired in 1855, to receive in England a meed of approbation not inferior to that of the most successful administrators. The great empire enjoyed a profound peace, which no enemy appeared capable of disturbing. A course of wise and enlightened internal policy had been inaugurated. The education of the natives, the development of the resources by public works and other facilities for commerce, the consolidation of a just and satisfactory settlement of the revenue,—these were some of the high objects on which it was fondly hoped his successor might concentrate his uninterrupted energies. There was never a season which seemed to glow with brighter prospects for India, than that which was destined to plunge her once more in gloom, and to shake the British empire to its foundations.

Beneath the general calm some causes for serious

apprehension had long been manifest to the more discerning. The reverses sustained in Affghanistan had tarnished the lustre of the British arms. The rapid progress of the annexation policy had excited the alarm of princes and chieftains, ambitious for personal ascendancy, and caring little for the general tranquillity and improvement. These feelings were diligently fomented by numbers of pensioned rulers and their discontented followers. The progress of European civilization was hateful to the old Hindu and Mohammedan bigots, who valued nothing so much as a rigid adherence to their decaying superstitions. A society was in active existence in Calcutta, called the Dhurma Sobah, established for the preservation of Hindu religion and caste against European innovations. By this society every effort of government at moral progress, every improvement in the law, every step in national education, was denounced as an attack on the social and religious institutions of their ancestors. These accusations were vented in public meetings, and widely disseminated by means of the native press.

Such elements of disturbance were naturally to be expected, and need have inspired no dismay; but they required a watchful eye, with a prompt and powerful arm. The discontented classes, though numerically insignificant, were active and resolute; the bulk of the population, to whom the improved administration gave increase of wealth and happiness, are proverbially apathetic. Submissive to all governments, they were never known to be zealous for any. Everything in India depends on the possession and the exhibition of POWER; and the British power was now again seriously called in question in the East.

An opinion had been widely spread that Russia was severely tasking all our resources in the Crimea. The court of Persia was again alive with intrigues, and corresponding with the Mohammedan princes in India. The expedition against that country in 1856 greatly weakened the European force at the disposal of the Indian government. No augmentation of the army had taken place proportionate to the increase of territory and population acquired in the Punjab, Pegu, and Oude; and serious apprehensions had been expressed by lord Dalhousie's government on this point, which were not sufficiently regarded by the ministers of the crown.

Meantime the native army, on which the main reliance was to be reposed, was itself, in Bengal, the object of no little uneasiness. A disposition to mutiny had often appeared in its ranks. Largely composed of Mohammedans, Brahmins, and Rajpoots, it was peculiarly open to the appeals of bigotry and fanaticism. An idea took possession of the sepoys that after reducing India under one authority, the British intended to reduce it to one religion. Every annexation lent strength to this notion. The sepoys were aware also of the weakness of the European force, and many symptoms indicated a disposition, sooner or later, to try their own strength.

The annexation of Oude, however just or unavoidable, might well fan the smouldering embers of discontent. The Bengal sepoys were mostly natives of that kingdom, and after serving their time returned thither in the enjoyment of pensions. Under the corrupt system of the native government the sepoys were allowed advantages in the courts of justice which British administration could never tolerate.

Again, the lax condition of the police had left every petty chief to maintain his own castle and retainers, and to these independent classes the restraints of British law could not but prove odious. A further effect of the annexation was the disbandment of two-thirds of the king's ragged and mutinous army, who, roaming the country in quest of employment, spread everywhere their own discontent.*

The inflammable elements might still, perhaps, with care and watchfulness have been subdued; but, unfortunately, lord Dalhousie, in the ardour of a high-principled reform, had announced the intention of early introducing the improved system of land revenue, and the announcement filled the great zemindars with alarm and indignation. In such a state as Oude these men are so inevitably powerful, that prudence might have dictated a longer toleration of their corruption and tyranny. Though subjected for so many centuries to Mussulman usurpation, Oude is still largely populated by Hindus, among whom the Brahmin and Kshatriya castes muster strong. It contains the oldest and probably the most warlike Hindu population in India, mixed with large numbers of haughty and intractable Mussulmans. Such men are not easily won to a foreign master, for unfortunately both Mussulman and Hindu are slow to appreciate public improvements, when purchased at the cost of private prerogative or prejudice.

* The country had been for generations the paradise of adventurers, the Alsatia of India, the nursing place and sanctuary of scoundrelism, such as is without a parallel on earth. When the fiat of lord Dalhousie went forth there were left standing in the country two hundred and forty-six forts, mounting four hundred and thirty-six guns, and having eight thousand gunners to work them. He took into our service about twelve thousand of the regular forces and five hundred artillerymen, and the rest, with arms in their hands, were sent adrift to seek their fortunes.—*The Sepoy Revolt*, by H. Mead.

How far any plot was formed for the overthrow of the British power is not at present satisfactorily ascertained. But predictions are said to have been afloat that the centenary anniversary of the battle of Plassey was destined to witness the destruction of the empire then founded in India. Such prophecies have a notorious tendency to fulfil themselves, and it is now certain that disaffection was alarmingly prevalent in the ranks of the Bengal army, before a suspicion of the impending danger had troubled the minds of the officers or the government.

In the year 1856 a new rifle, which had been introduced with effect into the British army, was ordered to be supplied also to the native troops. Depots of instruction in its use were opened at Dum Dum near Calcutta, at Umballa, and at Meerut. The cartridge used with this weapon, being of a peculiar construction, immediately attracted attention; report was spread that it was greased with the fat of bullocks and swine, in order to defile the sepoys, and destroy their caste. The rumour was at once noticed by the authorities: knowing the pertinacity with which the natives cling to suspicion, however unfounded, it was ordered (after explaining the falsehood of the report) that the cartridges should be supplied ungreased, and the sepoys apply the wax or oil themselves. The excitement still continuing, a change was made in the manual exercise, by which the end of the cartridge was torn off by the hand, so as to avoid its application to the mouth. Finally, the new cartridge and rifle, which had never been issued beyond the musketry depots, were altogether withdrawn, in deference to the wild unreasoning clamour which had extended itself through the country, though only a few of the sepoys had ever seen the cartridge, and not a single regiment had been supplied with them.

The temper of the troops had now grown heady and mutinous; the old cartridge also was viewed with suspicion; secret communications took place between the different regiments; private meetings were held, and plots began to be talked of, which, when they reached the ears of the European officers, were generally derided and disbelieved. Mutiny at last began to show itself at Barrackpore, in the neighbourhood of Calcutta. The adjutant of the 34th native infantry was fired upon by a sepoy, intoxicated with drugs, in the front of the main guard commanded by a jemadar, and not a man stirred to his rescue. The jemadar and the sepoy were both executed by sentence of court-martial, and the regiment was disbanded. The same penalty was inflicted upon another corps at the same time, but the mutiny continued to spread.

At Meerut, seventy troopers having refused their cartridges, general Anson, the commander-in-chief, an officer of no Indian experience and who had been absent from his seat in council during the investigations at Calcutta, ordered them to be tried by a court-martial composed of native officers. They were sentenced to ten years' imprisonment in irons. This severe penalty was confirmed by general Anson; but with singular imprudence, after the warnings already given, no precautions were taken for the safety of the cantonment in which it was promulgated. As might have been anticipated, the rest of the regiment rose and released the prisoners; then, being joined by other native troops, they commenced a murderous attack on the European officers. A regiment of dragoons, another of the line, and a squadron of European horse artillery were in the cantonment, but so awkwardly disposed and handled, that the mutineers were able to complete the massacre almost unchecked, and then made good their retreat to Delhi.

This fortified city, the centre of so many native traditions, the abode of the Mogul family, and the repository of vast stores of ammunition laid up by the British government, had been weakly confided to a garrison entirely composed of natives. The mutineers from Meerut reached the place, without molestation or pursuit from the large European force behind them. Crossing the Jumna by the bridge of boats which leads to the king's palace, they were, by his order, immediately admitted, and passed with cheers through the royal apartments into the city. The garrison joined them, and another frightful massacre of Europeans was perpetrated, followed by a scene of general pillage and plunder. With the royal city in their possession, the insurgents now proclaimed the descendant of Timour king, and issued invitations to the whole army to join the flag of the prophet. These transactions occurred on the 10th and 11th May, 1857.

The tidings were received in the several stations at first with doubt and misgiving; but as the intelligence was confirmed that Delhi was actually in the possession of the rebels, and the British government unable to recover it, the sepoys wavered; then regiment after regiment plunged into the mutiny, in most cases repeating the barbarous assassinations of their officers (with their wives and children) which had marked the first outbreak. In two months almost all the Bengal native army had disappeared; some by open mutiny, some by desertion, others by disbandment, while not a few were disarmed by government as matter of precaution. Still the rebellion was almost entirely confined to the army and the vile population which hangs about military cantonments, aided by the inmates of the jails released by the insurgents. A few of the petty chiefs seized the opportunity to kill and plunder on their own account, but none of the native states deserted the British cause, and hardly any of the village population were seduced into the revolt.

The danger and misery of the European residents were extreme. Scattered about the country in small societies, amid a population whom they had regarded with undoubting confidence, in the enjoyment of apparent security and the society of their wives and children, they suddenly found themselves menaced with dishonour and death. The most revolting cruelties, base inhuman outrages only conceivable to the filthy and brutal minds of Mussulmans and Hindus, were perpetrated without remorse upon defenceless ladies and children; often in the presence of their husbands and fathers. Death in most cases terminated their sufferings. Yet in these extremities the spirit of the English race was displayed in a manner that has filled Europe with admiration. By twos and threes the devoted victims turned to bay on their murderers. None disgraced their country, or denied their faith. Some confessed CHRIST in the language of martyrs; and one in particular must be mentioned, for the consolation of the many parents bereaved in this bloody insurrection. A young officer, named Marcus Arthur Cheek, was dragged wounded and faint into the presence of some rebel sepoys, at the moment that they had forced a native catechist upon his knees, and by threats of instant death were demanding his recantation of Christianity. "Whatever befalls," exclaimed the youthful officer, "never deny your Saviour." With these words he sank exhausted to the earth. Succour arrived at the moment; but the spirit of the gallant boy had passed in the exertion: he was at rest with One who will not deny him in the last day.

While examples of private courage and integrity were everywhere multiplied, the government exerted itself with prodigious energy to collect their European forces. Happily the Persian expedition was just returned to Bombay. Some troops destined for China were intercepted on their voyage, and brought to Calcutta. Further succours were obtained from Ceylon, the Mauritius, and the Cape of Good Hope. The most urgent requisitions were despatched to England, where the greatest promptitude was evinced as soon as the danger had been fully realized. Reinforcements were forwarded in large numbers, and by the month of October an army of eighty thousand British soldiers were in India, prepared to vindicate the authority of government and restore the country to tranquillity.

Before the first of these reinforcements landed, the torrent of insurrection had been stemmed and turned by the courage and conduct of the Company's officers. The utmost anxiety was evinced for the recovery of Delhi, since every day that it remained in the hands of the rebels gave vitality and extension to the insurrection. A force was assembled, under general Anson in person, but dying of cholera at Umballa he left the command to sir Henry Barnard. This general appeared before Delhi only to experience a similar removal by death, after gallantly driving in the rebels who ventured to meet him in the plain. General Reed succeeded in a state of health which soon obliged him to resign the command to general Wilson. Up to this time it had been thought practicable to carry the place by assault, though a regular siege was precluded by the vast superiority of the mutineers in numbers and material. General Wilson found the army too reduced on the 11th of July to justify the attempt. It was even feared that the force must be withdrawn; but this catastrophe was happily averted by the resolution of the general, aided by the skill and resources of the chief engineer, colonel Baird Smith.

The post was held till the 5th of September, when guns arrived for the siege. Fifty-six pieces were placed in battery, against upwards of three hundred in the possession of the rebels, whose practice was little inferior to the British. Two breaches were effected by the night of the 13th, and at sunrise on the 14th the assault was delivered at four points by about four thousand men. A third of the city was taken by nightfall. Twenty thousand sepoys still remained within the walls, where every house was a little fort, and they were in possession of the largest arsenal in India. Being pressed with equal judgment and resolution for five days, the remainder of the mutineers fled over the bridge of boats and left the city to their heroic conquerors. They were pursued and slain in great numbers. The old king was captured and placed in confinement till his complicity in the treason should be inquired into. His sons, who had commanded the rebels and taken part in the inhuman cruelties perpetrated on the Europeans, were shot upon the spot.

Foremost among the champions of his country's honour was general Havelock, of the Queen's army, rendering services second to none that sparkle in the military annals of India. At Cawnpore and at Lucknow the European garrisons, with large numbers of females and children, were beleaguered by masses of native troops, and lay in the most imminent peril of destruction. Havelock, at the head of two thousand men, was despatched to their assistance. Before his arrival, sir Hugh Wheeler commanding at Cawnpore had been compelled to capitulate to the Nana Sahib, (the suppposititious heir of Bajee Rao,) who had rushed from his stronghold at Bithoor to embrue his hands in English blood. The Mahratta swore with joined hands to protect the English and provide them boats to descend the Ganges. No sooner, however, were they embarked than he opened fire from the banks and sunk and destroyed them all, with the exception of some prisoners, mostly ladies and children, reserved for a more terrible fate. Being defeated by Havelock in the field, the villain sent for butchers from the shambles and commanded them to slaughter his prisoners. With cool, inhuman cruelty the Brahmin allowed the bonds of the chaplain to be loosed in order to read the funeral service for himself and his companions; and when Havelock entered Cawnpore the next day not one of the devoted victims was alive. The room in which the atrocious deed had been done was still swimming in human blood. Long tresses, with portions of ladies' garments, lay soaking in the gore, and a well was found choked with the bodies of the dead and dying indiscriminately thrown into it! Altogether it was computed that one thousand English lives fell a prey to the perfidy of this Mahratta Brahmin, who has never yet been found in the field, and whose means of doing mischief were wholly derived from the misplaced generosity of his betrayed and outraged benefactors.*

Havelock was more happy in his endeavour to reach Lucknow. Cutting his way through the sepoys who swarmed in thousands before the residency, he relieved the garrison at a most critical moment, and then found himself in turn beleaguered along with them by the rebel forces. Here he held out with astonishing bravery and skill for two months, when sir Colin Campbell, who had been sent from England as commander-in-chief, arriving with succours, succeeded in safely withdrawing the garrison. Havelock's work was now done, but his reward was not to be enjoyed on earth. On the day of this relief, wearied and worn with sickness, this truly Christian soldier breathed his last. While a grateful sovereign was consulting with an applauding country, to cover him with the honours of this world, he had gone to another, where a long course of devoted

* No less than sixty-three pages of *The London Gazette* were filled with the names of the persons murdered, killed in action, and otherwise cut off between the 10th of May and the middle of December, 1857. The list included three hundred and seventy-eight officers of the Queen's and Company's armies. One hundred and eighty-six Europeans fell in the massacre at Delhi; fifty-two at Gwalior, Indore, and Mhow; forty-one in the Allahabad division; thirty-one at Meerut; thirty-eight at Agra; thirty at Hissar; nineteen at Jhansi; while not less than seven hundred and two persons are known to have been murdered at Cawnpore exclusive of the soldiers and their families. Altogether the sad total is computed at about one thousand eight hundred men, women, and children, slain in this terrible mutiny.

piety justifies the hope that he will receive not a corruptible but an incorruptible crown.

The mutiny eventually involved nearly all the Bengal native army, regular and irregular, but it did not extend to the troops in Madras or Bombay, nor to the population generally, save in the province of Oude. The sepoys escaping in large numbers from Delhi had hastened to Lucknow, where their numbers compelled sir Colin Campbell to retire and place the women and sick in safety, while sir James Outram held post at Alumbagh till the return of the commander-in-chief. These arrangements were conducted with equal skill, fortitude, and daring; and on the 16th of March, 1858, Lucknow was retaken by a combined assault.

The mutineers were now beaten and dispersed at every focus of the insurrection. They have never shown any power of resistance in the field, and the superiority of British arms is unquestionable. The imminence of the danger may be considered as past, and, with the good blessing of God, India may yet again return to tranquillity under the British supremacy. But large masses of desperate men are still in arms. The fanaticism of caste is still rampant, and the most unremitting vigilance, caution, and courage, moral as well as physical, are demanded for the restoration of order.

CHAPTER XI.

PROGRESS OF CHRISTIANITY.

Introduction—St. Thomas—Syrian churches in Malabar—Treatment by the Portuguese—Compulsory perversions to Rome—Buchanan's researches—Intercourse with Church of England—Bishop Middleton and Church mission at Cottyam—Rupture—Present state—Xavier—De' Nobili—Jesuit mission in Madura—Monstrous frauds—Fathers turned Brahmins—Perjuries—Suppression of the mission—Apostasy of converts—Abbé Dubois—State of Romish Christianity in the South—English efforts—East India Company's chaplains—Danish missions, Ziegenbalg and Plutscho—British missions at Madras and Cuddalore—Government favour—Translations of Bible—Schwartz—Opposition of East India Company—American missionaries expelled from Calcutta—Parliamentary regulations—Ecclesiastical establishment—Missionary operations—The Press—Religious Tract Society—State of Protestant Christianity—Conclusion.

To this sketch of the rise and progress of secular empire in India it remains to add some brief notice of the progress of that kingdom which is not of this world. From the vagueness with which the term India was employed by the early ecclesiastical writers, it is difficult to decide when the gospel was first introduced into the region now bearing the appellation. The tradition which assigns the honour to St. Thomas, said to have been slain by the Brahmins at St. Thomé near Madras, is firmly held by the Syrian and Romanist Christians of India, but has no historical foundation. There is better evidence that the light of Christianity extended from Egypt, where it was kindled by St. Mark, through Persia towards the northern confines of India.

The only churches which survived to the period of

European observation were found on the coast of Malabar, where they still exist under the appellation of *Syrian*. They appear to have been planted in the fourth century, and probably by Thomas, a monk from that country, whose name has been confounded with that of the apostle. These churches continued for many centuries under the ecclesiastical rule of the patriarchs of Antioch and Mosul. They obtained not only toleration, but establishment and civil privileges, from the native princes, and in the ninth century were governed by a Christian *raja*.

The Portuguese, on arriving in this part of India, were surprised to find a numerous community professing the faith of Christ, but ignorant alike of the Latin language and the Roman pontiff. The determination was immediately taken to reduce them to papal obedience. The Syrian bishop was arrested and taken prisoner to Goa, from whence he was sent to Portugal. Here he was induced or compelled to acknowledge the papal supremacy, and returned to India to reduce his people to the same obedience. A new bishop had in the interval been received from Mosul, and a schism ensued, which was actively fomented by the Portuguese. More than once they seized and deported to Goa or Lisbon the prelates who ventured to defend their ecclesiastical liberties. A synod under archbishop Menezes, at Diamper, in 1599, decreed the destruction of all Syrian books on ecclesiastical subjects. The archbishop went round the church in procession chanting praises, while the ancient liturgies and other works were committed to the flames. Then calling the Jesuits to his assistance, he proceeded to enforce his authority by the most violent extremities.

A number of the defenceless churches were at last brought to adapt their ritual to the views of the Roman prelate, though retaining the Syrian language. Others, however, steadfastly adhering to their ancient rites, are known as the Syrian Christians, or the Christians of St. Thomas in Malabar. At the present time the Romish Syrians are computed at nearly one hundred thousand in number, and the Christians of St. Thomas at about half as many.

The Syrian churches were visited in 1806 by Dr. Claudius Buchanan, whose account of an independent ancient episcopal communion, still existing in avowed antagonism to the church of Rome, was received with considerable interest in England. Ten years later they were visited by bishop Middleton, who consulted the metran (or bishop) and some of his clergy on the assistance that might be afforded from England to the Syrian congregations. The proposal was cordially received by the metran. Without attempting a union with the Church of England, or in any way interfering with the local organization, the Syrian community thankfully agreed to accept translations of the Scriptures, (which they possessed only in Syriac, to them a dead language,) together with the counsel and co-operation of English agents in the instruction of the clergy and a general reformation of morals. A mission was ultimately planted at Cottyam in Malabar, by the Church Missionary Society, and a college established to aid in these designs.

A closer acquaintance with the Syrian churches tended greatly to abate the opinion which had prevailed respecting the purity of their doctrine, liturgy, and discipline. The English missionaries complained of many corruptions and abuses. Views and practices were discovered which they considered little short of the transubstantiation, purgatory, and saint-worship of Rome. The Syrian clergy, on the other hand, became jealous and suspicious of the English. The metran withdrew the permission given to the missionaries to preach and labour among his congregations, imposed an oath upon his clergy to hold no communication with them, and prohibited the deacons from attending the college. The separation between the two churches became complete in 1835. The English missionaries have since continued their labours for the good of the heathen and Mohammedans generally, and of individuals in the Romish-Syrian or Syrian communities, but in entire independence of the metran and his authority.

Since the separation, the conviction has become more general and decided of the corrupt condition of the Syrian Christians. Bishop Wilson, in 1843, declared that the grievous errors of transubstantiation, the sacrifice of the mass, purgatory, worship of the Virgin, adoration of the saints, extreme unction, and others of the same tendency, were generally believed and practised. At the same time it appears that few, if any, of these corruptions are sanctioned by their canons or articles of faith, and that, as a church, they hold no sinful terms of communion like the church of Rome.* They still reject the supremacy of the pope, acknowledge the supreme authority of the Holy Scriptures, and allow them to be freely translated and read by the people. They admit also of translations of the prayers, though the usual service is in Syriac. They allow no images in churches; and when that of the Virgin was first exhibited among them by a Jesuit priest, the whole con-

* See Appendix IV. to bishop of Calcutta's Metropolitical Charge, 1842-3.

gregation cried out, "Away with the idol; we are Christians." Like the Greek church, however, they admit of *paintings* while rejecting images; and on the whole, while the existence of these churches affords, like the Greek and other oriental independent communities, an irrefragable testimony against the claims of the Roman papacy, it is to be feared that their practical condition is one of great spiritual corruption.

The Portuguese invariably professed the spread of Christianity to be the great object of their discoveries and conquests in heathen lands. Religious missionaries of the different orders of the church of Rome sailed with all their expeditions. Churches were solemnly dedicated in every settlement. Portuguese colonies were founded, and the settlers were encouraged to intermarry with the natives on embracing the religion of the cross. By these means a professedly Christian population rapidly arose and increased. A permanency was given to their religious institutions by landed endowments, which have enabled them to survive the power that called them into existence. To the present day the "Portuguese" form a numerous class among the native population, and their convents, churches, episcopal sees, and other establishments, are respected, in common with other property, under the British rule.

The celebrated Francis Xavier landed at Goa A.D. 1542. He passed the first night alone in one of the churches, absorbed in meditation and prayer. Finding the state of religion very low, he set himself earnestly to inculcate a reformation of manners, with more frequent attendance on the sacraments. From Goa he proceeded to Cape Comorin, where, being in utter ignorance of the language and not provided with an interpreter, he occupied himself in baptizing children and attending the sick—"employments (as he simply remarks) which require no interpreter." He next procured the Lord's Prayer, the Ten Commandments, with some other passages of Scripture, to be translated into the vernacular tongue, and having learned them by heart, went about with a bell, gathering the natives, and reciting these elementary truths.

What amount of instruction, in faith or morals, was really communicated by these methods may be open to question; but the spirit they exhibited was manifestly of another kind from that of Menezes, and in one month Xavier baptized with his own hand ten thousand idolaters; nay, not unfrequently, this zealous missionary declares that he baptized a populous village in a single day. Such labours were, at all events, more evangelical than the office assigned to their author after their termination. Xavier died off the coast of China, but was interred at Goa, where he is now worshipped as the tutelar saint of the city, and "the protector of the Indies."* There is an old image of him near Cape Comorin, to which many Hindus and Roman Catholics go on pilgrimage.†

For two centuries the Portuguese continued to exert themselves with much vigour for the conversion of the natives. Their government adopted the work as essential to the duration of their power; and though Hindus and Mohammedans were allowed to reside in Goa, the public acts of either religion were forbidden under penalty of death. In Salsette they destroyed the pagodas and mosques, while the Inqui-

* This title was conferred upon Xavier nearly two hundred years after his death, when his name was inserted in the calendar of saints by pope Benedict XIV.

† Allen's India.

sition was established at Goa, to guard the purity of the doctrine so zealously propagated. Nor were these exertions confined to Portuguese settlements; missions were organized in the territories of the native princes; and where artifice seemed more available than force, it was resorted to with equal readiness.

The visits of the Goa fathers to the court of Akbar have already been mentioned. They resided on the first occasion for twelve years at Delhi, making two subsequent journeys for the same purpose by desire of the emperor, at intervals of eight and four years respectively. The inquisitive monarch received them with a great show of respect: successively bowing, kneeling, and falling prostrate before the crucifix, he adored the symbol after the Mohammedan, the Christian, and the Hindu modes of worship. A richly ornamented image of the Virgin Mary he declared to be a worthy representation of the queen of heaven; and when presented with a book, which purported to be the Bible in four languages, he received it with reverence, kissing it and placing it on his head. These openings, if sincere, were miserably abused by the papal emissaries. Being requested to prepare a history of Jesus Christ for the emperor's use, they had the folly and baseness to produce a book professing to be a "Compilation from the Holy Gospels and other Books of the Prophets;" but which in fact is filled (for the imposture is still in existence) with false legends of the Virgin Mary and St. Peter, proving that Christ was far from being the main object of Jesuit preaching. It is little surprising that Akbar, after perusing this work, and being treated by the infatuated fathers to a sight of their chapel, splendidly adorned with the borrowed finery of a Hindu temple, should cool in the ardour of his inquiries, and finally suffer the missionaries to leave him in despair.

Still more extraordinary, indeed pre-eminent in the annals of fraud, is the history of the Jesuit mission in Madura, headed by Robert de' Nobili, a nephew of cardinal Bellarmine. This man and his companions, after carefully studying the language and religion of the Hindu Shastras, assumed Sanscrit names and gave themselves out as European *Brahmins*, come to exchange ideas with their brethren in India. They adopted the yellow dress, wore the caste marks on their foreheads, and practised frequent ablutions. They observed also the vegetable diet of Brahmins, even exceeding the natives in the severity of their ascetic observances. To these deceptions de' Nobili scrupled not to add the forgery of a parchment in the ancient character, showing that the Roman Brahmins were older than those of India, and that the Jesuits were descended in a direct line from Brahma. These allegations he dared to confirm upon oath in an assembly of Brahmins at Madura. Nor was this the most audacious forgery resorted to by the Jesuits. Singular as the design appears, they actually compiled a *new Veda*, written in the ancient Sanscrit with extraordinary skill, and interweaving with other matter some account of Christianity. This remarkable production was palmed upon the natives as genuine, and becoming known in Europe was adduced by Voltaire as proving the superiority of the Vedas to the genuine Scriptures.

By these unjustifiable measures the Jesuits made proselytes of twelve eminent Brahmins, whose example and influence secured a large following of the people. To preserve the deception these Christian fathers carefully abstained from all intercourse with the lower orders which might violate their pretended caste. They visited the dying by night in the recesses of the jungle, with the strictest precautions to avoid discovery. The sick were carried into the open air to receive the sacraments, without polluting the priestly celebrant.* In short, instead of converting the Hindus to Christianity, the Jesuits became themselves Hindus and Brahmins, and were accused as such to the pope by some less astute Portuguese. The Jesuits defended themselves at Rome by delegates, who denied the facts, and with their usual audacity *swore* to the falsehood on the Holy Sacrament. A commissioner despatched by the pope to India was made away with by an arrangement with a native prince. At another time one of the missionaries, who was sent back from Rome with strict injunctions to abandon the practices complained of, took a solemn oath in the presence of the congregation that the pope had dismissed the charges, and justified the mission in every particular. The contest lasted for forty years; the Jesuits were then

* As the leaders of the mission were Brahmins, so they had missionaries of lower caste for the common people. One of them describes his own conduct in this way:—"Some time ago a catechist from the Madura mission begged me to go to Poulour, there to baptize some *pariar* catechumens, and to hear the confession of some new neophytes of that caste. The fear that Brahmins and shudras might come to learn the step I had taken, and thence look upon me as infamous and unworthy ever after of holding any intercourse with them, hindered me from going. *The words of the holy apostle Paul, which I had read that morning at the mass, determined me to take this resolution—'giving no offence to any one, that your ministry be not blamed'* (!) 2 Cor. vi. 3. I therefore made these poor people go to a retired place, about three leagues from here, where I myself joined them during the night, and with the most careful precautions there I baptized nine of them."

compelled to submit to the papal censure; but on endeavouring to introduce the prescribed reforms among their proselytes the greater part fell back into avowed heathenism.

The discovery of this gigantic fraud was quickly followed by the suppression of the order of Jesuits, and the poor remnant of their proselytes were left to native and incompetent teachers. Tippoo Sultan, in his ferocious zeal for Mohammedanism, seized as many as sixty thousand of these native Christians, and confined them in Seringapatam, with orders to submit to the initiatory rite of Islam. Not a single individual had courage to resist: the whole apostatized in a mass: but after the death of Tippoo, the majority returned to their nominal Christianity. "God preserve them," writes the abbé Dubois, from whom this account is derived, "from being exposed in future to the same trial: for should this happen, I have every reason (notwithstanding their solemn protestations when again reconciled to Christianity) to apprehend the same sad result: that is to say, a tame submission and a general apostasy."*

The abbé Dubois resided in the south of India for many years as a missionary of the church of Rome, and reckoned his flock by scores of thousands. On his return to Europe, he published a work declaring he had never seen a single native who was a sincere Christian. He adds his conviction that the time is past for the conversion of India, and that its millions have been consigned by the just sentence of the Almighty to hopeless reprobation!

The city of Goa still retains some religious importance, being the seat of a Portuguese archbishop, with

* Letters on Christianity in India.

a considerable staff of native clergy. There are also several other bishops, or vicars apostolic, in different parts of the country, mostly Italians by birth, though of late years the pope has conferred this authority on English and Irish agents. These are regarded with great jealousy by the "country born" priesthood, whose great anxiety appears to be to defend the endowments which yet remain to them from the grasp of the European intruders. On the whole, it can hardly be denied that with an outlay of money, zeal, and labour deserving the imitation of more evangelical communions, the church of Rome has effected little for the moral or social elevation of India, and still less for the diffusion of that knowledge which maketh "wise unto salvation."

It was to be expected that England, as being blessed with a purer form of Christianity than Portugal, would have exceeded her predecessor in zeal for its diffusion among the natives subjected to her dominion. But while the precepts of the gospel forbid the application of force to influence the conscience even for good, the principles of the British constitution place far less power and funds at the disposal of government than is enjoyed by despotic monarchs. The disposition of the English nation is to leave the diffusion of religious knowledge to the unfettered exertions of those who feel the Divine call to preach the gospel to every creature. This is unquestionably the method most resembling the apostolic preaching, and experience shows it to be not less successful in the end than the more concentrated efforts of government agencies.

The conversion of the natives, however, was not wholly disregarded by the rulers of British India. The original charter of the East India Company, dated

5th September, 1698, obliges them to maintain a minister in every garrison and superior factory, who shall apply themselves to the native language of the country where they shall reside, "the better to enable them to instruct the Gentoos that shall be servants or slaves of the same company or of their agents, in the Protestant religion." This was the origin of the ecclesiastical establishments, maintained by the Indian governments in each presidency, under the supervision of the bishops of Calcutta,* Madras,† and Bombay,† with their respective archdeacons.

The early chaplains paid much attention to their missionary duties, and some have continued to bear them in mind, regardless of a dogma often promulgated in India, that no person receiving a government salary "has a right to interfere with the religion of the natives." Still the number of resident chaplains has always been below the requirements of the charter, and the few appointed soon became so overwhelmed with the spiritual care of the army, and other European residents, that little time was left for missionary labours. The names of Brown, Buchanan, Martyn, Thomason, and Corrie,‡ all chaplains of the Company, attest the preservation of the original idea of their appointment, and

* Established by Act of Parliament on the renewal of the Company's privileges, in 1814.

† Appointed in like manner on the renewal in 1834.

‡ May it be permitted to the author in recording this name to recall his own brief connexion with its venerable owner? His first sermon in India was preached in the presence of bishop Corrie, on Sunday the 29th Jan., 1837. It was the last time the bishop ever attended the service of God below. The benediction at its close was the parting act of his brief episcopacy. The text was 1 Cor. i. 22—24. The bishop himself had preached on first landing from the kindred text, Gal. vi. 14; as he pressed the young preacher's hand at the conclusion, he solemnly blessed God for the glorious gospel thus continually prolonging itself in the land. On that day week the author preached at the good bishop's funeral.

in all the presidencies there have never failed some to co-operate with the missionary cause and promote the spread of Christianity. Dr. Allen, an American missionary, writes thus: "In the whole history of the propagation of Christianity in modern times, I know not where we can find more noble examples of Christian effort, liberality, and benevolence, than in the names which have been mentioned, and some others like them, among the East India Company's chaplains in India."*

By these labours foundations were laid in many parts of India, on which the missionaries of the Church of England were afterwards enabled to build. It was by the agents of a country, however, greatly inferior to Great Britain in power and responsibility, that the highway was first opened for the gospel to the heathen of India. The Danes had established a commercial settlement at Tranquebar, in the dominions of the raja of Tanjore, as early as 1621; and about the close of that century the king was urged by one of his chaplains (Dr. Lutkins) to make some provision for converting the heathen to Christianity. A couple of students were engaged from the University of Halle, and embarked for India in 1705. The names of these first pioneers of evangelical truth were Bartholomew Ziegenbalg and Henry Plutscho. The first fruits of their labours were five adult heathen slaves, belonging to Danish masters, whom they baptized after a public examination in the church at Tranquebar in less than a year from their arrival. Great jealousy was exhibited by the natives of their design, and a Brahmin whom they had prevailed upon to instruct them in the native language was thrown into jail by the raja, on a charge of betraying the

* Allen's India, p. 535.

mysteries of religion to the Christians. In two years more the missionaries preached publicly in Tamul and Portuguese to crowded congregations. Soon a little community of native Christians rewarded their exertions, and supplied the invaluable advantage of a *home* to future converts. This was the more necessary in a country where conversion entails the loss of all existing ties, social and domestic, followed by persecution, and in some instances by death itself.

In 1711 a translation of the New Testament was completed, and printed from type cast at Tranquebar. This early union of the press with the pulpit advanced the word of God, at a single step, to a position in India which the Roman Catholic missionaries had failed to attain for it in two centuries.

These efforts excited the deepest interest in the religious circles of England. As early as 1709 a postscript attached to the Report of the Society for Promoting Christian Knowledge notices the labours of Ziegenbalg and Plutscho. The former, returning to Europe for the benefit of his health in 1717, was invited to London, where he was received with marked distinction by the king (George II.), the prince of Wales, and several of the bishops and nobility. The society opened a fund in aid of the Tranquebar mission, and soon after entered more directly on the mission field. In consultation with the chaplain at Fort St. George it was determined to extend the Lutheran mission to some of the British settlements in that presidency.

The Rev. Mr. Schultze arrived at Madras for that purpose in 1728, and was received with the marked approval of the governor and leading officials. A similar mission was opened at Cuddalore (Fort

St. David) in 1738; and in 1734 a Gentoo* version of the Bible was produced by the "British missionaries of Fort St. George." This book was never printed, but copies written with an iron style on *cadjans* (leaves prepared for the purpose) were widely circulated.

During the general war that soon after broke out in Europe, Denmark became separated from her Indian possessions, and the missions were gladly sustained by the English society without interfering with the Lutheran system of doctrine or discipline. In 1742 the native Christians in the three missions numbered three thousand seven hundred and sixty-six souls, while about six thousand had been converted in all.

The further important step was then taken of admitting to the ministry two native catechists educated in the seminary at Madras. A collection of hymns translated into Tamul by the missionaries is noted as exercising a powerful influence; and this book, with its German titles and tunes, is still a favourite in the south of India. Prayer-books also and religious tracts, original and translated, were issued from a press sent out by the society from London, the influence of which was felt as far as Ceylon. In 1743, Philip Fabricius, who had shortly before arrived at Tranquebar, removed to Madras, and three years after published the Tamul translation of the Holy Scriptures, which is still regarded as the authorized version in most of the Protestant missions of the south. On the capture of Madras by the French in 1746 the missionaries were expelled in violation of the treaty, but they found

* Gentoo appears to be a mere corruption of Gentile. The term was generally applied to the population who spoke the Telugu or Wardoogoo language.

refuge in the Dutch settlement of Pulicat; and on the restoration of Madras (A.D. 1750), they were put in possession of a church erected by the French at Vepery, a suburb of Madras, where the mission is still flourishing.

Three additional missionaries sailed from Europe for Tranquebar in 1756, one of whom was the illustrious Schwartz, who, like Fabricius, soon passed into the society's employ as a "British" missionary. After many journeys through the country, Schwartz took up his abode at Trichinopoly, frequently visiting Tanjore, where he secured the esteem and protection of the raja. Gericke, a fellow-countryman and worthy fellow-labourer, was stationed at Cuddalore, and visited Negapatam and Vellore, while the Vepery mission extended itself to several places on the coast above and below Madras.

Through the labours of these zealous missionaries a large portion of southern India was early permeated by evangelical truth. Their simple and evangelical demeanour was so far from provoking the opposition of the natives, that no European in India possessed their esteem so completely as Schwartz. The government, far from dreading to give offence by employing a missionary, were glad to make use of his influence by despatching him on an important mission to Hyder Ali, when the roads were unsafe to any other emissary. This eminent servant of Christ terminated his labours on the 13th February, 1798, yielding up his spirit, in the seventy-second year of his age, with the following prayer:—"O Lord, hitherto thou hast preserved me, hitherto hast thou brought me, and hast bestowed innumerable benefits upon me; do what is pleasing in thy sight. I deliver my spirit into thy hands; cleanse and adorn it with the righteousness of my Redeemer, and receive me into the arms of thy love and mercy."

It seems astonishing that in the face of such results the East India Company should have set itself steadily to oppose the introduction of English missionaries, who now came forward to emulate the zeal of their German predecessors. Nor could the British legislature be induced, while regulating the Company's authority and privileges, to open a door for English missionaries in any part of India. An attempt which was made from America in 1812 proved equally unsuccessful. A party of missionaries who had arrived at Calcutta were compelled by the local government instantly to depart. Two of them went to Burmah; the others, resolving to make another trial on the west coast of India, were again sentenced to expulsion by the authorities at Bombay, though after a long struggle they were permitted to remain. At the review of Indian affairs in 1813, the zeal of the Christian public, now thoroughly awakened, triumphed over these unworthy restrictions, and the Company were directed by law to afford facilities for the resort of missionaries to India.

At the same time an ecclesiastical establishment was formed, consisting of a bishop and three archdeacons, for the better administration of episcopal discipline. This establishment was increased in 1833 by the erection of bishoprics at Madras and Bombay, subject to the bishop of Calcutta as metropolitan. The number of the Company's chaplains have also been augmented of late years. Churches have been built in every European station, and the general state of religion is greatly improved among the civil and military servants of the Company.

Meantime the missionary societies of England and

America have not been slow to embrace the opportunities afforded them of preaching the gospel to the millions of idolatrous India. Twenty-two Protestant missionary societies are now actively at work in the country, representing a considerable portion of the talent, piety, and learning of evangelical Christendom. A table of their several missions is given in the Appendix. The total number of missionaries is nearly four hundred. About one hundred thousand native Christians are in the enjoyment of their ministry, and nearly fifty thousand boys and twelve thousand girls are receiving Christian education in their schools.

The agency of the press, which lends to modern missions a power hardly inferior to that of miracles of old, has been largely exerted in India. Since the year 1813 the Religious Tract Society of London has actively reinforced this department of operations. One hundred and thirty standard works, besides many hundreds of tracts, have been issued from the press by its aid, and twenty-five millions of copies have been circulated among the people. The education of the native youth in the English language has been also liberally aided. Thousands of reams of paper, with hundreds of engravings, have been supplied to the mission stations, and the outlay of this society on its various labours in India has exceeded fifty thousand pounds.

The British and Foreign Bible Society also is largely labouring in India. Its publications and those of the Christian Knowledge Society, both in English and the native languages, are found in all government and many mission stations, and are assiduously distributed among the heathen. The whole Bible has been translated and printed in ten different languages, and the

New Testament in five more. School-book societies and other local associations for kindred purposes are in active operation at several important centres.

It has pleased many ignorant, and some prejudiced, persons to express an opinion that these Christian agencies have signally failed of their object, and that the native converts are at once inconsiderable in numbers and despicable in station and morals. The persons who disseminate this opinion are commonly Europeans, who have resided in India without the desire, and consequently without the opportunity, of acquainting themselves with the actual state of missions. European residents in general exhibit too little concern for the souls of the natives, seldom turning aside from the routine of official or mercantile employment to inquire into the spread of the gospel. It is not in the large towns and cantonments, where they principally dwell, that the missionaries reap their most abundant harvest. The gospel fares better in villages removed from the evil example of European vice, and the pernicious habits which are too often contracted from European intercourse.

It is indeed true of the native Christians of India, as it was of those of Corinth, that "not many wise men after the flesh, not many mighty, not many noble, are called." This would appear to be the usual condition of the gospel, on its first approach to a people already civilized, and possessed of high social organization. To barbarians, on the contrary, Christianity comes as the parent of civilization, and is accordingly first welcomed by the rulers and guides of the people. But while it is admitted that the bulk of native converts in India belong to the lower classes, attracted by the *sympathy* which caste makes it a merit to withhold; and while no faithful man will deny that the lamp of life burns, alas! too dimly in many a native, as in many a European, congregation,—no one having any practical acquaintance with the Protestant missions of India, will for a moment doubt that a great and blessed work has been there commenced.

The native Christians, as a general rule, will bear comparison in all moral and domestic virtues with the corresponding classes of society in England, and are decidedly *more religious*. They exhibit more frequent and devout attendance on Christian ordinances, a more intelligent appreciation of evangelical doctrine, and a more general readiness out of their deep poverty to contribute to the spread of the gospel. The author would be untrue to his own experience and convictions, if he did not close this brief sketch with a declaration that he has himself been acquainted with instances of piety, humility, self-denial, and earnest affection for the truth, among these despised native Christians, which would have shed a lustre on any station of life in England, and could only be produced in man's corrupt nature by the regenerating grace of God the Holy Spirit, and the influence of the saving and sanctifying truth of the gospel of salvation by Jesus Christ, through faith in his atoning and reconciling sacrifice.

It is not pretended that the existing agencies are at all proportioned to the extent and variety of the field of labour. Four hundred missionaries in the presence of one hundred and eighty millions of idolaters and Mohammedans is not a spectacle to be contemplated with satisfaction. Neither is it meant to extenuate the guilt of the Indian governments in obstructing, or the languor of the British public in sustaining, the missionary cause. All that is designed is to indicate the path which has been opened, and the undeserved measure of blessing vouchsafed to the few and feeble steps already taken. To investigate the practical effect of the successive governments to which the natives of India have been subjected, with their existing customs, social and religious, and the degree in which they may have yielded to the influence of Christianity, would indeed be an interesting and profitable undertaking. But it is one which must be reserved for another work. The present object has been attained in presenting a concise history of the several agencies, for evil and for good, which have operated on the native character;—in tracing the origin and growth of British power;—and in suggesting to the Christian reader the responsibilities imposed by its prevalence, on the nation, the church, and the individual. May He who has undoubtedly brought it to pass, that the millions of India should sit under the shadow of the English throne, now graciously fulfil his counsel, and direct its rule to the welfare of mankind and the praise of the glory of his grace.

APPENDIX I.

BRITISH INDIA—CHRONOLOGICAL TABLE OF TERRITORIAL ACQUISITIONS.

A.D.

1640. Site of Fort St. George in Madras granted by a native prince descended from the old rajas of Beejanuggur.

1650. Site of factories at Hooghly granted by Shah Jehan.

1661. Island of Bombay received from the Portuguese in dower of Charles II.'s queen; transferred to the East India Company A.D. 1668.

1700. Site of Fort William in Bengal, granted by the viceroy Azim, grandson of Aurungzebe.

UNDER THE GOVERNMENT OF LORD CLIVE.

1757. Twenty-four pergunnahs (districts round Calcutta) ceded by the nabob, confirmed by Shah Alum.

1759. Masulipatam and districts called "Northern Circars," conquered from the French, granted by the emperor Shah Alum, 1765; surrendered by the nizam, 1766.

1760. Burdwan, Midnapore, and Chittagong, ceded by the nabob Cossim Ali, confirmed by Shah Alum, 1765.

1765. Bengal, Bahar, and Orissa, granted by Shah Alum by the treaty of Allahabad (12th August).

„ Company's jaghire of Chingleput, near Madras, granted by the nabob of the Carnatic, Mohammed Ali.

UNDER WARREN HASTINGS.

1775. Benares—zemindarry ceded by the vizier of Oude.

„ Salsette Island conquered from Mahrattas; possession confirmed by treaty of Salbye, 1782.

1778. Guntoor, the last of the Northern Circars, surrendered by the nizam.

UNDER LORD CORNWALLIS.

1792. Malabar, Dindigul, Salem, Barahmal, etc., conquered from Tippoo Sultan, and ceded by treaty at the close of the first Mysore war.

UNDER MARQUESS WELLESLEY.

A.D.

1799. Coimbatoor, Canara, Wynaad, etc., conquered and retained in the partition of Tippoo Sultan's territories after the fall of Seringapatam.

,, Tanjore—administration transferred by rajah Serfojee; finally lapsed in default of heirs, 1855.

1800. "Ceded districts," acquired by Nizam from Tippoo 1792 and 1799, transferred in commutation of subsidy for British contingent in Hyderabad.

1801. Carnatic—administration surrendered by the Nabob; finally lapsed in default of heirs, 1855.

,, Goruckpore, Bareilly, and Lower Dooab, ceded by the vizier of Oude in commutation of subsidy for British contingent in Oude.

1802. Bundelcund and part of Guzerat exchanged by the Peishwah.

1803. Kuttack and Balasore conquered from Mahrattas, and ceded by treaty with Dowlut Rao Scindia.

,, Upper Dooab, Delhi, Ahmednuggur, conquered from Mahrattas and ceded by treaty with raja of Berar.

1805. Districts in Guzerat (Baroda, etc.) ceded by the Guicowar.

UNDER THE MARQUESS OF HASTINGS.

1815. Kumaon and part of the Terai conquered from the Ghoorkas and ceded by treaty at the close of the Nepal war.

1817. Saugor and Nerbudda territory ceded by the Peishwah in treaty of June 13th; surrendered by the raja of Berar, 1818, in commutation of subsidy for British contingent; confirmed by treaty, 1826.

1818. Kandeish, conquered from Mahrattas, ceded by treaty with Holcar.

,, Ajmere ditto ditto Dowlut Rao Scindia.

,, Poona, Concan, and Southern Mahratta country, conquered from the Peishwah, and ceded by treaty on the surrender and deposition of Bajee Row.

1820. Southern Concan, conquered in 1819 from the piratical chief of Sawant Warree, confirmed by treaty.

UNDER LORD AMHERST.

1826. Assam, Arracan, and Tenasserim provinces, conquered from the Burmese, and ceded by treaty at conclusion of the first war.

UNDER LORD WILLIAM BENTINCK.

1830. South Cachar, lapsed on death of raja without heirs.

1834. Koorg conquered from the raja, who was deposed after murdering all his male heirs.

1835. Jyntees, a small state in the Cossya hills (Assam), taken from the raja, who had kidnapped four British subjects for a human sacrifice.

1836. Loodiana and Ferozepore, Cis-Sutlej territories, lapsed in default of heirs to deceased rulers.

A.D.

1840. Jaloun, in Bundelcund, lapsed in default of heirs to the nana Govind Rao, recognized as hereditary ruler on the overthrow of the Peishwah.

1841. Kurnoul, on the southern bank of the Kistna, taken from the nawab for conspiring against the British government.

UNDER LORD ELLENBOROUGH.

1843. Sindh conquered from the Ameers.

UNDER LORD HARDINGE.

1845. Danish settlements of Serampore and Tranquebar purchased.

1846. Julinder Dooab (between the Beas and the Sutlej) conquered in the first Sikh war, and ceded by treaty of Lahore (9th March).

UNDER THE MARQUIS DALHOUSIE.

1848. Sattara lapsed in default of heirs to the raja.

1849. The Punjab conquered and annexed at the close of the second Sikh war.

,, Jeitpore, in Bundelcund, lapsed in default of heirs.

1850. Sumbhulpore (south-west frontier of Bengal), ditto ditto.

1852. Pegu and Martaban conquered and annexed at the close of the second Burmese war.

,, Khyber, in Sindh, resumed from Ali Morad.

1853. North Cachar resumed from the rebel chief Toola Ram Sennaputtee.

,, Odeipore (south-west frontier of Bengal) lapsed in default of heirs.

,, Berar or Nagpore lapsed on death of raja without heirs, 11th December.

1854. Jhansi, in Bundelcund, lapsed in default of heirs.

1855. Boodawul, in Kandeish, ditto.

1856. Oude—Wajid Ali dethroned for misgovernment, and territory annexed by proclamation.

APPENDIX II.

NATIVE STATES.

NAME.	LOCALITY.	AREA in Square Miles.	POPULATION.
BENGAL.			
Allee Mohun or Rajpoor Ali	Malwa, or Central India	708	69,384
Amjherra	Ditto	584	57,232
Bahadoorgurh	Adjacent to Delhi.	48	14,400
Bhawlpore	Cis-Sutlej	25,200	925,000
Bhopal	Central India	6,764	663,656
Bhurtpore	Adjacent to Agra	1,978	600,000
Bullubgurh	Adjacent to Delhi.	190	57,000
Bundelcund — (thirty-two States)	Central India	8,394	879,800
Burwanee	Ditto	1,380	13,800
Cooch Behar	N. E. Frontier	1,364	136,400
Cossya and Garrow Hills	Ditto	4,347	65,205
Cuttack Mehals — (six States)	Orissa	16,929	761,805
Deojana	Near Delhi	71	6,390
Dewas	Central India.	256	25,088
Dhar	Central India	1,070	104,860
Dholpore	Banks of the Chumbul	1,626	550,000
Furrucknuggur	Adjacent to Delhi	22	4,400
Golab Sing's Dominions	Cashmere	60,000	3,000,000
Gwalior (Scindia's Possessions)	Central India	33,119	3,228,512
Hill States — (twenty-five States)	Cis-Sutlej	5,000	430,713
Ditto (three States)	Trans-Sutlej	4,718	285,442
Hyderabad, or Nizam's Dominions	The Deccan	95,337	10,666,080
Indore:—			
Holcar's Possessions	Central India	8,318	815,164
Jaboon, including Borai, or Boree, and Jucknowda	Ditto	1,348	132,104
Jhujhur	Adjacent to Delhi	1,230	110,700
Joura	Central India	872	85,456
Koorwaee	Ditto	200	19,600
Kupoortullah	Trans-Sutlej	598	212,721
Loharoo	Near to Delhi	200	18,000
Munneepoor	N. E. Frontier	7,584	75,840
Nepal	Northern Bengal	54,500	1,940,000
Omutwarra—(two States)	Central India	1,348	132,104
Patowdee	Near Delhi	74	6,660
Rajpoot States — (fifteen States)	Rajpootana	114,391	7,412,426
Rampore	Rohilcund	720	320,400
Rutlam	Central India	936	91,728
Saugor and Nerbudda Territories—(six States)	Ditto	12,244	1,560,000
Seeta Mow	Ditto	208	20,348
Sikh Protected States—(nine States)	Cis-Sutlej	7,366	1,894,800

NAME.	LOCALITY.	AREA in Square Miles.	POPULATION.
South-West Frontier of Bengal—(sixteen States)	Orissa . . .	23,125	1,111,919
Sickkim	Northern Bengal .	1,670	61,766
Tonk, and other Dependencies of Ameer Khan .	Central India .	1,864	182,672
Tipperah	Adjacent to Burmah	7,632	not known.
Total Bengal (148 States) . .		515,533	38,749,575
MADRAS.			
Cochin	Coast of Malabar .	1,988	288,176
Jeypoor and the Hill Zemindars	Orissa . . .	13,041	391,230
Mysore	Southern India .	30,886	3,460,696
Poodoocottah (Rajah) Tondiman's Dominions . .	Ditto . . .	1,165	61,745
Travancore	Ditto . . .	4,722	1,011,824
Total Madras (5 States) . . .		51,802	5,213,671
BOMBAY.			
Balasinore	Guzerat . .	258	19,092
Bansda	Ditto . . .	325	24,057
Baroda (Dominions of the Guicowar)	Ditto . . .	4,399	325,526
Cambay	Ditto . . .	500	37,000
Cutch	Western India .	6,764	500,536
Daung Rajas	Guzerat . .	950	70,300
Dhurrumpore	Ditto . . .	225	16,650
Guzerat Petty States—(eleven States) . .	Ditto . . .	4,580	240,800
Kattywar Petty Chiefs .	Ditto . . .	19,850	1,468,900
Khyrpore	Sindh	6,000	105,000
Kolapore	Southern Mahratta country . .	3,445	500,000
Myhee Caunta . . .	Guzerat . .	3,400	150,000
Peint and Hursool . .	Adjacent to Ahmednuggur . .	750	55,500
Rewa Caunta—(six States)	Guzerat . .	4,879	361,046
Sawunt Warree	South Concan .	800	120,000
Southern Mahratta Jaghires	Southern Mahratta country . .	3,700	410,470
Sucheen	Guzerat . .	300	22,200
Wusravee (Bheel Chiefs) .	Ditto . .	450	33,300
Total Bombay (33 States) . .		60,575	4,460,370
Total number of Native States . 186		627,910	48,423,616

APPENDIX III.

CHRISTIAN CHURCHES AND MISSIONS IN INDIA.

MINISTERS.	BENGAL.		MADRAS.		BOMBAY.		TOTAL.	
	EU.	NA.	EU.	NA.	EU.	NA.	EU.	NA.
Church of England, Bishops	1	...	1	...	1	...	3	...
Ditto, Government Chaplains	54	...	41	...	29	...	124	...
Ditto, Incorporated Society for the Propagation of the Gospel	13	5	32	6	...	...	45	11
Ditto, Church Missionary Society	42	1	38	9	12	4	92	14
Ditto, other clergymen	18	...	11	2	...	...	29	2
Church of Scotland Government Chaplains	2	...	2	...	2	...	6	...
Ditto Field Chaplains, Missionaries, etc.	7	1	3	...	1	...	11	1
Free Church of Scotland	6	3	9	3	10	2	25	8
London Missionary Society	13	...	31	1	4	...	48	1
Wesleyan Missionary Society	...	...	14	...	...	...	14	...
Baptist Missionary Society	34	...	...	...	...	...	34	...
Orissa Baptist Mission	7	...	...	...	...	...	7	...
Baptist Anglo-Indian Mission	2	...	...	...	...	...	2	...
Irish Presbyterian Mission	...	...	...	...	6	1	6	1
Welsh Mission in Sylhet	2	...	...	...	...	...	2	...
Lutherans.—Church Missionary Society	3	...	...	...	...	...	3	...
Ditto, German Lutheran Mission	7	...	...	...	...	...	7	...
Ditto, Leipsic Evangelical Mission	10	...	...	...	...	...	10	...
Ditto, American Evangelical Mission	5	...	5	...	...	...	10	...
Episcopal Church of Moravians	3	...	...	...	...	...	3	...
German Evangelical Missions	...	...	30	...	27	...	57	...
American Board of Missions (Presbyterian)	19	...	18	...	13	...	50	...
Ditto, Baptist Missionary Unions in Assam, Pegu, and Tenasserim	24	3	...	...	...	...	24	3
Ditto, North Orissa Free Baptist Mission	4	...	...	...	...	...	4	...
Tezpoor Mission, evangelical, of no particular denomination	1	...	...	...	...	...	1	...
Total (Protestant)	277	13	235	21	105	7	617	41
Church of Rome in the Papal obedience—								
Bishops	4	...	1	...	1	...	6	...
Vicars Apostolic	1	...	9	...	...	...	10	...
Priests	81	...	210	...	44	...	335	...
Portuguese Church under Archbishop of Goa—								
Bishops	...	...	...	...	1	...	1	...
Episcopal Governors	1	...	1	...	...	...	2	...
Priests	9	...	33	...	57	...	99	...
Armenian Church—								
Priests	6	...	...	...	...	...	6	...
Greek Church—								
Priests	1	...	...	...	...	...	1	...
Total (Romish, &c.)	103	...	254	...	103	...	460	...

*** The numbers of the Syriac and Syro-Romish Ministers have not been ascertained.

STATIONS (PROTESTANT.)

STATION.	DISTRICT OR DIVISION.	PRESIDENCY.
Agra	Agra	North-West Provinces.
Agurparah	Calcutta	Bengal.
Ahmedabad	Guzerat	Bombay.
Ahmednuggur	Ahmednuggur	Bombay.
Akyab	Arracan	Bengal.
Alipore	Calcutta	Bengal.
Allahabad	Allahabad	North-West Provinces.
Allepie	Travancore	Madras (Native State).
Almanda	Coorg	Madras.
Almorah	Kumaon	North-West Provinces.
Alvarneri	Tinneveily	Madras.
Anarkullee	Lahore	Supreme Government.
Aneycadoo	Tanjore.	Madras.
Aniappen	Tanjore	Madras.
Arcot	Carnatic	Madras.
Arnee	Carnatic	Madras.
Asirvathapuram	Tinnevelly	Madras.
Azimghur	Allahabad	North-West Provinces.
Balasore	Orissa	Bengal.
Banda	Bundelcund	North-West Provinces.
Bangalore	Mysore	Madras (Native States).
Bansberia	. . .	Bengal.
Baraset	Baraset	Bengal.
Bareilly	Bareilly	North-West Provinces.
Barisal	Backergunge	Bengal.
Baroda	Guzerat	Bombay.
Barrackpore	Calcutta	Bengal.
Barripore	Calcutta	Bengal.
Bassein	Pegu	Supreme Government.
Battalagundu	Madura	Madras.
Beerbhoom	Bahar	Bengal.
Belgaum	Belgaum	Bombay.
Bellary	Ceded District	Madras.
Benares	Benares	North-West Provinces.
Berhampore	Ganjam	Madras.
Bettigherry	South Mahratta	Bombay.
Bezwarah	Travancore	Madras (Native State).
Bhaugulpore	Bhaugulpore	Bengal.
Bhollobpur	Nuddea	Bengal.

STATION.	DISTRICT OR DIVISION.	PRESIDENCY.
Bhooj	Cutch	Bombay.
Bhowanepore	Calcutta	Bengal.
Bishop's College	Calcutta	Bengal.
Bishtopore	Calcutta	Bengal.
Black Town	Madras	Madras.
Bombay	Bombay	Bombay.
Burdwan	Jessore	Bengal.
Burhampore	Moorshedabad	Bengal.
Buxar	Shahabad	Bengal.
Byculla	Bombay	Bombay.
Calcutta	24 Pergunnahs	Bengal.
Calicut	Malabar	Madras.
Canandagoody	Tanjore	Madras.
Cannanore	Malabar	Madras.
Cawnpore	Allahabad	North-West Provinces.
Chaga	Orissa	Bengal.
Chaterpore	Vizagapatam	Madras.
Chicacole	Ganjam	Madras.
Chinsurah	Hooghly	Bengal.
Chintadrepettah	Madras	Madras.
Chitoura	Agra	North-West Provinces.
Chittagong	Chittagong	Bengal.
Chittoor	Arcot	Madras.
Chombala	Malabar	Madras.
Christianagram	Tinnevelly	Madras.
Chunar	Mirzapore	North-West Provinces.
Chupra	Nuddea	Bengal.
Cochin	Travancore	Madras (Native State).
Coimbatore	Coimbatore	Madras.
Colingah, South	Calcutta	Bengal.
Combaconum	Tanjore	Madras.
Coonghul	Mysore	Madras (Native State).
Coonoor	Neilgherries	Madras.
Cottayam	Travancore	Madras (Native State).
Cuddalore	Carnatic	Madras.
Cuddapah	Cuddapah	Madras.
Culna	. . . .	Bengal.
Cuttack	Orissa	Bengal.
Cutwa	Burdwan	Bengal.
Dacca	Dacca	Bengal
Darjeeling	Darjeeling	Bengal.
Debrooghur	Assam	Bengal.
Deesa	Guzerat, Guicowar's Dominions	Bombay (Native State).
Dehra	Dehra Doon	North-West Provinces.
Delhi	Delhi	North-West Provinces.

STATION.	DISTRICT OR DIVISION.	PRESIDENCY.
Dharwar . . .	South Mahratta . .	Bombay.
Dinagepore . . .	Bhaugulpore . .	Bengal.
Dinapore . . .	Patna	Bengal.
Dindigul . . .	Madura . . .	Madras.
Dohnavoor . . .	Tinnevelly . . .	Madras.
Dugshai . . .	Punjab . . .	Supreme Government.
Dum Dum . . .	Calcutta . . .	Bengal.
Edeyencoody . .	Tinnevelly . .	Madras.
Ellore	Masulipatam . .	Madras.
Erungalore . . .	Tanjore . . .	Madras.
Farm	Benares . . .	North-West Provinces.
Ferozepore . . .	Sirhind	North-West Provinces.
Furruckabad . . .	Agra	North-West Provinces.
Futtehgur . . .	Agra	North-West Provinces.
Futtehpore . . .	Allahabad . . .	North-West Provinces.
Ghazepoor . . .	Allahabad . . .	North-West Provinces.
Gogo	Kattywar, Guzerat .	Bombay.
Gooby	Mysore . . .	Madras (Native State).
Goojranwallah . .	Punjab . . .	Supreme Government.
Gorruckpore . .	Benares . . .	North-West Provinces.
Gowahati . . .	Assam	Bengal.
Guledagudda . . .	South Mahratta . .	Bombay.
Guptapara . . .	Pegu	Supreme Government.
Gyah	Bahar	Bengal.
Henzadu . . .	Pegu	Supreme Government.
Hooghly . . .	Hooghly . .	Bengal.
Howrah . . .	Calcutta . .	Bengal.
Hubly	South Mahratta . .	Bombay.
Hyderabad . . .	Scinde	Bombay.
Indore	Gwalior . . .	North-West Provinces.
Intally, South Road .	Calcutta . . .	Bengal.
Jackatallah . . .	Neilgherries . .	Madras.
Jaulnah . . .	Nizam's Dominions .	Madras.
Jellasore . . .	Orissa	Bengal.
Jessore	Jessore . . .	Bengal.
Jhelum	Punjab . . .	Supreme Government.
Joginda	Nuddea . . .	Bengal.
Juanpur . . .	Benares . . .	North-West Provinces.
Jubbulpore . . .	Jubbulpore . .	Bengal.
Julindar . . .	Punjab	North-West Provinces.
Junir	Ahmednuggur . .	Bombay.
Kapasdanga . . .	Kishnagur . . .	Bengal.
Kadatchapuram . .	Tinnevelly . . .	Madras.
Kaira	Kaira	Bombay.
Kaity	Neilgherries . .	Madras.
Kamptee . .	Nagpore Territory, or Berar . . .	Supreme Government.

STATION.	DISTRICT OR DIVISION.	PRESIDENCY.
Kemmendine	Pegu	Supreme Government.
Khari	Calcutta	Bengal.
Khokar	Ahmednuggur	Bombay.
Khundittur	Orissa	Bengal.
Kidderpore	Calcutta	Bengal.
Kirkee	Poonah	Bombay.
Kishnagur	Nuddea	Bengal.
Kolapore	South Mahratta	Bombay.
Kolga	Himalaya	
Koteghur	Simla	Supreme Government.
Kote Kangra	Punjab	Supreme Government.
Kunnankullam	Travancore	Madras (Native State).
Kurrachee	Scinde	Bombay.
Kussowlie	Simla	Supreme Government.
Kyelang	Kangra (Punjab)	Supreme Government.
Lahore	Punjab	North-West Provinces.
Lakhyantipore	Calcutta	Bengal.
Lal Bazar	Calcutta	Bengal.
Landour	Dehra Doon	North-West Provinces.
Loodianah	Sirhind (Cis-Sutlej States)	North-West Provinces.
Madras	Madras	Madras.
Madura	Madura	Madras.
Mahanad	. . . . . .	Bengal.
Mahi-Kantha	Guzerat	Bombay.
Malasamudra	South Mahratta	Bombay.
Malayapur	Calcutta	Bengal.
Malcolm-Peth	Sattara	Bombay.
Mallapalli	Travancore	Madras (Native State).
Malliapooram	Calicut	Madras.
Malligaum	Candeish	Bombay.
Malur	Madura	Madras.
Mandakayam	Travancore	Madras (Native State).
Mandapasalie	Madura	Madras.
Mangalore	South Canara	Madras.
Marinargoody	Carnatic	Madras.
Masulipatam	Northern Circars	Madras.
Mausmalie	Madura	Madras.
Mavelicare	Travancore	Madras (Native State).
Mayaveram	Tinnevelly	Madras.
Mean Meer	Lahore	Punjab.
Meerut	Meerut	North-West Provinces.
Mengnanapuram	Tinnevelly	Madras.
Mercara	Coorg	Madras.
Mhow	Gwalior	North-West Provinces.
Mirzapore	Mirzapore	North-West Provinces.

STATION.	DISTRICT OR DIVISION.	PRESIDENCY.
Mogra Hât	Calcutta	Bengal.
Monghir	Bhaugulpore	Bengal.
Moodaloor	Tinnevelly	Madras.
Mooltan	Punjab	Supreme Government.
Moradabad	Kumaon	North-West Provinces.
Moulmein	Tenasserim	Supreme Government.
Mozuffernuggur	Saharanpoore	North-West Provinces.
Mozufferpore	Tirhoot	Bengal.
Mulki	South Canara	Madras.
Murree	Punjab	North-West Provinces.
Mussoorie	Dehra Doon	North-West Provinces.
Muttra	Agra	North-West Provinces.
Mynpoorie	Agra	North-West Provinces.
Mysore	Mysore	Madras (Native State).
Nagercoil	Travancore	Madras (Native State).
Nagpore	Berar	Supreme Government.
Nangoor	Tanjore	Madras.
Narsigdarchoke	Calcutta	Bengal.
Nasik	Ahmednuggur	Bombay
Nazareth	Tinnevelly	Madras.
Negapatam	Tanjore	Madras.
Nellore	Nellore	Madras.
Neyoor	Travancore	Madras (Native State).
Nowgong	Assam	Bengal.
Nuddea	Jessore	Bengal.
Nundial	Cuddapah	Madras.
Nynee Tal	Kumaon	North-West Provinces.
Ootacamund	Neilgherries	Madras.
Palamcottah	Tinnevelly	Madras.
Palaveram	Chingleput	Madras.
Pullam	Travancore	Madras
Panneikullam	Tinnevelly	Madras.
Panneivilli	Tinnevelly	Madras.
Pareychaley	Travancore	Madras (Native State).
Partianur	Madura	Madras.
Pasumalie	Madura	Madras.
Patna	Patna	Bengal.
Pavoor	Tinnevelly	Madras.
Periaculum	Madura	Madras.
Peshawur	Punjab	Supreme Government.
Piplee	Orissa	Bengal.
Poonah	Poonah	Bombay.
Poonamallee	Madras	Madras.
Pooree	Orissa	Bengal.
Poreiar		
Pragassapuram	Tinnevelly	Madras.

STATION.	DISTRICT OR DIVISION.	PRESIDENCY.
Prome	Pegu	Supreme Government.
Pulney Hills	Madura	Madras.
Purtapura	Agra	North-West Provinces.
Puthiamputtur	Tinnevelly	Madras.
Puthukotie	Tinnevelly	Madras.
Quilon	Travancore	Madras (Native State).
Rajahmundry	Northern Circars	Madras.
Rajkoti	. . . . .	Bombay.
Ramnad	Tinnevelly	Madras.
Raneegunge	Bancoora	Bengal.
Rangoon	Pegu	Supreme Government.
Rawul Pindee	Punjab	Supreme Government.
Roorkee	Saharunpore	North-West Provinces.
Rosh Kali	Calcutta	Bengal.
Rottenpur	Nuddea	Bengal.
Russool Mahmoud Choke	Calcutta	Bengal.
Ryapuram	Madras	Madras.
Sabathu	Cis-Sutlej	North-West Provinces.
Sadras	Chingleput	Madras.
Saharunpore	Saharunpore	North-West Provinces.
Salem	Salem	Madras.
Santhapuram	Travancore	Madras (Native State).
Santipore	Nuddea	Bengal.
Sarandei	Tinnevelly	Madras.
Sattankullum	Tinnevelly	Madras.
Sattara	Sattara	Bombay.
Saugor	Nerbudda	North-West Provinces.
Savagasi	Tinnevelly	Madras.
Saveshapuram	Tinnevelly	Madras.
Sawyerpooram	Tinnevelly	Madras.
Sealcote	Lahore, Punjab	Supreme Government.
Secunderabad	Nizam of Hydrabad's Dominions	Madras (Native State).
Seebsagoor	Assam	Bengal.
Seetabuldee	Nagpore	Supreme Government.
Serampore	Hooghly	Bengal.
Seroor	Ahmednuggur	Bombay.
Sheemoogah	Malabar	Madras.
Shevaroy Hills	Salem	Madras.
Shikarpore	Scinde	North-West Provinces.
Sholapore	Sholapore	Bombay.
Shway Gyeen	Tenasserim	Supreme Government.
Sibsagor	Assam	Bengal.
Silhet	Silhet	Bengal.
Simla	Punjab	Supreme Government.

STATION.	DISTRICT OR DIVISION.	PRESIDENCY.
Sitabaldi . . .	Nagpore Territory .	Supreme Government.
Sivagasi	Tinnevelly . . .	Madras.
Sivagunga . . .	Madura . . .	Madras.
Solo	Nuddea . . .	Bengal.
Sooree	Birbhoom . . .	Bengal.
St. Thomè . . .	Madras . . .	Madras.
St. Thomas's Mount .	Madras . .	Madras.
Sunawur . . .	Kussowlie . . .	North-West Provinces.
Surandei . . .	Tinnevelly . . .	Madras.
Surat	Surat	Bombay.
Tallygunge . . .	Calcutta . . .	Bengal.
Tanjore	Tanjore . . .	Madras.
Tannah	Bombay . . .	Bombay.
Tavoy	Tenasserim . . .	Supreme Government.
Tellicherry . . .	Malabar . . .	Madras.
Tezpoor	Assam	Bengal.
Thakerpuker . .	Calcutta . . .	Bengal.
Thayet-Myo . .	Pegu	Supreme Government.
Tinnevelly . . .	Tinnevelly . . .	Madras.
Tirumungalum . .	Madura . . .	Madras.
Tirupuvanum . .	Madura . . .	Madras.
Tiruwalla . . .	Travancore . . .	Madras (Native State).
Tonghoo . . .	Pegu	Supreme Government.
Toomkoor . . .	Mysore . . .	Madras (Native State).
Tranquebar . . .	Tanjore . . .	Madras.
Trevandrum . . .	Travancore . . .	Madras.
Trichinopoly . . .	Trichinopoly . .	Madras.
Trichoor . . .	Travancore . . .	Madras.
Tripassore . . .	. . . . . .	Madras.
Trivaloor . . .	Chingleput . . .	Madras.
Udapi	South Canara . .	North-West Provinces.
Umballah . . .	Sirhind	North-West Provinces.
Umritsur . . .	Lahore, Punjab . .	Supreme Government.
Usulumputty . . .	Madura . . .	Madras.
Vediarpooram . .	Tanjore . . .	Madras.
Vellore	Arcot	Madras.
Vepery	Madras . . .	Madras.
Vizagapatam . .	Northern Circars . .	Madras.
Vizianagrum . .	Vizagapatam . .	Madras.
Wadale . . .	Ahmednuggur . .	Bombay.